AN INTRODUCTION TO
GREEN CRIMINOLOGY
& ENVIRONMENTAL JUSTICE

SAGE was founded in 1965 by Sara Miller McCune to support the dissemination of usable knowledge by publishing innovative and high-quality research and teaching content. Today, we publish over 900 journals, including those of more than 400 learned societies, more than 800 new books per year, and a growing range of library products including archives, data, case studies, reports, and video. SAGE remains majority-owned by our founder, and after Sara's lifetime will become owned by a charitable trust that secures our continued independence.

Los Angeles | London | New Delhi | Singapore | Washington DC

AN INTRODUCTION TO
GREEN CRIMINOLOGY
ENVIRONMENTAL
& JUSTICE

ANGUS NURSE

Los Angeles | London | New Delhi
Singapore | Washington DC

Los Angeles | London | New Delhi
Singapore | Washington DC

SAGE Publications Ltd
1 Oliver's Yard
55 City Road
London EC1Y 1SP

SAGE Publications Inc.
2455 Teller Road
Thousand Oaks, California 91320

SAGE Publications India Pvt Ltd
B 1/I 1 Mohan Cooperative Industrial Area
Mathura Road
New Delhi 110 044

SAGE Publications Asia-Pacific Pte Ltd
3 Church Street
#10-04 Samsung Hub
Singapore 049483

Editor: Amy Jarrold
Editorial assistant: George Knowles
Production editor: Sarah Cooke
Marketing manager: Sally Ransom
Cover design: Stephanie Guyaz
Typeset by: C&M Digitals (P) Ltd, Chennai, India
Printed and bound by CPI Group (UK) Ltd,
Croydon, CR0 4YY

Library of Congress Control Number: 2015940441

British Library Cataloguing in Publication data

A catalogue record for this book is available from
the British Library

ISBN 978-1-47390-809-3
ISBN 978-1-47390-810-9 (pbk)

CONTENTS

CONTENTS

CONTENTS

ABOUT THE AUTHOR

Angus Nurse is Senior Lecturer in Criminology at Middlesex University School of Law where he teaches and researches criminology and law and is Programme Leader for the MA Criminology. Angus has research interests in green criminology, corporate environmental criminality, critical criminal justice, animal and human rights law and anti-social behaviour. He is particularly interested in animal law and its enforcement and the reasons why people commit environmental crimes and crimes against animals. Angus has also researched and published on the links between violence towards animals and human violence. His first book *Animal Harm: Perspectives on why People Harm and Kill Animals* was published by Ashgate in 2013, his second; *Policing Wildlife: Perspectives on the Enforcement of Wildlife Legislation* was published by Palgrave Macmillan in 2015.

Angus is co-editor of Palgrave Macmillan's *Palgrave Studies in Green Criminology* book series (with Rob White from the University of Tasmania and Melissa Jarrell from Texas A & M University at Corpus Christi). Together with Becky Milne (University of Portsmouth) and Sam Poyser (Nottingham Trent University) he is currently working on a book on miscarriages of justice, a subject on which he has contributed to two essay collections from the Justice Gap.

PREFACE

This book developed to serve two disparate functions; first, the need for an introductory easily digestible text providing an introduction to the concepts of green criminology and environmental justice for both students and practitioners. Second, a research-based volume that provides discussion of contemporary issues and debates in green crime and environmental harm. The research on which this book is based has taken place over more than 15 years but is far from complete given ongoing developments in environmental crime policy and practice and in the field of environmental law and its enforcement.

Green crime is a fast-moving and somewhat contested area in which academics, policymakers and practitioners frequently disagree not only on how green crimes should be defined but also on: the nature of the criminality involved; potential solutions to problems of green crime; and the content and priorities of policy. Within ecological justice discourse, debates continue over whether green crimes are best addressed through criminal justice systems or via civil or administrative mechanisms. Indeed, a central discussion within green criminology is that of whether environmental *harm* rather than environmental crime should be its focus, with the environmental harm perspective currently dominating green criminological discourse. In essence, there is ongoing fundamental debate over whether green crimes should be seen as the focus of mainstream criminal justice and dealt with by core criminal justice agencies such as the police, or whether they should be considered as being beyond the mainstream. The argument for this harm perspective is dominated by the often transnational nature of environmental 'crimes', their location within government environmental policy departments rather than criminal justice ones and the fact that environmental harms are often dealt with by specialist environmental agencies (in)appropriately constituted (and resourced) to deal with the specifics of green offending. It should, however, be noted from the outset that much environmental harm is regulatory in nature rather than actually being categorized as crimes. Put another way, much of what we may think of as green crime is not in fact defined as crime and is dealt with other than by criminal justice agencies.

For those new to the field of green criminology these debates risk becoming a distraction from the core issues of understanding the current problems facing the environment and ecosystems and the manner in which justice systems deal with these. The purpose of this book is to provide an introduction to key concepts in green criminology and to discuss the nature of environmental harms (including crimes against animals) within a broad justice framework. However, it is also intended to provide for discussion of the complexities of contemporary harms and issues relating to illegal environmental activity. In particular, corporate environmental 'crime' and the role of the state in dealing with transnational environmental crime and the use of civil and administrative law mechanisms where criminal justice processes prove ineffective. The central questions running through this book are a) how can a green perspective be applied to contemporary criminal justice? and b) how should distinctly green crimes be dealt with in order to both address offending behaviour and repair the harm caused by environmental offending?

While the focus of this text is predominantly on crime and criminality, it is not purely an environmental crime book. There are many excellent books that deal with transnational and environmental crime problems such as Situ and Emmons' (2000) *Environmental Crime*; a text covering the context in which environmental crimes are dealt with by criminal justice systems and that helps define their nature. Rob White's (2008) *Crimes Against Nature* is a seminal work in applying criminological theory to green problems and in developing green criminological thought, and Piers Beirne and Nigel South's (2007) *Issues in Green Criminology* brings together a number of leading scholars in an exploration of green crimes as diverse as animal abuse, food crime, radioactive waste and climate change and its bearing on women's vulnerability towards violence. I have at one time or another recommended all of these books to students, also using them as sources for various research projects. However, this book's objective is slightly different and falls into the category of green criminology as a tool for studying, analysing and dealing with environmental crimes. Its primary focus is on activity prohibited by law, although it extends beyond examining just the criminal law and considers civil and administrative law and regulatory justice systems. The purpose of doing so is to primarily consider how legal systems and public policy currently deal with environmental offences. This makes the book of interest not just to students studying green criminology as a theoretical discipline but also those studying green criminology within criminal justice, criminal investigation, environmental law and environmental politics degrees. Its intention is also to allow students to consider the best mechanisms for dealing with environmental offences not just in terms of punishing offenders (the core focus of criminal justice) but also in respect of remedying environmental and wildlife damage caused by environmental offending.

Selection of Topics

The topics in this book have been selected to incorporate discussion of the importance of environmental justice and green criminology within international criminal justice. While there is inevitably some bias towards discussing the position in the United Kingdom (UK) and European Union (EU), where the majority of my original field research and policy analysis takes place, this book is international in scope; its topics having been selected to incorporate discussion of the international context of environmental crime and the transnational nature of much of its criminality. Much environmental crime crosses state boundaries and as a result highlights the difficulties of international enforcement in an era of uncertainty over the efficacy of international criminal justice systems and existing international law enforcement regimes that still rely predominantly on agreements between national policing systems. The book also explicitly considers the practical enforcement of environmental law within a green criminological context concerned with what should be done about environmental harms when they occur, as well as with how they might be prevented. In the Non-Governmental Organization (NGO) sector, policy analysts and investigators increasingly adopt a transnational approach and facilitate exchange of information and intelligence between countries using a number of umbrella agencies (e.g. WWF, TRAFFIC, Birdlife International). Rather than there being a single integrated international environmental law system, agreements between various organizations are often integral to ensuring effective environmental law enforcement. The monitoring of environmental harms; investigation and prosecution of environmental crimes; and regulatory justice systems are all covered by this book. It also explores the role of various enforcement agencies including those NGOs who are actively involved in policy development and practical enforcement activity. A central issue considered within this text is the role of the state in dealing with environmental crimes and the public policy response to offending, which also varies between jurisdictions such that in some countries, certain environmental harms are dealt with as criminal offences whereas in other countries these are dealt with as technical or regulatory breaches. This is particularly the case where corporate activity is involved, given the general unwillingness of governments to deal with corporations as criminal entities. Indeed in some jurisdictions it is difficult to prosecute a corporation as the legal entity responsible for environmental offending, requiring investigators and prosecutors to identify an individual who can be deemed responsible for the environmental harm caused. Frequently such individuals are at the 'lower end' of the offender scale, the working man rather than the company manager or director who some might consider should be held responsible for any corporate environmental damage.

This book seeks to examine this wide range of issues relating to environmental crime and harm and explore the different aspects of green crime and green criminology. In doing so it explores a range of activities, including: theories of green criminology; the causes of environmental crime; the protection of wildlife and illegal wildlife trade; the criminal exploitation of natural resources; the green movement and the role of NGOs in investigating wildlife crime; the role of the courts and alternative dispute resolution (ADR) that seeks to deal with environmental harms outside of the court process or through restorative means. In examining these issues it explicitly considers the green criminological perspective on repairing environmental harms and the general failure of justice systems to achieve this.

I said at the beginning that this book is intended to serve as an introductory textbook; by which I mean this book hopefully serves as a general course reader applicable to a wide range of green criminology or environmental crime modules within undergraduate degree courses. Green criminology is taught at a range of levels within criminology programmes and specialist green criminology modules generally appear after the first year at undergraduate level as well as at Masters level. The selection of topics and manner in which they are presented was deliberately chosen to make the text accessible for this wide range of courses and thus there may well be specific topics covered on individual courses that are not covered here, particularly in respect of those courses that deal more with harm and less with crime and criminal justice. While broad in scope the book is not intended to be a comprehensive handbook as this would require a much longer book. Thus there are undoubtedly some environmental crime or harm activities that should perhaps be discussed but which have not been included, either for reasons of space, because they represent specialist topics not generally taught across the green criminological spectrum or because they merit later or exclusive coverage given their inclusion in current and ongoing research projects. Any errors or omissions are my own and it should be noted that references to law and case law reflect the position as of August 2015, given the fast-moving nature of developments in environmental law and its enforcement. But as this text develops to meet changing needs in the green criminological curriculum I look forward to updating and revising its content in light of comments from students, instructors and practitioners alike.

Angus Nurse

Middlesex University, UK

ACKNOWLEDGEMENTS

This book would not have been possible without the support and assistance of several colleagues whose enthusiasm and constructive criticism has assisted greatly in refining many of the original ideas. Matthew Cremin and David Wilson, colleagues at Birmingham City University were instrumental in shaping and constructively criticizing some of the original ideas on wildlife crime that are presented here. Katerina Gachevska, of Leeds Beckett University helped considerably in developing some of the ideas about corporate crime and the negative impact corporations have on the environment. Nic Groombridge of St Mary's University Twickenham lent his considerable expertise to the examination and questioning of some of the material on masculinities and wildlife crime and Jennifer Maher of South Wales University also provided insight and perspective on animal abuse issues. I'm also grateful to Melissa Jarrell of Texas A & M University at Corpus Christi for her editorship of *The Monthly*, the online journal of the International Green Criminology Working Group (IGCWG) that published an initial article on the future protection of wildlife from which Chapter 4 derives. I'm also grateful to a number of colleagues who commented on draft versions of some of the chapters and who also examined and peer-reviewed some of the original wildlife crime research updated here. I am also grateful to students of Birmingham City University and Middlesex University who studied the green criminology modules I taught at each institution and who provided invaluable feedback on their needs as new and developing scholars and individuals wishing to develop careers in environmental justice and policy. Their views on what works (and what doesn't) has considerably shaped my green criminology teaching and learning agenda and considerably influenced the writing of this text and the topics included. Any errors in the material are, of course, my own.

Green criminology continues to grow as a global discipline yet it remains under-represented in university curricula and is often an option subject rather than a core, compulsory one. Yet it is also a subject that students find stimulating and challenging and taps into contemporary environmentalism, a core interest of university students concerned with corporate environmental wrongdoing, animal abuse and threats to endangered species. I am grateful to SAGE and its editors for their support for this project.

ACRONYMS

ASPCA	American Society for the Prevention of Cruelty to Animals
CITES	The Convention on International Trade in Endangered Species of Wild Fauna and Flora
CPS	Crown Prosecution Service
DEFRA	Department for Environment, Food and Rural Affairs
EIA	Environmental Investigation Agency
EPA	Environmental Protection Agency (US)
EU	European Union
HSUS	Humane Society of the United States
IFAW	International Fund for Animal Welfare
IUCN	International Union for the Conservation of Nature
LACS	League Against Cruel Sports
NGO	Non-Governmental Organization
PETA	People for the Ethical Treatment of Animals
RSPB	Royal Society for the Protection of Birds
RSPCA	Royal Society for the Prevention of Cruelty to Animals
SSPCA	Scottish Society for the Prevention of Cruelty to Animals
TRAFFIC	The world conservation monitoring body (CITES trade monitors)
UN	United Nations
UNEP	United Nations Environment Programme
UNODC	United Nations Office on Drugs and Crime
WEMS	Wildlife Enforcement Monitoring Network
WAP	World Animal Protection
WWF	World Wide Fund for Nature

PART I
INTRODUCTION AND THEORY

1

AN INTRODUCTION TO GREEN CRIMINOLOGICAL THEORIES

By the end of this chapter you should:

- Have a firm understanding of the principles of green criminology and the various meanings ascribed to the term.
- Understand the core concepts of 'environmental justice', 'ecological justice', 'species justice' and 'environmental harm' that underpin green criminology.
- Understand the rationale for a green criminology and an eco-global perspective on criminology, as well as some of the criticisms that might be made of green criminology.
- Understand green criminology's place within critical criminology and comparative criminology, as well as its importance within socio-legal study.

Introduction

Criminologists have increasingly become involved and interested in environmental issues to the extent that the term 'Green Criminology' is now recognized as describing a distinct subgenre of criminology. Within this unique area of scholarly activity researchers consider not just harms to the environment, but also the links between green crimes and other forms of crime, including organized crime's movement into the illegal trade in wildlife. A wide conception of the interplay between green crimes and mainstream crimes are also considered, such as the links between domestic animal abuse and spousal abuse or more serious forms of offending such as serial killing (Linzey, 2009; Nurse, 2013a). Within green criminology, scholars focus on various issues of importance to environmental and social harm from a green perspective. In doing so, they have exposed environmental and ecological injustice as well as identifying areas where mainstream criminal justice could benefit from a green perspective while also examining where 'general' criminal justice techniques can be applied to green crimes.

This introductory chapter sets out to explain what green criminology is and to discuss some of its theoretical underpinning.

Contextualizing Green Criminology

Green criminology is not easily categorized given that it draws together a number of different perspectives as well as theoretical and ideological conceptions. Thus rather than there being one distinct green criminology, it is rather an umbrella term for a criminology concerned with the general neglect of ecological issues within criminology (Lynch and Stretesky, 2014: 1) as well as the incorporation of green perspectives within mainstream criminology. Indeed as Lynch and Stretesky succinctly state:

> As criminologists we are not simply concerned that our discipline continues to neglect green issues, we are disturbed by the fact that, as a discipline, criminology is unable to perceive the wisdom of taking green harms more seriously, and the need to reorient itself in ways that make it part of the solution to the large global environmental problems we now face as the species that produces those problems.
>
> (2014: 2)

This overview goes some way to explaining both the importance of green criminology as well as the problems that a green criminology hopes to overcome. Traditional criminology is primarily concerned with the day-to-day business of 'ordinary crimes' described by Lea and Young in their classic work *What Is To Be Done About Law and Order?* as 'street crime, burglary, inter-personal violence—the crimes of the lower working class' (1993: 89). This continues to be the case for mainstream criminology where restrictive notions of police and policing by state institutions and of crime as being solely that determined as such by the criminal law dominate. Green criminology, however, extends beyond the focus on street and interpersonal crimes to encompass consideration of 'the destructive effects of human activities on local and global ecosystems' (South and Beirne, 1998: 147). In doing so green criminology considers not just questions of crime as defined by a strict legalist/criminal law conception (Situ and Emmons, 2000), but also questions concerning rights, justice, morals, victimization, criminality and the use of administrative, civil and regulatory justice systems.

Green criminology also examines the actions of non-state criminal justice actors such as Non-Governmental Organizations (NGOs) and civil society organizations. Crucially, green criminology considers the role of such organizations as active participants in justice systems as well as being monitors of justice system failings. As leading green criminologist Nigel South once wrote, addressing environmental harms and injustice requires 'a new academic way of looking at the world but also a new global politics' (2010: 242).

In part, green criminology contends that the historical approach of criminal justice systems to dealing with crime is inadequate to deal with crimes of larger significance and those which involve non-traditional crime victims. In doing so it challenges traditional conceptions of crime, injustice and victimhood as well as approaches to crime and criminality that may not reflect the contemporary reality of global harms.

Much of this book is concerned with environmental crime, primarily those acts prohibited by the law and defined as crime but also incorporating regulatory offences; 'technical' breaches of the law that may not be defined as crimes but which nevertheless are the subject of some form of sanction and punishment. The reality is that many practices that cause environmental harm are ostensibly legal and there is an argument that only those things defined by criminal law as offences can really be classed as green crimes. Situ and Emmons (2000: 2) define this as follows:

> The strict legalist perspective emphasizes that crime is whatever the criminal code says it is. Many works in criminology define crime as behaviour that is prohibited by the criminal code and criminals as persons who have behaved in some way prohibited by the law.

In short, the strict legalist view is that crime only exists where the criminal law defines it as such by prohibition of certain acts under the law. An alternative approach to animal and environmental legislation sometimes advocated by activists is the social legal perspective which argues that some acts, especially by corporations, 'may not violate the criminal law yet are so violent in their expression or harmful in their effects to merit definition as crimes' (Situ and Emmons, 2000: 3). This approach 'focuses on the construction of crime definitions by various segments of society and the political process by which some gain ascendancy, becoming embodied in the law' (Situ and Emmons, 2000: 3). For example, industrial pollution events are often regulatory breaches rather than actual crimes but are considered so serious in their impacts that green criminology would argue they constitute environmental crime (Lynch and Stretesky, 2014). However, a central focus of green criminology is the notion of environmental harm, a conception that incorporates the victimization and degradation of environments and harm caused to nonhuman animals. Lynch and Stretesky (2014: 8) argue that environmental harms are more important than the personal harms of street and property crimes both in terms of being more extensive and damaging. They argue that 'the environment around us is under expanded assault, that is it is routinely harmed and damaged by humans' (2014: 9).

The reality of environmental harm is that its consequences are wide-reaching, affecting more than just the direct victims of street crime and impacting negatively on ecosystems, future generations and the survival of many human and nonhuman animal species. Hall (2013) identifies that environmental harm has the potential for long-term negative impacts on human health (citing examples such as Bhopal, Chernobyl and the Deepwater Horizon Gulf oil spill where direct human harm was a consequence). Environmental harm also has negative long-term economic, social and security implications and is thus worthy of consideration by criminologists as both direct and indirect threat to human populations. Both Hall (2013) and Lynch and Stretesky (2014) identify that environmental harm is often a focus of neoliberal markets and the exploitation of natural resources by corporations and states, but much harm is entirely legal or at least distinctly not criminal. This theme is explored by a range of other writers (Stallworthy, 2008; Walters et al., 2013) and is a core part of green criminology's claim for developing justice systems and research enquiries that extend beyond concentration on criminal justice systems and the use of the criminal law, something which this book explores in its discussion of various aspects of green criminology. Accordingly the term 'environmental harm' is referred to repeatedly throughout this chapter and the remainder of the book and has importance not just in discussing *criminal* harms but also in discussing green criminology's approach to wider harms.

What is Green Criminology?

Defining green criminology requires embracing a range of different conceptions not just on what green criminology is, but also on: what it seeks to achieve; what perspectives should (and should not) be included; and also contrasting perspectives on what it means to be 'green' (Lynch and Stretesky, 2003). Rob White (2013b: 25) identifies differences within green criminology on the distinction between 'harm' and 'crime', partly linked to debates around legal/illegal, but also in relation to conflicting perspectives on victimization and 'varying conceptions of justice'.

Green criminology's focus on the notion of addressing harm extends beyond criminal prosecution as a default response to offences and includes the use of civil sanctions and alternatives to criminal justice as applied to wildlife (Vincent, 2014). Rob White identifies that concern with environmental crime requires considering the local and the global 'and to ponder the ways in which such harms transcend the normal boundaries of jurisdiction, geography and social divide' (2012d: 15). In this context, green criminology falls squarely within critical criminological discourse; that body of criminology concerned with challenges to orthodox criminological thinking and which views crime as the product of social conflict; unequal power and social relations (Welch, 1996). However Halsey (2004) was critical of green criminology's failure to clearly define itself, the nature of environmental harm and the types of regulatory structures needed to address environmental problems. Steve Tombs (Waddington, 2013) has also questioned the necessity for a green criminology (amongst other sub-disciplines) arguing instead for a zemiological approach (Hillyard and Tombs, 2011) based on the notion of social harm being inextricably linked to social and economic inequalities that are at the heart of a liberal state. In Tombs' conception, many criminological problems are best understood by understanding the contexts in which harm is most likely to occur; the patterns and extent of harm; and the characteristics of those most likely to experience harm. Arguably only by examining these issues can solutions to crime problems, most of which are actually social harm problems, be achieved. Tombs further argues that as criminology already encompasses a wide range of study and green crimes are merely another form of harm, there is no need for distinct subgenres of criminology. In principle Tombs' argument holds merit; given that criminology already incorporates study of social harms there is an argument that a distinct green criminology is conceptually redundant. However, successive green criminologists (Lynch and Stretesky, 2014; White and Heckenberg, 2014; Nurse, 2012, 2013a; Beirne, 2009; Wellsmith, 2011) have identified that mainstream criminology routinely ignores or marginalizes environmental and wildlife crimes, many of which fall outside the remit of criminal justice systems and are dealt with by regulatory, administrative or civil justice systems (Nurse, 2014; Stallworthy, 2008). Given that criminal justice systems primarily operate on the basis of a strict socio-legal definition of crime as defined by criminal legislation (Situ and Emmons, 2000), the much wider and more serious harms that green criminology deals with, compared with mainstream crime's street and personal crime focus, require detailed study. Accordingly, there is a need for dedicated, sustained consideration of the nature of environmental harms and the justice systems and policy mechanisms that address these as well as direct consideration of solutions to environmental crime problems.

Green criminology has developed considerably since Halsey's original criticisms, into a globally diverse movement of academics, practitioners and policy professionals. Beirne and South identified that 'movements in green environmentalism and in animal rights arose at about the same time, in the early to mid-1960s [although] only quite recently have they explicitly started to forge a common agenda' (2007: xiii). The term 'green criminology' dates back to the 1990s (Lynch, 1990) when it originated 'to describe a critical and sustained approach to the study of environmental crime' (White and Heckenberg, 2014: 7). Lynch and Stretesky (2014) identify that growing awareness among criminologists of the extent of environmental harm and degradation and the failure of mainstream criminology and criminal justice policy to address these issues led to some criminologists focusing their attention on these issues. A green criminological 'movement' began in the 1990s and has gathered pace ever since.

A 1998 special 'green' issue of the journal *Theoretical Criminology* brought together a range of criminologists exploring issues as diverse as:

- rights and justice
- causes of animal abuse
- ecofeminism
- masculinities and environmental crime
- the ecological impact of illicit drug cultivation.

This illustrates a broad range of green scholarship and the development of green criminology since this time, which is evidenced by the existence of green conference panels, numerous books, journals and specialist green criminology book series and the willingness of research councils to fund green criminological research, is indicative of a healthy field renewing itself and seeking to make sense of a wider range of social harms than criminology has traditionally concerned itself with. Green criminology incorporates a critique of an anthropocentric perspective and integration of biocentric and ecocentric perspectives on crime, criminal justice and social harm.

Beirne and South describe green criminology thus:

> At its most abstract level, green criminology refers to the study of those harms against humanity, against the environment (including space) and against non-human animals committed both by powerful institutions (e.g. governments, transnational corporations, military apparatuses) and also by ordinary people.

> (2007: xiii)

By (slight) contrast, White and Heckenberg describe green criminology as a distinctive critical form of criminology as follows:

> The term can refer to a specific focus on environmental crimes or harms: that is a particular topic for sustained criminological analysis (such as poaching of parrots). Alternatively it may refer to a conceptual approach premised upon certain notions of justice and particular moral frameworks, such as environmental justice or species justice. It may involve 'old' (that is conventional) theories and perspectives (general strain theory for example) applied to new areas (such as climate change) as well as 'new' methods and approaches (such as horizon scanning) applied to old areas (e.g. illegal waste disposal).

> (2014: 7)

Both definitions identify green criminology as an umbrella term for a number of theoretical or conceptual approaches that combine to provide a means of applying a green perspective to crime. White and Heckenberg argue that green criminology should be defined as widely as possible to arrange for the broadest diversion of conceptual and empirical insights to be incorporated under its umbrella (2014: 7). This is certainly the case in contemporary green criminology where scholars consider a wide range of both distinctly green and mainstream topics broadly falling within the following categories:

- Environmental Criminology
- Environmental Justice
- Ecological Justice (including species justice albeit there is an argument for this to be considered as its own category).

The focus of green criminology thus extends beyond pure definitions of 'crime' to consider the nature and extent of environmental harm and the negative impact of human action on the environment. These conceptions identify that defining green crimes can be problematic not just because of the wording of legislation, but also because of socially constructed notions of the acceptable use or exploitation of nature and natural resources. What is illegal environmental exploitation in one state may be acceptable use of natural resources in another. Walters et al. identify that 'non-anthropocentric concepts of justice are fundamental to the uniqueness of green criminology and to its ability to enhance the criminological gaze' (2013: 4). White and Heckenberg (2014) also explicitly note that green criminology may be defined by networks and collaborations between scholars or by the objective content of research. Or put another way, conceptually green criminology may be about environmental scholars and activists collaborating on specific problems and applying a green perspective to traditional crime(s) or specifically green crime, or it may be about enquiry into green problems (objectively defined). The environmental justice, ecological justice and species justice conceptions thus include theoretical and ideological considerations on the protection of nature because of its intrinsic value and the right of nonhuman species to be protected from human interference and/or to be given rights that are upheld by justice systems and environmental laws. Each of these conceptions contains additional theoretical approaches, which are discussed in more detail in the following sections.

Environmental Criminology

White and Heckenberg suggest that environmental criminology is primarily concerned with situational crime prevention and might be more usefully described as 'place-based criminology' (2014: 19). In this context, environmental criminology considers the links between the occurrence of crime and specific geographical or location-based circumstances that allow crime to occur. Brantingham and Brantingham (1991) developed a criminological conception of environmental and context factors that influence criminal activity on the basis of five key factors:

- space (geography)
- time
- law
- offender
- target or victim.

Environmental criminology is, thus, concerned with a conventional criminological approach to dealing with crime as legally defined (White and Heckenberg, 2014: 19) and understanding breaches of legislation committed by human actors. However, environmental criminology, as applied to environmental harm and offences against the environment and nonhuman animals, also provides a means for examining the place and time in which crime occurs. Theoretically, sufficient understanding of crime patterns provides a means through which crime can be prevented by applying situational crime prevention techniques of target hardening, reducing opportunity, reducing reward and so on. But crucially, environmental criminology has also 'led to new interests, new conceptualisations and new techniques of analysis' (White, 2008: 9). In part this is because criminologists concerned with environmental harm and the location of human activities that harm the environment have become interested in what Rob White (2008) refers to as the *interconnectedness* of social and environmental issues. Thus a range of social factors such as poverty, health, indigenous people's rights, the functioning of law and the exploitation of nature are seen as being inseparable.

Thus, while the approach to much green crime is reactive and based on a policing and regulatory response that relies on the law enforcement perspective of detection, apprehension and punishment (Bright, 1993; Nurse, 2013a) environmental criminology considers preventative mechanisms for dealing with crime including:

- situational crime prevention
- market reduction approaches
- future prevention.

Applying Brantingham and Brantingham's (1991) five conceptions, theorizing the 'how', 'why', 'when' and 'who' of environmental crime becomes possible as does taking action to actively prevent certain environmental crimes. As later chapters of this book discuss, particularly in relation to the illegal exploitation of wildlife, environmental criminology is able to consider where situational factors such as the environment (e.g. easy access to unprotected wildlife) can make crime more likely to occur at a particular time and place.

White and Heckenberg, for example, discuss specific circumstances where modification to the environment of game preservation areas, national parks and wildlife reserves intends to provide situational crime prevention benefits, including:

- use of pilotless drones, closure of logging roads and DNA coding of ivory to prevent elephant poaching;
- protecting nests during the breeding season, use of CCTV surveillance, road blocks and market interventions to prevent the illegal trade in parrots; and
- increased use of rangers and ground patrols to prevent rhinoceros poaching.

(2014: 281–6)

In addition, crime mapping that identifies some areas as crime hot spots, i.e. areas with an 'abnormal' concentration of crime, allows for identification of situational factors that help explain why a particular environment is problematic and attractive to potential offenders. In the case of wildlife or forest crime (discussed in later chapters) it may be that the environment is poorly supervised, lacks effective 'place management', has unusually high concentrations of rare items (e.g. rhinos and their horns, unique populations of endangered wildlife, prized species of timber) or other characteristics. Akella and Allan argue that 'anti-poaching patrols and other frontline deterrence efforts are critical to preventing wildlife crime' (2012: 7). Thus situational measures to reduce the likelihood of wildlife poaching taking place might include:

- a combination of walls and fences (increased effort);
- armed guards and other security counter measures (increased risk);
- the moving of wildlife to increasingly remote areas (reduced provocation);
- concerted action to address wildlife markets and provide alternative sources of revenue for local communities (removal of excuses).

The environmental crime approach may also inform measures to reduce future offending considering both supply and demand issues. The demand and wealth of (urban) consumers of wildlife and forest products can be a strong driver of illegal wildlife and forest activities, thus Schneider (2008) suggests a market reduction approach to wildlife crime. Besides users on the supply side, such as local subsistence users, commercial hunters and forest concessionaires, a diverse group of users exists on the demand side. These include consumptive end-users in markets and restaurants, and non-consumptive users, such as tourists, as well as Western consumers who unwittingly through demand for goods such as natural wood products may drive demand for suppliers to fulfil such demand through unlawful means. Schneider's market reduction approach consists of identifying 'hot' products and market-based analysis of these products to iden-tify who is involved in their criminal exploitation and subsequent analysis of the reasons for their involvement. Schneider (2008) identifies ivory, rhino horns, and animal skins and parts as status symbols prized by wealthy custom-ers around the world who are not traditionally the subject of law enforcement attention. CITES (the enforcement Secretariat for the CITES Convention) has also recognized demand reduction as a key element in addressing poaching, specifically that of illegal rhino horn, adopting at its 62nd Standing Committee meeting, a strategy for developing ideas for demand reduction for rhino horn, which includes the following objectives:

- influencing consumer behaviour to eliminate consumption of illegal rhino horn products through effective demand reduction strategies;
- identifying specific messaging approaches and methods for dealing with consumption by specific target audiences;
- strengthening legal and enforcement deterrent effectiveness by raising awareness of legal protection and penalties for sale and consumption of rhino products;
- raising awareness of the negative consequences and impact on populations of poaching and consumption of rhino products.

(CITES, 2013)

Thus market-based approaches address the demand for and supply of wildlife products targeting prices and markets for wildlife products and substitutes such as sustainable harvested resources. Linked to an environmental crime assess-ment of supply hot spots, common, market-based strategies to prevent illegal trade in wildlife products include the following tactics:

- imposing taxes or other levies to raise consumer prices or reduce producer profitability;
- lowering tax rates on (sustainable) substitute products;
- increasing the profitability of sustainable-harvested production through subsidies, value adding, and certification and labelling.

(UNODC, 2012: 346)

However, market-based instruments rely on clearly established property rights, a contested issue in many source countries for wildlife products and the coop-eration of governments to apply financial and economic instruments to the wildlife trade. Thus, certification measures and trade regulations (both interna-tional and domestic) provide a means through which social crime prevention might be attempted by addressing consumer and retailer behaviour.

Green criminologists have historically been critical of the failure to employ crime prevention techniques to environmental (particularly wildlife) crime problems (Wellsmith, 2010, 2011; Nurse, 2012). Environmental criminology, however, provides a means through which preventative techniques can be applied to wildlife crime and other environmental crime problems.

Environmental Justice

The environmental justice conception refers to the distribution of environments in terms of access to and use of natural resources. Rob White identifies environmental justice as being concerned with:

- environmental rights as an extension of human or social rights;
- intergenerational responsibility;
- environmental justice: equity for present and future generations;
- environmental harm, an idea constructed in relation to human centred notions of value and use.

(2008: 15)

This conception of environmental justice identifies human beings as being at the centre of analysis in an anthropocentric notion that sees humans as both the focus of environmental issues (as victims perhaps of a poor environment) but also as the key instigators of environmental damage. In one sense, environmental justice considers that humans matter and that where there are conflicts between human interests and environmental ones, human interests generally win out (Stallworthy, 2008). However, one conception of environmental justice is that there is uneven access to environmental resources and environmental rights (where these can be said to exist). Thus environmental justice is in part concerned with equity and deals with the marginalization of those historically denied access to environmental resources and the benefits derived from exploiting these.

In the US context, Schlosberg identifies the term environmental justice as 'used to cover at least two overlapping parts of the grassroots environmental movement; the antitoxics movement and the movement against environmental racism' (2007: 46).

Within environmental justice discourse, various commentators have used the term 'environmental racism' to denote the manner in which ethnic minority groups and indigenous people disproportionately suffer from lack of access to environmental resources. Ethnic minority groups are also disproportionately affected by the location of toxic factories, pollution and waste sites in their neighbourhoods and the degradation of their environment. Environmental racism contends that negative environmental consequences of business impacts communities of colour more than Caucasians. Thus environmental racism can be defined as:

> Racial discrimination in environmental policy making and the enforcement of regulations and laws; the deliberate targeting of people of color communities for toxic and hazardous waste facilities; the official sanctioning of the life-threatening presence of poisons and pollutants in our communities; and the history of excluding people of colour from the leadership of the environmental movement.

(Chavis, 1991)

Similarly the Earth Justice Legal Defense Fund in an oral intervention at the 55th Session of the United Nations Commission on Human Rights defined environmental racism as being 'any government, institutional, or industry action, or failure to act, that has a negative environmental impact which disproportionately harms—*whether intentionally or unintentionally*—individuals, groups, or communities based on race or colour' (emphasis in original, United Nations, 1999). Environmental racism discourse is thus concerned with race-linked theory and action, which means considering positive racially oriented action to combat discrimination. Green scholars working within environmental racism discourse advocate for the elimination of exposure to dangerous products and practices for all and the elimination of racial discrimination in environmental decisions. Here, green criminology extends beyond pure academic pursuit into action intended to influence and develop the policy agenda in ways that bring positive benefits for marginalized groups. Separate from environmental racism, a Red-green Movement exists which relates economic oppression to environmental degradation. It argues that in a class society, environmental problems are more likely to impact the working class and the poor.

Within environmental justice discourse ecofeminism has also criticized capitalist profit-growth orientation and the patriarchy. Cudworth (2005) describes ecofeminism as a theoretical construction that connects the domination and exploitation of nature with the domination and exploitation of women, arguing that women are more concerned with survival than men. By analysing contemporary ecologism and green social theory, Cudworth proposes a concept of 'anthroparchy' (human domination of 'nature') which argues that understanding the interrelations between different types of social domination are integral to dealing with environmental problems. As with other theoretical conceptions on green criminology, there is no single definition of ecofeminism. Instead it is an umbrella term for examining relationships between gender, nature, culture, other formations of difference and ecological crime issues. Within environmental justice discourse ecofeminism contributes to an understanding of inequality and discrimination by exploring masculine and feminist perspectives, exploring the manner in which marginalization of feminist perspectives and women in decision-making is a factor in environmental crime. This issue is explored in more detail in a later chapter that examines the role of masculinities and crime, noting that much environmental crime is committed by men and that patriarchal perspectives are a significant factor in attempts to exert dominion over nature and the resultant environmental harms.

It is worth pointing out that there is also a European conception of environmental justice based around providing distinct access to information about the environment and mechanisms to challenge public decisions that have negative environmental consequences. The Convention on Access to Information, Public Participation in Decision-making and Access to Justice in Environmental Matters (the Aarhus Convention) entered into force in 2001. The Convention, adopted under the auspices of the United Nations, recognizes every person's right to a healthy environment – as well as his or her duty to protect it. In doing so it puts forward a specific theoretical concept of environmental justice; that which seeks to ensure that every individual lives in an environment adequate for his or her health and well-being. This conception applies to future generations as well as current ones. In doing so it embodies green criminology's notion of environmental justice as ending environmental discrimination (White, 2008) but encompassing this within a legal framework that specifies environmental justice as being based on three pillars:

- the right to know
- the right to participate
- the right of access to environmental justice.

Within these pillars, the Aarhus Convention effectively defines environmental justice as including the right of everyone to receive environmental information held by public authorities which incorporates information on the state of the environment, but also on policies or measures being taken in respect of the environment (UNECE/UNEP, 2006). Aarhus provides that effective environmental justice involves ensuring that the public have sufficient information on decisions that affect the environment that they can question such decisions and participate in decision making. Thus Aarhus ensures that the public has access to review procedures that will allow them to challenge public decisions that have been made without respecting the public's right to know or right to participate or which otherwise would appear to contravene or fail to comply with environmental law in general. Aarhus thus requires signatory states to track pollution from industrial sites and other pollution sources and to inform the 'concerned' public of activity or specific projects that could adversely affect the environment. The Convention explicitly recognizes every person's right to live in a healthy environment, something lacking in other areas of environmental law. The Convention also recognizes the role of NGOs as having a role in allowing the public to access environmental justice and by ensuring that the public has recourse to the law also requires that there must be some form of remedy mechanism available to those affected by decisions and projects that could adversely affect the environment. The UK, as a member of the Convention, has chosen its judicial review procedure as its mechanism for providing the public with the scrutiny and redress tools required by Aarhus. Judicial review is primarily concerned with the proper exercise of powers rather than the merits of a decision but (subject to restrictions) provides a scrutiny mechanism through which any person with 'sufficient interest' in a public decision can examine whether this was the case. In essence judicial review is concerned with whether:

- laws have been correctly interpreted;
- any discretion allowed to a decision-making body has been properly exercised;
- the decision-maker has acted fairly;
- the use of power by a public body has not infringed human rights.

(Barnett, 2011: 545)

Remedies on successful judicial review can include gaining an injunction that prevents a decision from being acted upon or a declaration by the courts that a decision was unlawful. Thus, in respect of environmental decisions, this can be a powerful means of securing environmental justice through the courts, notwithstanding the limited grounds on which judicial review can be brought and the costs involved in doing so.

Ecological Justice

This perspective acknowledges that human beings are only one part of the planet and that any system of justice needs to consider the wider biosphere and species that depend on nature. Within an ecological justice perspective there is scope to incorporate what is referred to as a consequentialist ethic, a theoretical conception concerned with goodness or badness as being more important than 'rightness' or 'wrongness' (Brennan and Lo, 2008). Jeremy Bentham's (1748–1832) and John Stuart Mill's (1806–73) writings on utilitarianism argue that consequences are the measure of whether an action is right or wrong and that the 'value' of consequences can be measured by how much happiness or well-being is caused by an action. But utilitarianism is also noted for the idea that doing the right thing means that everybody has an equal share in happiness and no individual's happiness has greater value than another's.

Utilitarianism is consequentialism in action. It suggests that animals and nonhuman nature are no less deserving of protection and respect than humans. Bentham went so far as to suggest that pleasure and pain could be calculated and valued in terms of intensity, duration, certain or uncertainty and proximity or remoteness. While this is a simplified explanation of Bentham's theory, in effect he argued that one could weigh up the sum of pleasure and the sum of pain for everybody and that one could decide, on balance, whether an action or decision was good or bad on the basis of the outcome and its consequences for the greatest number of people. Mill, developing Bentham's concept, argued that people would prefer to exercise intellectual capabilities even if experiencing some pain in the process rather than having unlimited physical pleasure with no intellectual or spiritual benefit.

While these may seem complex notions, in essence the utilitarian notion is a means of deciding that decisions should be made on the basis of positive outcomes for the greatest number of people and those which promote a sense of well-being, this is rather than making decisions based on an anthropocentric notion of human pleasure and benefit which ignores unpleasant or painful consequences. Thus, employing a utilitarian and consequentialist perspective should lead one to conclude that wherever possible, human actions which negatively impact on the environment and nonhuman animals should be avoided, even where this causes some inconvenience to human interests. This reasoning forms the basis of *species justice*, a theoretical construction found within ecological justice.

Species justice considers the responsibility man owes to other species as part of broader ecological concerns. The principal idea is that man, as the dominant species on the planet, has considerable potential to destroy nonhuman animals, or, through effective laws and criminal justice regimes, to provide for effective animal protection and so has a responsibility to do so. This includes animal rights, aspects of animal protection and criminality involving a range of nonhuman animals. Benton suggests that 'it is widely recognized that members of other animal species and the rest of non-human nature urgently need to be protected from destructive human activities' (1998: 149). If this is true then contemporary criminal justice needs to extend beyond traditional human ideals of justice as a punitive or rehabilitative ideal, to incorporate shared concepts of reparative and restorative justice between humans and nonhuman animals. In effect, the criminal justice system needs to be modified to provide for a broad criminal justice perspective, justice for all sentient beings, not just for humans.

Social theorists and theologians argue that man's dominant position on the planet necessitates living in harmony with the environment and 'nonhuman' animals (Singer, 1975; Benton, 1998; Linzey, 2009). Thus violence and cruelty towards animals makes society poorer because it demeans us as individuals and increases the acceptance of violence within society. Within the species justice literature, especially its animal rights discourse, there are complex arguments about the moral imperative to respect and promote animal welfare and the consequences of cruelty to animals for society. Piers Beirne argues that the sources of animal abuse are not just in individualized one-on-one cruelty 'but also in various institutionalised social practices where animal abuse is seen as socially acceptable' (2007: 55). One aspect of species justice discourse concerns the social and legal changes needed so that animals are not viewed as 'things' entirely subject to human interest and control. Animal rights discourse contains complex debates about the form that animal rights should take.

Questions persist concerning whether effective animal protection and an end to animal cruelty necessitates providing animals with legal personhood (Wise, 2000; Singer, 1975) or whether effective species justice can be achieved through better animal protection laws and increased use of the existing criminal law. These species justice questions are also explored in more detail in later chapters.

The Purpose of Green Criminology: The Green and the Mainstream

White and Heckenberg identify that the term 'environmental crime' embodies a certain ambiguity and is a concept consistently undervalued in law (2014: 9). In part this is because of a persistent approach within criminology and crime policy of seeing environmental issues as being outside of the mainstream of criminal justice systems and, instead, of being the responsibility of nature conservation or environmental protection departments rather than criminal justice ones (Nurse, 2012). Enforcement of environmental crimes can be problematic where criminal justice systems prove inadequate to the task of dealing with particular offence types. Corporate environmental crimes, for example, are of particular concern given the difficulty of either identifying specific individuals within a corporation who are culpable for the offence or in taking enforcement action against a corporate body. Given green criminology's generally critical approach, such crimes are also of interest in examining the distinction between the legal and the illegal. Much environmental crime is carried out by ostensibly legal actors operating within neoliberal markets (Doyon, 2014; White and Heckenberg, 2014; Lynch and Stretesky, 2014). However, the extent to which governments and legal systems are generally unwilling to consider corporations as criminal entities is an area where green criminologists and mainstream criminologists have a shared interest. Green criminology's strength is its ability to apply ideas about mainstream crime to green issues, while also applying green perspectives to mainstream criminological concerns. In doing so it develops criminological discourse.

Potter (2010: 10) argues that the link between environmental issues and criminology takes place on three levels:

- First, we can identify a range of crime and criminal justice activity relating directly to environmental issues.
- Second, we can see the study of environmental harm in general as an extension of the well-established (and indeed fundamental) tradition within both sociology and criminology of critically questioning the very definition of crime and the core subject matter of criminology.

- Finally, it is possible to identify a number of areas where environmentalists can benefit from the experience of sociologists and criminologists working within more traditional notions of crime.

Potter's conception suggests that green criminology is concerned not just with distinctly environmental crimes but also with how studying green crimes can help to improve criminology. Environmental laws are often dealt with via administrative or civil law systems rather than criminal justice ones. Wildlife law is often a fringe area of policing whose public policy response is significantly influenced by NGOs (Nurse, 2012) and which continues to rely on NGOs as an integral part of the enforcement regime. White (2012b) identifies that third parties such as NGOs often play a significant role in investigating and exposing environmental harm and offending and have become a necessity for effective environmental law enforcement. As a result, green criminology provides a means for examining fringe areas of policing and criminality and applying critical thought to these areas. Green criminologists are, therefore, often in the position of challenging contemporary criminal justice ideas and their theories provide a new way of looking at contemporary criminal justice problems. Green criminology's value is, thus, in part, its contribution to a broader and deeper understanding of crime and criminal behaviour. Engagement with NGOs and other practitioners is integral to green criminology's continued development beyond Halsey's (2004) criticism; it is a discipline that not only theorizes about green crimes but also takes active steps to contribute towards policy and practice that addresses environmental harms.

At its best, green criminology attempts to both challenge and indeed overturn many common-sense notions of crime to reveal and challenge the reality of harms with wider social impact and negative consequences for the environment and human relations (Nurse, 2013a). Green criminology suggests that we reappraise more traditional notions of crimes, offences and injurious behaviours and start to examine the role that societies (including corporations and governments) play in generating environmental degradation. Thus, like other crimes, green crimes are a social construction influenced by:

- social locations
- power relations in society
- definitions of environmental crimes
- media
- political process.

Symbiotic green crime is crime that grows out of the flouting of rules that seek to regulate environmental disasters. There are, for instance, numerous minor and major examples of governments breaking their own regulations and contributing to environmental harms.

How the justice system should deal with these issues is a core concern of green criminology. Rob White (2008) identifies the following three approaches:

1. **The Socio-legal Approach** – which emphasizes use of the current criminal law and attempts to improve the quality of investigation, law enforcement, prosecution and conviction of illegal, environmentally related activity.
2. **The Regulatory Approach** – an emphasis on social regulation, using many different means as the key mechanism to prevent and curtail environmental harm. This attempts to reform existing systems of production and consumption using enforced self-regulation and bringing NGOs into the regulatory process.
3. **Social Action Approach** – emphasis on need for social change predominantly through democratic institutions and citizen participation.

These approaches are discussed in more detail throughout this book in relation to specific green crime and environmental harm issues outlined in individual chapters.

Summary

White (2008: 8) has described the term green or environmental criminology as that which 'basically refers to the study of environmental harm, environmental laws and environmental regulation by criminologists'. However, as this chapter has discussed, this basic formulation, while undoubtedly correct, considerably downplays the complex reality of green criminology as a diverse study that includes the study of environmental harms, laws and regulation but goes much further. There is no single definition of green criminology, although White and Heckenberg's 2014 conception is fairly comprehensive. Instead there are a number of criminologists concerned with environmental harm and/or the operation of environmental laws (including those which protect nonhuman animals) and criminologists applying green perspectives to mainstream crime. Some do both, but, as with mainstream criminology, green criminologists have their specialisms and may focus on specific aspects of environmental harm or environmental crimes and can operate from distinct ideological and theoretical positions.

The distinctive nature of green criminology is a conception of crime that extends beyond the pure socio-legal consideration of crime as being defined by the criminal law. Lynch and Stretesky argue that 'green harms are the most important considerations in modern society because they cause the most harm, violence, damage and loss' (2014: 7). In illustrating this point they identify that much corporate environmental damage such as pollution from lawful emissions is entirely legal—that is, not a violation of the law—but can have long-term harmful consequences such as damage to water courses, acceleration of global warming and exposing citizens to harmful toxins. Only when the permitted emission limits are exceeded or an upset accident such as a chemical spill or other discharge occurs might the incident be seen as a crime. It should be noted, however, that many environmental offences are dealt with as regulatory breaches and are not seen as crimes attracting only fines or administrative sanctions rather than the punitive response of the criminal justice system (Stallworthy, 2008). Thus, incidents of global importance affecting humans, nonhuman animals, plants and ecosystems can sometimes be treated more 'leniently' than interpersonal crimes, which while serious, have less far-reaching consequences.

Green criminology in the theoretical conceptions discussed within this chapter considers such issues and broadly argues that at least conceptually there should be a wider definition of crime that incorporates harms not currently defined as crimes. As Lynch and Stretesky state: 'the form of criminal justice criminologists ordinarily examine to discuss the control of crime is a narrow form of justice' (2014: 7). Conceiving an effective form of justice means considering more than just individual victims of crime (Benton, 1998) and requires exploration of a wider range of criminal behaviour than just that of the rationally driven offender (Nurse, 2013a). Green criminology attempts this both in theory and in practice by reconceptualizing definitions of crime to focus on the impact of behaviour on the environment. Green criminology also considers the extent to which actions that infringe existing legislation are deserving of a response commensurate with the idea of what criminal sanctions are intended to achieve: punishment, reparation and rehabilitation or changed behaviour. These ideas are explored in more detail in later chapters.

Self-study Questions

1. What is green criminology and why is it important as a way of looking at crime?
2. In what ways can a green perspective be applied to contemporary criminal justice problems?
3. What types of distinctly green crimes exist and what problems exist in developing a criminal justice system that deals with green crime?
4. There are a variety of different approaches to dealing with crime and criminality. Rob White contends that 'there is no green criminological *theory* as such' (2008: 14) but there is instead a green 'perspective' that explicitly considers environmental issues (broadly construed) as part of criminology. Explain the different aspects of this 'green perspective' and their different approaches to dealing with crime and criminality.

2

SPECIES JUSTICE: ANIMAL RIGHTS, ANIMAL ABUSE AND VIOLENCE TOWARDS HUMANS

By the end of this chapter you should:

- Have a firm understanding of species justice arguments which contend that justice systems need to consider the rights and protection of nonhuman animals.
- Understand conceptual arguments that animals should have rights and some of the different conceptions on how such rights can be realised in legal systems.
- Have a firm understanding of the basis of animal protection through criminal law systems and awareness of some contemporary debates concerning these.
- Understand the link between animal abuse and interpersonal violence and related arguments that suggest that animal abuse and human violence are inextricably linked.

Introduction

This chapter examines a range of issues relating to animal rights, animal abuse and the links between animal abuse and interpersonal (human) violence. Animal rights are a core area for green criminology, primarily linked to the concepts of ecological justice and species justice that were introduced in Chapter 1 (Beirne, 2007). Green criminology's ecological justice perspective contends that justice systems need to consider not just human victims of crime, but also crimes committed against the environment and nonhuman animals. The specific issue of whether and how wild or domestic animals should be protected through the criminal law is also a core concern of species justice (Benton, 1998; White, 2008) particularly in respect of recognizing that legal systems often reduce animals to property (Wise, 2000). Thus, generally animals are not recognized as victims even where they are direct targets of violence and criminality. However, green criminological consideration of species justice goes beyond merely considering whether animals should have rights and the nature of such rights. Debates in theology, criminology and the study of animal law address the rights of animals and the moral wrong of inflicting harm on other sentient beings, the relationship between man and nonhuman animals, the need for legal rights for animals, and issues of animal abuse and the need for increased standards of animal welfare (see, for example, Wise, 2000; Scruton, 2006; Sunstein and Nussbaum, 2004; Ascione, 2008). Green criminology, by contextualizing crime and justice systems through a green lens, goes further and considers the benefits to mainstream criminology of better integrating enforcement of animal laws into justice systems. In doing so, consideration is given to the extent to which animal abuse and human violence are linked, both in terms of exploring the commonality between criminality (Linzey, 2009; Nurse, 2013a) and considering how animal abuse contributes to wider social harms.

This chapter explores these issues in some detail, first considering the case for animal rights and contemporary discussions in green criminology concerning species justice, next considering contemporary perspectives on animal law and animal abuse and finally considering the links between animal abuse and interpersonal violence. A central theme of this chapter is that there are compelling arguments for viewing animal crime as part of the criminal law and viewing cruelty to animals as part of an overall offending profile rather than as solely an animal welfare or animal rights issue. These are complex ideas exploring contested and sometimes controversial arguments surrounding the status of animals in society. Thus, crimes affecting animals are dealt with across two chapters. This chapter considers theoretical conceptions on animal protection and rights and explores some issues relating to companion animals. Chapter 4 examines wildlife crimes as a separate issue, exploring illegal wildlife trafficking and the future protection of wildlife.

The Case for Animal Rights

Students of environmental crime and green criminology are likely to be aware that considerable academic scholarship has examined the concept of animal rights, recognizing that animals' status is often that of property. Thus, despite being sentient beings, animals generally lack their own rights (Kean, 1998) and are often protected under the law only insofar as such protection is considered to be commensurate with human interests (Nurse, 2013a). Regan (2004: xiv) argues that animal rights 'is more than a philosophical idea; it is also part of the name of a burgeoning social justice movement, the animal rights movement'. Kean (1998) identifies that animals have become news in the context of being the subject of discussion by legislators, media coverage, social protest and public interest. Animal protection has become a legitimate interest of government, legislators and law enforcement and is a developing area of law in the form of both anti-cruelty statutes and laws designed to promote animal welfare and prohibit certain specified actions considered to be harmful to animals.

Noting the importance of the animal rights movement, Beirne (2007: 65) also comments:

> Since the mid-1960s support for animal rights has grown into a large-scale, well-publicised and theoretically informed social movement. In some parts of the more developed world the movement's gains seem to have been extraordinary. In some societies among its achievements might be counted the movement's contribution to state regulation of the production, transport and slaughter of cattle and poultry; a gradual decline in the consumption of meat, and a concomitant rise in the consumption of grains, fruit and vegetables; stricter controls on animal shelters, zoos, circuses and aquaria; greater restrictions on the use of vivisection in scientific and commercial laboratories and in schools; a drastic reduction in sales of animal skins and fur; and the protection of endangered species, especially exotica such as whales, wolves, and raptors.

Beirne's list represents a litany of animal abuse, identifying that animals are used for 'entertainment', food, experimentation and research and are traded as commodities commensurate with their status as property subservient to human needs. Animal rights policies seek to redress this balance, providing animals with a certain level of protection from over-exploitation (and in some cases to prevent their use altogether) as well as providing appropriate levels of protection in the form of good animal welfare standards. Animal rights policies are primarily contextualized within utilitarianism and questions of whether animals can suffer (see Bentham, 1789; Singer, 1975) encompassed in the belief that suffering in animals often causes humans to suffer. The principal argument is that it is immoral to allow animals to suffer or to cause harm to animals, even if the animal itself is not provided with any legal rights or moral status. Animal rights exponents may also argue that animals as sentient beings can feel pain and on this basis should not suffer harm given their interest in avoiding pain and suffering and, as sentient beings, should also be given legal rights.

Animal rights have also become an issue of specific interest to criminology scholars. Beirne (1999) argues that animal cruelty should be drawn into the realm of criminological inquiry as its importance can be determined at several levels, as follows:

> animal cruelty may signify other actual or potential interpersonal violence;
>
> animal cruelty is, in many forms prohibited by criminal law;
>
> violence against animals is part of the utilitarian calculus on minimization of pain and suffering (the public good);
>
> animal cruelty is a violation of rights; and
>
> violence against animals is one among several forms of oppression that contribute, as a whole, to a violent society.

> (Beirne, 1999; Nurse, 2013a: 35)

Beirne thus identifies that for criminologists and those interested in reducing or addressing crime justice and violence in society, animal rights and animal cruelty are worthy topics of consideration not solely to be seen as animal protection issues but as policy and justice concerns that touch across different areas of public policy and justice systems' responses to violence. However, discussion of animal rights requires consideration of a range of different concepts:

- protection from harm
- legal rights
- rights of personhood and not to be considered a thing?
- citizenship
- legal protection from unnecessary suffering.

Thus at this stage it is important to question what are animal rights, and what mechanisms need to be included in justice systems before it can be determined that animal rights have been provided? Rollin (2006) in attempting to define animal rights argued that animals have a right to have their interests considered by humans and that as sentient beings in possession of a life they also have a right to that life and an interest in avoiding suffering. To illustrate this he argued:

> As a very simple example to which most people would agree, we might point out that a captive giraffe has a right to a cage in which it can stand straight up. (Assume for the moment that we have a right to keep animals captive at all.) Or a bird surely has a right to fly, and keeping a bird captive in a small cage that prevents this is immoral in much the same way as is not allowing a person to express himself or herself verbally (humans being linguistic beings by their nature).

> (2006: 118)

Rollin's argument acknowledges that animal rights are not absolute. He accepts, for example, that animal use might be permitted in some circumstances but identifies that where this is the case 'such use must take cognizance of the animal's nature into account' (Rollin, 2006: 188). The mechanics of doing so, often require codification of animal rights through the law and associated regulations, although currently there is no agreed upon binding definition of animal rights (Nurse, 2013a). The 1975 Universal Declaration of Animal Rights attempted to have specific rights for animals codified into international law via recommendations that animals should have:

- Legal Rights, specifically:

  o Right to live
  o Right to freedom
  o Right to home (for wild animals)
  o Freedom from cruel or inhumane treatment
  o Freedom of expression rights
  o Minimum standards of animal welfare
  o Governmental responsibility for animal rights
  o The outlawing of animal experimentation.

The original declaration failed although a revised Declaration of Animal Rights written in 2011 by Aylam Orian seeks to expand on and update these rights. (The full text of the declaration is available online at: http://declarationofar. org). In addition to the original rights outlined earlier, the new declaration proclaims that:

- All animals have the right to eat, sleep, be physically and psychologically comfortable, be mobile, healthy, safe, and fulfil all their natural and essential needs. As such, all animals are to be free from hunger, thirst, and malnutrition; physical discomfort and exhaustion; confinement against their will, bad treatment, abusive or cruel actions; pain, injury and disease; fear and distress; and free to express their normal patterns of behaviour.
- All animals have the right to reproduce, live with their offspring, families, tribes or communities, and maintain a natural social life. They have the right to live in their natural environment, grow to a rhythm natural to their species, and maintain a life that corresponds to their natural longevity.
- Animals are not the property or commodity of humans, and are not theirs to use for their benefit or sustenance. Therefore, they are to be free from slavery, exploitation, oppression, victimization, brutality, abuse, and any other treatment that disregards their safety, own free will and dignity. They should not be slaughtered for food, killed for their skins, experimented on, killed for religious purposes, used for forced labour, abused and killed for sport and entertainment, abused for commercial profit, hunted, persecuted or exterminated for human pleasure, need, or other ends.

- Humans shall do whatever is within their means to protect all animals. Any animal who is dependent on a human, has the right to proper sustenance and care, and shall not be neglected, abandoned, or killed.
- Animals that have died must be treated with respect and dignity, as humans are.

Thus the proposed contemporary declaration not only provides for basic freedoms for animals and protection from cruelty, it also considers whether animals are deserving of some form of legal personhood status that gives them rights that should, and could, be actively upheld. The following sections discuss these ideas in more detail, and the subsequent section on animal protection law considers the extent to which such ideas are becoming enshrined in law through the imposition of duties to provide animal welfare and the creation of offences relating to a failure to consider animals' needs (Nurse and Ryland, 2014; Schaffner, 2011).

Legal Rights, Legal Personhood and Animal Welfare Protections

While animal rights are often spoken of as being legal rights commensurate with legal personhood, it is worth distinguishing between giving animals the same rights as humans, and a distinct form of legal personhood and the recognition of certain rights that animals may have which are arguably already enshrined in law. The argument for giving animals legal personhood is fairly well established. Wise (2000: 49) argues that:

> Every human has the basic legal right to bodily integrity. We are all legally disabled from invading each other's bodies without consent. Every human has the basic right to bodily liberty as well, so that we're legally disabled from enslaving and kidnapping each other … But no nonhuman has these rights.

In part, Wise's argument is that animals, legally classified as property or things, are unable to assert rights or have them properly protected on their behalf. Arguably, resolving this issue requires providing animals with legal status such that they acquire rights as legal persons. Currently, for example, animals cannot be victims of a crime because they lack the required legal status for their suffering to be recognized within contemporary justice systems' perceptions of victimhood (Hall, 2013; Nurse, 2013a). Sunstein (2004: 7) argues that laws might be reformed so that 'animals would be represented by human beings, just like any other litigant who lacks ordinary (human) competence; for example, the interests of children are protected by prosecutors, and also by trustees and guardians in private litigation brought on children's behalf.' In the context of discussing crimes against animals, Sunstein's argument makes sense. That animals do not have direct recourse through the law for the harms visited upon them is speciesist (Beirne, 2007; Sollund, 2012) and represents a form of discrimination against a crime or harm victim purely on the grounds that the victim is nonhuman. Thus justice systems arguably fail to provide redress for all victims of crime. Yet a question remains concerning whether legal personhood is the only mechanism through which animal harms and abuse might be addressed.

In *The Case for Animal Rights* (2004) Tom Regan distinguishes legal rights from moral rights but effectively argues that animals should be granted the same (or similar) rights to humans because they have value. Regan contests the basic assumption that animals do not have rights in his 2007 argument on the case for the abolition of vivisection. Here, Regan compared the experimentation on the children of Willowbrook State Mental Hospital to experimentation on animals and observed that poor standards of treatment and welfare are sometimes 'justified' on the basis that the victims are not fully aware and thus lack possession of and capability to exercise the appropriate rights. But in comparing experimentation on the seriously mentally retarded children of Willowbrook Mental Hospital to experiments on animals, Regan suggested that 'logically we cannot claim that harms done to the children violate their rights, but the harms done to these animals do not' (Regan, 2007: 131). Regan's point was that both child abuse and animal abuse represent a violation of rights that requires a remedy given that both children and animals are subjects-of-a-life with similar interests in avoiding suffering. However, Sunstein observes that in many cases, animal abuse provides for action to be taken under existing law (discussed later in this chapter) albeit the offence that might be prosecuted relates not to specific animal rights but instead to committing a prohibited act (e.g. torture, cruelty or even damage to another's property when involving a companion animal). Although, such anti-cruelty or property laws provide a form of protection in respect of prohibiting animal abuse and either providing a means of punishing an offender through the criminal law or allowing an animal 'owner' to take action for damage or harm caused to a companion animal. 'Owner' is, however, a somewhat contested term in relation to human—animal relationships although its use is widespread within animal protection law. Species justice discourse generally prefers the term 'companion' and to use 'companion animal' rather than 'pet' to describe those nonhumans that share a home with a human.

Sunstein (2004: 4–5) observes that in relation to defining the nature of animal rights and animal protection, two camps exist:

> Some people insist on the protection of *animal welfare*. Others seek *animal rights*. [Emphasis in original] Animal welfare advocates argue for stronger laws preventing cruelty and requiring humane treatments. The American Society for the Prevention

of Cruelty to Animals is committed to this basic approach. By contrast, animal rights advocates oppose any and all human 'use' of animals. They invoke the Kantian idea that human beings should be treated as ends, not means – but they extend the idea to animals, so as to challenge a wide range of current practices.

Sunstein (2004) identifies that this latter conception on animal rights promotes an end to rodeos, circuses, zoos and use of animals in agriculture by enshrining in law the legal status of animals to be considered entities in their own right and free from human subjugation. Thus animal rights theories argue that it is only through providing animals with *actual* rights that animal abuse and cruelty would be ended despite the fact that each US state has an animal anti-cruelty statute and animal welfare and anti-cruelty laws exist in most Western or Global North jurisdictions. Tannenbaum (1995: 167) has argued that anti-cruelty pro-visions in these laws 'create legal duties to nonhuman animals. They therefore afford legal rights to nonhuman animals', although this is clearer in jurisdic-tions that recognize animals as sentient beings (Nurse and Ryland, 2014). It should be noted however that there are problems with enforcing these rights and there are numerous limitations and exemptions. Frasch (2000) explains that the principle behind much of the legislation is concern for the human actor and the wider community because denying animals rights and the subse-quent cruelty and abuse that is permitted due to the absence of rights might lead to violence towards humans (discussed later in this chapter).

The UK's Animal Welfare Act 2006 arguably comes close to providing animal rights by enshrining a duty to provide animal welfare in the law (Nurse and Ryland, 2014). The Act requires companion-animal owners to consider the needs of their individual animal rather than adopting a standard approach to companion animals. In doing so it provides for a new form of owner/compan-ion relationship. The Act requires owners and those 'responsible' for companion animals to know how their companions should behave when healthy so that they tailor their homes to suit the needs of any companion where possible. Indeed UK government guidance makes clear the responsibilities to provide for a suitable environment, suitable diet, and the ability to exhibit normal behaviour patterns and to be protected from pain, suffering and disease (Nurse and Ryland, 2014). In passing the Animal Welfare Act 2006 the UK recognizes that animals are sentient beings, not merely commodities, and has confirmed its commitment to the highest possible standards of animal welfare. Yet despite the UK having some of the strongest animal welfare legislation in the world, it has yet to provide animals with actual legal personhood. However, efforts to do this are currently taking place in the Americas, shining a spotlight on the com-plexity of Western animal protection laws that offer high levels of protection from cruelty but which generally still treat animals as property. Here are two recent cases, arguably with very different outcomes, that illustrate contempo-rary debates on providing legal personhood for animals, a notion generally resisted by legislators and jurists (Wise, 2000).

Case Study 2.1 Nonhuman Rights Project Inc. vs Lavery Appellate Court Hearing 518336

This case, usually referred to as the 'Tommy the Chimp' case, was heard by the New York Supreme Court in late 2014. The case was brought by the Nonhuman Rights Project (NhRP)[1] who petitioned the court to issue a writ of habeas corpus granting Tommy the chimp the right to bodily liberty. Tommy is a chimpanzee who, at time of writing, is kept caged within a warehouse in Johnstown, New York. The NhRP argues that Tommy is being unlawfully imprisoned and therefore being deprived of his fundamental legal right to bodily liberty.

Arguing for legal rights for Tommy is essentially about arguing whether Tommy can be legally classed as a 'person'. Importantly, this is not necessarily the same as arguing that Tommy as a sentient being is *exactly* the same as a human, but is about whether Tommy as a sentient being should have the same rights as other legal persons. The presentation of this case in New York relates to the New York Court of Appeals having previously concluded that 'legal personhood' is not synonymous with being a human being. However, legal personhood means that the entity counts in civil law and can have their interests protected, NhRP identifies that there are examples of other legal persons that are not human beings including a river, a religious holy book, and a mosque.

The 'Tommy' case is one of three cases filed by the NhRP in December 2013 as the first ever lawsuits filed on behalf of captive chimpanzees. The three suits relate to: Tommy, a 26-year-old chimpanzee; Kiko, also a 26-year-old chimpanzee who is caged in private property in Niagara Falls; and Hercules and Leo, two chimpanzees owned by New Iberia Research Centre and used in biomedical research. NhRP has brought the cases supported by scientific evidence in the form of affidavits demonstrating that chimpanzees are self-aware and autonomous. The scientific evidence argues that chimpanzees have sufficient understanding of their situation and an awareness of their needs to know that they don't want to be caged for life. The cases argue that given their sentience and understanding they are entitled to be recognized as 'legal persons' with certain fundamental legal rights, including a common law right not to be imprisoned. Arguably the situation is similar to that of other groups such as slaves who were previously denied rights on the grounds that they were considered to be property, 'lesser beings' and undeserving of the rights granted to mainstream society. The lawsuits ask the judges to grant the chimpanzees the

---

[1]http://www.nonhumanrightsproject.org/

right to bodily liberty and order that they be moved to a North American Primate Sanctuary Alliance sanctuary member. Alternatively NhRP argue that they should go to Save the Chimps, the world's largest chimpanzee sanctuary located in Fort Pierce, Florida, where they can live out their days with others of their kind in an environment as close to the wild as is possible in North America.

Steven Wise acting for the NhRP commented in his 8 October 2014 closing arguments on Tommy's case that: 'The uncontroverted facts demonstrate that chimpanzees possess the autonomy and self-determination that are supreme common law values that the writ of habeas corpus was constructed to protect. Both common law liberty and equality entitle him to common law habeas corpus personhood' (Mountain, 2014).

In bringing the Tommy case, the NhRP acknowledged that while the case could result in the New York judges deciding that Tommy is a legal person, this was not the only possible outcome. Lawyer Steven Wise has recognized that as this is an appeal, judges could decide that Tommy *could* be a person and refer this issue back to a trial court to decide (Wise, 2014). The court could also decide that Tommy is not a person and never could be, but this opens the door both for a further appeal and for other avenues to be explored. For example, a case could be brought under state law that allows courts to release a privately owned animal if its owner does not maintain conditions required by law. This is similar to provisions in UK law where animals can be seized from persons guilty of animal welfare offences who can also be banned from owning animals in the future. Bodies like the RSPCA who are engaged in animal welfare prosecutions regularly ask for such banning orders (RSPCA, 2015).

Historically, animal cruelty in both the UK and USA has been dealt with by the passing of anti-cruelty legislation rather than by applying existing legal arguments and principles to animals. As the New York state judges have observed, effective animal protection can often be achieved without giving them the same rights as people (Wiessner, 2014). However, as the lawsuits by NhRP quite reasonably ask, why should there be a need for new legislation when existing legal principles can be applied to property (the chimps) as has been the case in the past?

The New York Appeals Court concluded that chimpanzees are not legal persons and so cannot receive the same rights as humans, denying legal personhood to Tommy. The NhRP sought leave to appeal which, at time of writing, has yet to be decided. Early in January 2015 a second New York Appeal Court ruled that habeas corpus was not available in Kiko's case but gave different reasons from those provided in Tommy's case. At time of

(Continued)

(Continued)

writing, the Kiko case is also the subject of an NhRP Motion for leave to appeal to the Court of Appeals. The NhRP has also indicated an intention to pursue appeals in the Hercules and Leo case, which also failed, largely on the grounds that the judge was bound by precedent arising from the Tommy case. However, Wise (2015) notes that New York County Supreme Court Justice Barbara Jaffe's rulings in the Hercules and Leo case are important in a variety of ways, not least in determining 'that a human or corporation (the NhRP) had "standing" to bring a lawsuit directly on behalf of a nonhuman animal without having to allege any injury to human interests'.

Case Study 2.2   Sandra the Orang-utan

In December 2014 an Argentine court was widely reported as having ruled that Sandra the Orang-utan is a 'non-human person' with a legal right to freedom. The case was brought by Argentina's Association of Professional Lawyers for Animal Rights (AFADA) who filed a writ of habeas corpus aiming to end Sandra the Orang-utan's confinement in a Buenos Aires zoo. The legal arguments identified that Sandra possessed cognitive abilities which included 'perception of time, self-awareness, emotional relationships and frustration due to her 20-year confinement in the zoo' (Farone, 2014). Possession of these abilities, as clear evidence of sentience, was argued to provide evidence that Sandra should be considered a person rather than a thing, albeit a 'non-human person'. The court's statement of 18 December 2014 issued by Judges Alejandro W. Slokar and Angela E. Ledesma Esq., stated that 'on a dynamic rather than static interpretation of the law it is necessary to recognize the animal as a subject of rights, because non-human beings (animals) are entitled to rights'.

While it was widely reported in the media that the court's judgment meant that Sandra would be released (see for example Lough, 2014; Reuters, 2014), closer reading of the Argentine judgment suggests that the court did not actually order Sandra's release but gave a judicial opinion that the law could or should be read 'dynamically' so as to give the orang-utan nonhuman legal personhood. This reflects a contemporary judicial application of animal protection laws and other law that arguably now needs to be interpreted in the light of changed social conditions which acknowledge animals' changed status in society. (Justice Jaffe in the Hercules and Leo case similarly cited recent gay marriage case law as evidence on how rights are now extended to a wide range of groups, and concluded that efforts to extend legal rights to chimpanzees are understandable.) Despite the fact that Sandra was not released, the confirmation that judges consider that habeas corpus laws need to be read so as to apply to nonhumans is potentially a significant step forward in respect of the concept of legal personhood for animals.

Garrett (2012: 49) identifies habeas corpus as being 'the "great writ of liberty" that allows a judge to inquire into the legality of a prisoner's detention'. Its use is often linked to discussions of due process, or the requirement to respect a person's legal rights, which in US law is linked to the Due Process Clauses of the Fifth and Fourteenth Amendments, which state that no person shall be deprived of life, liberty, or property 'without due process of law' (Garrett, 2012: 49). In the UK, constitutional scholar Dicey's (1915) concept and rules of the constitution state that a man can be imprisoned for breach of the law but cannot be imprisoned for anything else. Dicey states:

> Liberty is not secure unless the law, in addition to punishing every kind of interference with a man's lawful freedom, provides adequate security that every one who without legal justification is placed in confinement shall be able to get free. This security is provided by the celebrated writ of habeas corpus…

> (Dicey [1915] 1982: 128)

While Dicey's focus was on human liberty, reasonable given that his original text was published in 1885, the principle that 'every one' rather than 'every man' should be able to seek freedom when unlawfully confined, is one that animal rights scholars have embraced when making legal arguments. Applying for writs of habeas corpus represents a legitimate legal tactic to allow the courts to address the concept of legal personhood and unlawful imprisonment without necessarily equating animals with humans. Indeed, as the two cases discussed in this chapter illustrate, the legal argument is not that animals and humans are *exactly* the same, but that animals as sentient beings aware of their surroundings have their own conception of their imprisonment. What the courts must decide is whether this is sufficient that imprisonment of animals in poor conditions is an interference with their freedom or rights while potentially accepting that they are animals not humans. Thus animals may become 'legal persons' and be granted rights while not necessarily being granted the same legal status as human beings. Separate from this, they may be given a form of legal rights and legal protection as the next section illustrates.

Contemporary Animal Protection Law

The reality is that most legal systems provide legal protection for companion animals and livestock, thus it could be argued that some form of species justice and a limited form of rights already exists via animal welfare and anti-cruelty law (Nurse, 2013a). Within the UK, some (but not all) wildlife and animal protection law comes within the remit of the criminal law. In other words, offences against animals form part of the public law and are, in theory at least, prosecuted by the state as crimes.

But questions of how far animals should be protected by the law and how justice systems should respond to both domestic animal abuse and wildlife crime are topics of debate with species-justice discourse as well as by animal law scholars. Schaffner (2011: 10) notes that:

> As a general matter, animals are characterized as 'things' under the law in most countries. Notably the European Union in the Treaty of Amsterdam and most recently in the Lisbon Treaty defined animals as 'sentient beings.' However, other countries, including the United States, have not legally recognized animals as sentient beings. In these countries, animals may be owned and used by humans solely for human purposes. This fact is critical to an understanding of the legal treatment of animals in every respect.

Schaffner's point is illustrated by the reality that in practice much animal protection and wildlife law is enforced on a voluntary basis or as non-mainstream crime, relying on NGOs to carry out much of the enforcement work and generally carrying lower penalties than mainstream crimes against the person or property. Yet crimes against animals are sometimes linked to crimes against humans (see p. 37–40) and can involve considerable cruelty and violence. As a result, animal offenders are precisely the kind of violent offender that society needs to be protected against and some notions of species justice contend that an effective system of species justice is essential as part of protecting wider society not just animals (see for example, Sollund, 2012; Beirne, 2007).

As this chapter illustrates, some animal rights theorists argue that animals should have the same legal rights as humans, whereas others argue that animals should be protected only so far as animal needs correspond with human ones. There are also complex questions concerning how to deal with the criminality involved given that there are different types of animal offender (Nurse, 2013a) and that some crimes against animals are committed at a state level. Nurse (2013a: 7) summarizes the general legal position as follows:

> International law sets out the obligations on states in respect of legal standards for animal protection. The primary international law mechanisms are treaties and conventions (Schaffner 2011). Yet at present there is no binding international treaty for the protection of animals and thus no clear international legal standard on animal protection. Instead, it is down to individual states to decide the content of their

animal protection laws either through public or private law mechanisms, which either consider animals to be worthy of state protection and public enforcement of animal harm (via public law) or as property subject to civil law allowing individuals rather than the state to resolve potential animal harm problems (via private law). Thus levels of animal protection vary from country to country or even on a regional basis where municipal authorities have law-making powers (e.g. state or province laws within the United States, Canada and Australia) dependent on the legislative approach taken and the extent to which cultural perspectives on animal harm are incorporated into legislation.

Contemporary animal protection law is primarily concerned with preventing cruelty to animals and applying animal welfare standards to the relationship between humans and animals, particularly in respect of companion animals and livestock. Radford (2001: 7) argues that the central thread running through UK animal protection legislation is the offence of 'unnecessary' suffering. Schaffner, primarily examining the position in the USA agrees, stating that 'the United States anti-cruelty laws are criminal laws and comprise the most basic and fundamental legal protection for animals. As the least controversial of the animal protection laws, these laws protect animals from the intentional and gratuitous infliction of pain and suffering at the hands of humans' (2011: 22). While Schaffner notes that animals used for food and research and wild animals (discussed further in Chapter 4) are generally exempt from anti-cruelty laws, generally these laws protect animals from pain and suffering whether inflicted deliberately or as a result of an act of omission. The specific wording of anti-cruelty legislation in the USA varies by state, but is broadly commensurate with the historical definition of unnecessary suffering used in UK legislation that relates to physical pain. Thus, anti-cruelty statutes generally prohibit:

- torture
- the causing of physical pain, for example by hitting, kicking or stabbing an animal
- starving, dehydrating or suffocating an animal
- keeping an animal in unsuitable conditions that negatively impact on its health
- abandonment
- overworking an animal.

The list of factors generally applies in a manner that provides that the causing of pain and suffering to animals should be actively avoided except in those cases where a limited amount of suffering is accepted as integral to a permitted activity. So, for example, necessary veterinary treatment may cause some temporary pain or discomfort to an animal and would be permitted by both UK and US anti-cruelty or animal protection law, as would animal suffering that occurs during 'normal' animal husbandry practices. As indicated earlier in this chapter, Nurse and Ryland (2014) have observed that whereas most anti-cruelty laws are prohibitive or negative (they specify what you *cannot* do to animals) the UK's Animal Welfare Act 2006 imposes a *positive* duty to provide animal welfare. Thus as Nurse and Ryland indicate (2014: 3) owners or those responsible for companion animals now have a positive obligation to ensure their welfare and to provide for each of their animal's basic needs, which includes: providing adequate food and water; veterinary treatment; and an appropriate environment in which to live. UK law now also extends the definition of unnecessary suffering to include both the active and passive nature of an offence. Nurse and Ryland's analysis concludes that the UK concept of unnecessary suffering 'is wide in scope and includes mental as well as physical suffering. Thus it is an offence unnecessarily to infuriate or terrify a protected animal in addition to, or instead of, causing physical pain' (2014: 2). Schaffner identifies that in considering animal suffering under the Animal Welfare Act 2006 a range of factors need to be taken into account in determining whether the suffering was 'unnecessary' as follows:

- whether the suffering could have been reduced or avoided;
- whether any suffering was the result of conduct carried out in compliance with the law or a regulated practice;
- whether the suffering was the result of a legitimate purpose which includes veterinary treatment but also the protection of another person or animal;
- whether the suffering was proportionate to the purpose for which it occurred;
- whether the conduct causing the suffering was that of a reasonably competent and humane person.

(2011: 26–7)

As indicated earlier, these considerations apply not just to the care of animals in the home but also to animals undergoing veterinary treatment. Where animals are being used for scientific research, states generally license this activity requiring researchers to keep animals in appropriate conditions that are often subject to inspection with the possibility of revoking a licence where appropriate standards are not maintained. Thus even officially 'endorsed' animal use might give rise to offences and be subject to regulatory control that provides animals with some protection, albeit continued use of animals for scientific and medical research frustrates the principle of animals as having legal rights that provides them with freedom from suffering and human exploitation.

Consideration of animal abuse identifies wider species justice concerns and the importance of animal abuse to mainstream justice. Green criminologists (e.g. Benton, 1998; Beirne, 1999; White, 2007) have recognized the link between environmental and animal protection laws and societal concerns over violence towards human subjects; a core interest of mainstream criminology and justice systems. Criminological research has shown that there is a link between animal cruelty and violence towards nonhuman animals and violence towards humans. Promoting good animal welfare and preventing animal cruelty thus has benefits for society not only in preventing possible violence towards humans but also in protecting and improving society by improving the way we protect and live in harmony with the environment and create a strongly institutionalized protection of universal civil liberties (Nurse, 2013a).

The Link between Animal Abuse and Interpersonal Violence

Despite the anti-cruelty legislation mentioned earlier in this chapter, animal abuse remains a significant societal concern and a core issue in animal crime. Latest figures from the UK's Royal Society for the Prevention of Cruelty to Animals (RSPCA) show an increase in the number of people convicted of animal cruelty and neglect in England and Wales in 2013. The RSPCA reports that it secured 3961 convictions in 2013 and investigated 153,770 cruelty complaints, while over a million and a quarter calls (1,327,849) were received (RSPCA, 2015). Figures from the Australian RSPCA show a total of 58,591 cruelty complaints investigated in the financial year 2013–14, an increase over 2012's figure of 49,861 (RSPCA Australia, 2014). In both jurisdictions, the actual scale of animal abuse is likely much higher. As with other forms of crime, only a percentage of the total amount of abuse is likely to be reported to official agencies while a larger amount of crime that is known to those involved will be kept secret and dealt with (which sometimes means covered up) within the family.

The rising levels of both convictions and calls are significant because animal abuse has societal implications beyond the direct harm caused to the animals involved. The reality of animal abuse is that much of its investigation and prosecution is still carried out by NGOs like the respective RSPCA's rather than mainstream criminal justice agencies, despite the fact that animal abuse constitutes criminal behaviour. Researchers in the USA and UK have determined that there are clear links between animal abuse and other forms of interpersonal violence, to the extent that many of those who begin by abusing animals go on to commit crimes against humans (Linzey, 2009).

However, the relationship between offences against animals and human violence is complex and is not as simple as saying that animal abusers will automatically become violent offenders or serial killers; albeit media discourse frequently reports the link as near absolute. There are several different elements to the link between animal abuse and human violence so that some animal abusers may also engage in child abuse, some in spousal abuse and some in stranger violence. Others may confine their offending activities to animal abuse especially where their abuse is linked to employment (Nurse, 2011).

Thus when considering the nature and impact of animal abuse and its links with other forms of crime it becomes necessary to consider the type of abuse, the cause of the abuse and the setting in which it occurs.

The Progression Thesis and Domestic Violence

The basic context of the link between animal abuse and human violence is one of progression; an escalation from animal abuse to interpersonal violence. Consideration of good standards of animal welfare and anti-cruelty laws within a species justice and green criminological context requires examining 'what such treatment indicates about the abuser – namely a propensity to violence that might ultimately lead to violence against humans' (Lubinski, 2004). The progression thesis effectively requires a combination of two separate causal propositions:

1. those who abuse animals are more likely to commit interpersonal violence towards humans; and
2. those who commit interpersonal violence are more likely to have previously abused animals.

In that regard, one important perspective often overlooked in the debate on animal welfare is that promoting good animal welfare and respect for animals has the 'tangible' benefit of preventing violence towards humans and anti-social behaviour that has a negative impact on society (Nurse, 2013a). This perspective has become an increasingly important consideration in US public policy where the FBI and other law enforcement agencies use animal cruelty as one indicator of *possible* further offending in dangerousness assessments, particularly when assessing anti-social and psychopathic personality disorders. In some US states, social services and other healthcare and social policy professionals are now involved in interventions designed to prevent juvenile offenders involved in animal cruelty offences from escalating to other forms of violence (Linzey, 2009). The public policy objective pursued by such studies and policy interventions in the USA is that dealing with animal welfare offenders and strictly enforcing animal cruelty laws benefits society by preventing further crimes against society. Some US states also hold animal abuse registers, viewing animal offenders in the same category as paedophiles (Nurse, 2013a).

Theorists from different perspectives within animal rights debates have identified that: the reduction of animal cruelty, prevention of animal abuse and provision of equal consideration for animals and humans alike benefits society by creating a society that is increasingly cruelty free. Thus, cruelty towards both nonhuman animals and humans is less likely to occur and is not tolerated when it does. In some respects this mirrors criminological *control* theory, which argues that some crime is prevented due to the formal and informal controls that operate within a community, so that crime which harms the community is not tolerated and the community actively engages with law enforcement agencies to prevent crime. Thus, criminologists and law enforcement professionals have increasingly become interested in animal welfare issues (specifically animal abuse and animal cruelty) as a potential risk factor in violence towards humans. Thus, returning to Beirne's (1999) assessment of the importance of animal abuse; its value to criminological enquiry is that it could identify those who potentially present a threat to human populations in addition to the danger they pose to nonhuman animals.

Patterson (2002) theorizes that 'since violence begets violence, the enslavement of animals injected a higher level of domination and coercion into human history by creating oppressive hierarchical societies and unleashing large-scale warfare never seen before.' His thinking, commensurate with the progression thesis, asks whether human '"enslavement"' of animals was the first step on the road to the Holocaust. In this respect, Patterson effectively argues that better treatment of animals and effective animal welfare laws are necessary to minimize breakdowns in society. However, the argument that individuals' progress in their offending from animals to humans, that crime is individualistic and is often characterized by an escalation from minor offending to serious offending is potentially too simplistic. Beirne (2004) argues that the progression thesis is actually two separate propositions; one is that 'those who abuse animals must be more likely than those who do not subsequently to act violently toward humans. In the other, those who act violently toward humans must be more likely than those who do not previously to have abused animals' (2004: 40). Beirne's qualification identifies that it is not always the case that those who abuse animals progress on to human violence (Nurse, 2013a) but that in some circumstances this is a likely outcome. The characteristics of the offender and the specific circumstances in which the violence is taking place are all factors in determining when and whether animal abuse escalates into human violence (Henry, 2004).

Nurse (2013a: 93) describes how in a landmark 1963 article in the *American Journal of Psychiatry*, 'Macdonald identified three specific behavioural characteristics associated with sociopathic behaviour; animal cruelty, obsession with fire starting and bedwetting (past age five). The "MacDonald Triad" was instrumental in linking these activities to violent behaviours, particularly homicide; identifying cruelty to animals as a *possible* indicator of future violent behaviour.' Nurse further identifies that subsequent studies 'have confirmed that cruelty to animals is a common behaviour in children and adolescents who grow up to become violent criminals and, in the case of adults who abuse animals, it can indicate a violent or abusive family dynamic, where harm is inflicted on weaker or more vulnerable family members who may be unable to defend themselves'

(Nurse, 2013a: 93). Particularly in the case of domestic violence, acts of animal abuse might be used to intimidate, control or coerce women and children within an abusive relationship either to accede to a perpetrator's demands or desires or to keep silent about the abuse they are suffering.

Beyond the conception of animal abuse as an indicator of future offending, it is also worth considering what animal abuse indicates in relation to other offending that might be present within a domestic setting. The neglect or harm inherent in animal abuse so frequently occurs in the abuse of other family members to the extent that where animal abuse occurs it is more *likely* that other forms of abuse will also be happening (Clawson, 2009; Arluke and Luke, 1997; Hutton, 1997; Ascione, 1993). For example, US research published in 1997 which sampled around 50 battered women's shelters found that 84% of the shelters surveyed confirmed that women who came to the shelters talked about incidents of pet abuse, 63% confirmed that children who came to the shelters talked about pet abuse and 83% of the shelters confirmed the coexistence of domestic abuse and pet abuse (Ascione et al., 1997). Other researchers have drawn similar conclusions and the US researchers also found that some women experiencing domestic abuse were reluctant to leave the family home in those cases where a shelter was unable to take a pet, as this would mean leaving a vulnerable companion animal behind to suffer further abuse. As Mumsnet and the Women's Alliance were reported as saying in *The Guardian* recently (Doward, 2012), the vast majority of women suffering domestic violence do not go into refuges and for many it is a last resort.

In addition, the effect of animal abuse and domestic violence on children is such that children may become involved in animal abuse not just in respect of their own propensity to commit violence (Felthous and Kellert, 1987; Ascione, 1993) but also as a reaction to the violence they observe and are subject to. Children learn appropriate behaviours from observing adults, thus witnessing domestic violence and companion animal abuse may compromise children's psychological (and moral) development and normalize a propensity for interpersonal violence and cruelty to animals. Weber (1964) identified the hierarchical nature of power within the family and its association with distinct family roles, primarily based around the father as the central power conduit within families (Nurse 2013a: 94). While contemporary family dynamics have developed, male power and masculinities remain significant factors in domestic violence and animal abuse. Thus children's animal abuse can be a reaction to domestic violence and animal abuse and may be a form of stress offending, as acting out and externalizing witnessed violence are mechanisms through which children deal with the stress of having witnessed marital violence, make sense of what they have witnessed or seek the attention of the adults engaged in marital violence. Thus, in some contexts, child animal abusers are themselves victims; their animal abuse providing an indicator of other forms of existing domestic violence.

Summary

This chapter identifies animal abuse and animal protection as core concerns of criminal justice systems. Despite the fact that animal crimes often remain at the margins of criminal justice, much animal abuse is prohibited by law and forms part of the criminal law in various jurisdictions where it constitutes a criminal offence. While Schaffner (2011) indicates that much animal law continues to treat animals as property, Nurse and Ryland (2014) indicate a changing conception in animals' status, typified by the EU's acceptance of animals as sentient beings, and further enshrined in the UK's Animal Welfare Act 2006 that requires consideration of the needs of the individual animal.

However, there remains a distinction between animal rights and animal welfare such that while legal systems generally provide animals with protection from unnecessary suffering and acts of cruelty (by act or omission) this is not quite the same as providing animals with *actual* rights. While in some contexts the difference is a technical one given that animal protection laws target the same actions as might be targeted by rights proponents, Wise (2000) and the lawsuits of the NhRP illustrate that welfare protection fails to provide for freedoms and bodily liberty. Thus while protected from excessive cruelty, animals are still subject to human control and exploitation, something that can arguably only be resolved by granting legal personhood.

This chapter also identifies that species justice (Nurse, 2013a; Beirne, 2007, 1999; Benton, 1998) goes beyond purely animal concerns and has significant overlap with human ones. Despite the evidence of a growing body of research that consistently shows clear links between animal abuse and other forms of domestic abuse such as spousal or child abuse, animal abuse continues to be seen as an animal welfare problem, at least in the UK. There are complex questions concerning the extent to which animal abuse serves as an indicator for criminal justice and social welfare organizations that there are likely other forms of harm present which indicate that animal abuse should be dealt with as mainstream criminal justice by the courts, the police and the public.

However, the FBI and selected other justice agencies now recognize animal abuse as an indicator of anti-social behaviour and there is evidence that some criminal justice agencies accept the progression thesis and incorporate it into their offender assessments, although others question its validity. Thus questions remain over how best to deal with animal abusers and the importance attached to animal abuse by criminal justice systems. In particular:

- Should animal abuse by young offenders be the subject of early intervention by the criminal justice system and social welfare or health professionals?
- What form should any criminal justice intervention or 'treatment' of animal abusers take?

- How can the links between animal abuse and other forms of domestic abuse be addressed and given the range of 'justice' agencies already involved in these areas who should take the lead?
- How should legal systems deal with animal abuse and how does it link in with other areas of law?

These and other questions are at the heart of social policy and criminal justice discussions about the importance of animal abuse. However, there is evidence that criminal justice systems are increasingly embracing the importance of animal abuse as a specific area of crime and within contemporary discourse on applying a green perspective to crime and justice.

Self-study Questions

1. Critically evaluate the links between animal abuse and violence towards humans. What evidence exists that animal abuse and human violence are linked and what are the links?
2. What are the primary causes of violence towards animals? Consider theory in your answer and discuss the extent to which animal abuse is about animals or raises other concerns/issues.
3. 'Animal abuse is an animal welfare issue that should be the subject of attention by animal welfare charities.' Critically evaluate this statement and consider the social implications of animal abuse in doing so.
4. Some US states have begun to introduce animal abuse registers identifying animal abusers in much the same way as they do sex offenders. Discuss the value of this 'naming and shaming' approach and its likely success in dealing with animal abuse. In doing so, consider the progression thesis.

3

THE CAUSES OF ENVIRONMENTAL CRIME AND CRIMINALITY

By the end of this chapter you should:

- Understand the varied nature of environmental criminality and its causes.
- Have a firm understanding of the key theories that explain environmental offending and the contexts in which they can and should be applied.
- Understand key debates concerning environmental criminality and its causes.
- Understand key debates on environmental offending as deliberate, accidental or unintended and on non-compliance as a form of entrepreneurship.
- Understand the distinction between criminality and regulatory or technical breaches and how behaviour that infringes different types of legislation are viewed.

Introduction

This chapter discusses the causes of environmental criminality by examining key debates concerning the reasons why environmental crimes occur, as well as theoretical discussions on environmental offending. Conventional criminology is perhaps dominated by discussions of street crime and serious offending related to crimes of violence, sexual offences and the activities of organized crime; particularly in the areas of drugs, weapons and people trafficking

(Lea and Young, 1993). As Chapter 1 indicates, much mainstream criminological discourse is concerned with individualistic offending and is anthropocentric in nature, dominated by human concerns and human victims.

By contrast, much environmental crime is corporate in nature and concerns the behaviour of legal actors, legitimate corporations engaged in lawful, state-supported activities. Thus immediate differences can be found between environmental crime and mainstream crime in conceptions of both offender and criminality. Offenders in mainstream crime are generally regarded as deviants by both society and criminal justice agencies, whereas corporate environmental offenders are frequently characterized as having committed technical, regulatory offences and are often not subject to the attention of mainstream criminal justice agencies.

Chapter 3 discusses these issues, noting that the distinction between the legal and illegal is sometimes blurred, but also noting that the legal often facilitates the illegal. This chapter primarily considers corporate environmental offending in respect of pollution and hazardous and toxic waste although brief preliminary mention is made of the causes of wildlife crime, albeit that topic is dealt with in more detail in Chapter 4, while criminality associated with the oil and gas extraction industries, the timber trade and biopiracy is dealt with in Chapter 6.

Protecting the Environment

There are a number of international environmental conventions, mechanisms put in place requiring states to provide for effective environmental protection, which create broad environmental protection regimes and are designed to prevent environmental crimes. Nurse (2015a) identifies that such international laws represent a consensus among nation states that, despite arguably belonging to no one, the environment and natural resources should be protected both for their intrinsic value and for the benefit of future (human) generations. This requires mechanisms that implement protection of the environment as benefiting communities where natural resource exploitation occurs, often through human rights mechanisms as well as environmental ones. Voiculescu and Yanacopulos (2011) identify the United Nations (UN) as being at the forefront of devising universally acceptable standards to embed 'respect for human rights norms and abstention from corrupt practices' into business and transnational corporations' operating practices (2011: 4). Their observation is based on the idea that environmental damage is predominantly committed by corporations who fall outside the remit of much criminal law and are subject only to civil or administrative sanctions. However, despite such international agreements, the reality is that environmental protection in practice is implemented via state law (discussed further in Chapter 5). Thus, taking cultural and social differences into account, different countries have different laws and 'frequently quite different approaches to dealing with environmental crime' (White, 2007: 184). Environmental crime is also not always dealt with by mainstream criminal justice agencies such as the police, and in many countries falls within the jurisdiction of the enforcement arm of the state environment department, rather than being integrated into mainstream criminal justice (Nurse, 2015a, 2013b).

Western conceptions of environmentalism and the need to protect the planet and criminalize environmentally damaging actions are not universally shared and the concept of criminal environmental activity is a relatively new concept. As Nurse (2013a) observes, Brown Weiss (1993) identified that until the 1960s environmental issues were viewed as state concerns and there was a lack of appreciation of the need for international environmental agreements. The Convention on International Trade in Endangered Species of Flora and Fauna (CITES) was one of the first and oldest international legal agreements on environmental issues; it provided a framework for future wildlife and animal protection measures (Zimmerman, 2003). Attempting to provide a framework for international environmental protection, the UN General Assembly adopted a World Charter for Nature in 1982, which contains the following five principles of conservation:

- Nature shall be respected and its essential processes should be unimpaired.
- Population levels of wild and domesticated species should be at least sufficient for their survival and habitats should be safeguarded to ensure this.
- Special protection should be given to the habitats of rare and endangered species and the five principles of conservation should apply to all areas of land and sea.
- Man's utilization of land and marine resources should be sustainable and should not endanger the integrity or survival of other species.
- Nature shall be secured against degradation caused by warfare or other hostile activities.

In principle, the UN Charter provides a mechanism for protecting the environment (and animals) from harm by providing a conservation framework that requires active protection of nature. However, in practice, implementation of the Charter relies on national environmental protection and biodiversity laws that contain enforcement mechanisms and provide a framework for conservation enforcement. Nevertheless, Sections 21–24 of the Charter provide authority for individuals to enforce international conservation laws that could provide for some environmental protection and has been used by NGOs as a basis on which to conduct direct action to prevent animal harm (Nurse, 2013a; Roeschke, 2009).

Regional environmental legislation also exists. For example, the Treaty on the Functioning of the European Union (TFEU) provides a framework for environmental protection across the EU, dictating minimum penalties for environmental offences in accordance with Article 175 of the Treaty establishing the European Community. TFEU requires Member States to treat certain intentional or seriously negligent acts which breach Community rules on protecting the environment as criminal offences. EU legislation includes provisions prohibiting the following:

- the unauthorised discharge of hydrocarbons, waste oils or sewage sludge into water and the emission of a certain quantity of dangerous substances into the air, soil or water;
- the treatment, transport, storage and elimination of hazardous waste;
- the discharge of waste on or into land or into water, including the improper operation of a landfill site;
- the possession and taking of, or trading in protected wild fauna and flora species;
- the deterioration of a protected habitat;
- trade in ozone-depleting substances.

The EU requires criminal penalties to be effective, proportionate and dissuasive and to apply both to persons convicted of breaching Community law as well as persons involved in such offences or inciting others to commit them (Nurse 2015a: 52–3). Thus an obligation exists on states to ensure effective environmental protection and which arguably regulates Member State environmental protection and failure to provide such protection. This is discussed further in Chapter 5 although the quality and nature of regulation is of relevance to this chapter's discussion of the causes of environmental crime.

As Chapter 2 illustrates, green laws, and particularly protective laws, often specify prohibited activities, while this chapter indicates that international law sets out the obligations on states in respect of legal standards, with the primary international law mechanisms being treaties and conventions (Schaffner, 2011). In the field of environmental law, a range of different laws both national and international prohibit specific action deemed to harm the environment. However, environmental laws also incorporate the idea of *sustainability*, a concept which identifies that use of natural resources is permitted only so far as those resources (including wildlife) are not exhausted. Chapter 5 details the obligations on states where environmental protection is concerned and also discusses how state wrongdoing or failures in environmental protection might be addressed. However, for the purposes of this chapter's discussion of environmental crime causes, it is worth noting that, generally, states have an obligation to prevent environmental crime and to create a system of sanctions (or punishments) in respect of environmental crime. States should also provide for a system of monitoring and investigating environmental offences (discussed in Chapter 9). The extent to which a state has effective environmental law, regulation and enforcement systems is crucial in its level of environmental crime given that weak enforcement regimes are considered a primary cause of environmental crime (Situ and Emmons, 2000).

Quinney's idea of crime as a social construction identified that acts defined as crime are, for the most part, behaviours undertaken by relatively powerless social actors (Quinney, 1970). But the response to these actions and the way that knowledge and understanding of them is collected, collated and disseminated by different groups determines our understanding of crime. However, environmental crime is often a crime of the powerful, committed by corporations, organized crime groups and others who constitute powerful social actors with access to capital and the benefits of globalized markets (Lynch and Stretsky, 2014; South and Wyatt, 2011). Situ and Emmons (2000) identify that environmental crime is predominantly a civil matter; in other words fines and administrative penalties are the main technique for dealing with environmental crime. The reason given for this is a perceived lack of effective international law and the reliance on national (state) legislators to define what environmental crime is and how it should be dealt with. The result is often that it is not seen as a priority criminal justice issue. However, Lynch and Stretsky (2014: 7) point out that 'green harms are the most important concerns in modern society because they cause the most harm, violence, damage and loss'. While acknowledging that much environmental harm is the result of lawful activity, or at least activity not defined or controlled by the criminal law, Lynch and Stretsky argue that the very nature of environmental harm as activity that has wide-reaching impacts makes it worthy of dedicated criminological attention which it seldom receives. Implicit in their analysis is a criticism of traditional criminology's limitations dictated by narrow concerns of 'crime' as solely being activities defined as such by the criminal law and of justice systems' failure to deal with major environmental harms such as pollution.

Pollution and Waste Offences

White and Heckenberg define pollution as 'contamination of the soil, water or the atmosphere by the discharge of harmful substances that adversely affect the environment' (2014: 157). Their definition acknowledges that pollution can be deliberate or accidental and may be the incidental by-product of otherwise lawful operations. Indeed they go so far as to identify that global capitalism is inherently polluting; given the extent of globalized production and consumption. Lynch and Stretsky (2014) echo this idea; identifying that human industrial and consumerist activity generates an extraordinary amount of pollution seemingly without due regard to the consequences of such activity on ecosystems and future generations.

However, this chapter's concern is primarily with the causes of *illegal* pollution; offences against regulatory mechanisms and existing legislation, rather than the wider harms caused by polluting human activities, which are, in part, dealt with in Chapter 7's discussion of climate change and global warming as areas of criminological concern. As with animal and wildlife offences, most Global North jurisdictions have some form of legislation dealing with pollution. For example, both the USA and UK have Clean Air Acts designed to maintain acceptable levels of air quality. The UK Clean Air Act 1993 is particularly concerned with 'dark smoke' and emissions produced by burning non-organic, especially carbon-containing manufactured materials and items such as:

- plastics
- tyres
- foams
- treated, impregnated and painted items (windows, doors)
- glued and bonded items (particle board)
- paints, resins and thinners
- bituminous materials (roof felt, roof sealant).

The US Clean Air Act 1990 (which consolidates and updates clean air provisions originally passed in 1970) is also concerned with smog and other pollutants. Both US and UK acts create offences in relation to their respective concerns with air quality and emissions. The UK Clean Air Act 1993 provides for a fine of up to £20,000 for each offence in relation to 'dark' smoke. In the USA the Environmental Protection Agency (EPA) is able to use both civil and criminal sanctions to deal with Clean Air Act offences. The Agency explains that 'when EPA finds that a violation has occurred, the agency can issue an order requiring the violator to comply, issue an administrative penalty order (use EPA administrative authority to force payment of a penalty), or bring a civil judicial action (sue the violator in court)' (EPA, 2014). EPA enforcement of the Clean Air Act 1990 (and regulations issued under it) can, therefore, result in offenders being given a chance to prevent further offending, settlement of a case or prosecution that can result in prison. Other legislation covering pollutants and toxic waste is designed to either prevent uncontrolled pollution or to provide for some form of remediation when it occurs. White and Heckenberg argue that 'the rise of the chemical industries means that many different types of toxic waste are produced, gathered up and put together into the same dump sites (e.g. rivers and lakes and ocean outlets)' (2014: 159). Clapp (2001) argues that both legal and illegal transfers of toxic waste create social vulnerabilities and impact negatively on a range of communities. Walters (2007: 188) identifies that illegal actions involving radioactive waste including dumping at sea have been well documented. Walters (2007: 188) cites Parmenter (1999) as having identified that the nuclear and chemical industries in both the USA and Europe routinely illegally burned or dumped waste at sea. These illegal actions were a consequence of a perceived corporate view that environmental regulations were impossible to comply with or placed an unnecessary burden on business (2007: 188). Thus, one cause of such environmental crime is a rational choice decision taken by corporate offenders to subvert regulations considered likely to impact negatively on corporate profits. Consumer pressure and concern over pollutants is another factor. As Chapter 1 indicates, polluting industries and harmful activities arising from lawful business activities, routinely impact negatively on vulnerable and marginal communities. Particularly in respect of toxic waste, there are demands that such harmful chemicals should not be disposed of in urban affluent areas. However, pollution offences can also occur as a result of 'upset' accidents such as equipment malfunctions, failures in processes and accidents as the following case study illustrates.

Case Study 3.1 Thames Water and the River Wandle (R v Thames Water Utilities Ltd. [2010] EWCA Crim 202)

Thames Water is one of the largest suppliers of water and sewage services in the United Kingdom. It is regulated by the Environment Agency and has an annual operating profit in the region of £278 million. This case concerns Thames Water's sewage treatment processing at the Beddington Sewage plant where treated effluent exits the works via the main effluent carrier, which is a concrete channel some 2.3 kilometres long forming a tributary of the River Wandle. The court heard that at the point of confluence, the effluent from the works amounts to about 80% of the water in the river, which eventually flows into the River Thames.

The court also heard that in the two years leading up to the offence, Thames Water had invested over £15 million in the equipment at Beddington Works, in order to further its continuing effort to improve the quality of the effluent. As part of this improvement, four large filter tanks were purchased from the manufacturer Norsk Hydro, and were installed at the Beddington Works in about 2005/6. The tanks supplemented the already existing primary and secondary sewage treatment plants at the Works by together providing a tertiary treatment plant for the removal of any remaining small pieces of solid waste, before the effluent flowed into the main effluent carrier, and thus finally into the river. The tertiary treatment plant came on line in early 2007. Effluent from the

(Continued)

(Continued)

secondary treatment plant flowed to the tertiary treatment plant where it was diverted into the tanks, exiting each tank over a weir, and then into the main effluent carrier.

Planned maintenance at the site included periodic cleaning of the inside of the tanks, involving two processes being carried out, about a fortnight apart, by the manufacturer Norsk Hydro. In the first process, hydrochloric acid was to be used to remove limescale build up. The second process involved about 1,600 litres of sodium hypochlorite (bleach) being poured into each tank to remove any biological matter. Cleaning involved closing the penstock valve to the tank in order to prevent the flow of effluent into the tank and also any risk that the cleaning chemical (bleach) would be flushed into the river. Norsk Hydro completed the first ever hydrochloric acid cleaning in the weeks leading up to 17 September 2007 but was unavailable to carry out the second process, a sodium hypochlorite cleaning process, until the end of October 2007. Wanting to ensure optimum performance of the tanks Thames Water decided not to wait on Norsk Hydro's availability and decided to carry out the cleaning itself.

The cleaning operation resulted in discharge of bleach into the river. In its assessment of the facts (paragraphs 14 to 15) the court stated that Thames Water failed to carry out a risk assessment, used untrained and unsupervised staff and that while the first three tanks were cleaned without incident:

> When the penstock valve to the fourth tank was closed it registered as being fully shut. However it was not, and effluent continued to flow into the tank. No dipstick test was carried out as to the level inside the tank, nor was a lookout posted on the weir, and therefore the two employees failed to notice the continuing ingress of effluent. Mr Barnard for the Appellant conceded that a moment's reflection would have revealed the need for safeguards, and that the mistake in failing to post a lookout on the weir was a 'juvenile' one. Thus when the 1,600 litres of sodium hypochlorite was poured into the tank, the great majority of it was flushed out over the weir and into the main effluent carrier. Although the employees realised that some of the chemical had been flushed out, it appears that they thought that it was only a small proportion, and thus the matter was not reported.

The court also commented that within half an hour local residents noticed a strong and nauseating smell of bleach. As a result of the discharge, the river turned milky white and began to bubble and fish died along a 5 kilometre stretch of river. Police were called and the public needed to be kept back from the edge of the river for their own safety. Police visited Thames Water and the incident was reported to regulator the Environment Agency who tested the water, confirming that the bleach discharge was 150 miligrams of bleach per litre, well above the Environment Agency's recommended limit of 0.005 miligrams per litre.

A significant clean-up operation followed over several days involving Thames Water's contractors, the Environment Agency, local angling clubs and the public. Subsequently Thames Water was originally fined £125,000 for causing polluting matter to enter controlled waters (i.e. spilling a form of bleach into the River Wandle) contrary to Section 85 of the Water Resources Act 1991. However, on appeal, judges ruled that the fine imposed in January 2009 was 'manifestly excessive' and cut it to £50,000 (BBC News Online, 2010). However, Thames Water had also entered into an agreement with the Angler's Conservation Association (ACA) where it had agreed to resolve problems at the river via the following actions:

- provide £7,000 project funding for a local education project;
- pay £10,000 in compensation for two affected local angling clubs;
- pay £30,000 to meet the costs of restocking and an ongoing survey to assess damage to the river's ecology;
- provide £200,000 core funding for the Wandle Trust to include support for the cost of an employee who will raise additional project funding to deliver access and habitat improvements along the length of the river;
- pay £250,000 over 5 years for a restoration fund to support local projects to improve the river environment;
- investment in failsafe measures at Beddington Sewage Treatment works to prevent a future occurrence of such pollution.

The River Wandle case indicates how corporate offending, albeit in this case accidental offending, can impact on a range of victims. Victims include: the river itself; local angling clubs who are users of the natural resource; the fish; and the wider public as all affected by an incident where significant environmental harm was caused by an illegal act committed by a legal actor otherwise providing an essential service. Situ and Emmons (2000) argue that the type of corporate environmental offending generally typified by waste and pollution offences is characterized by motivation, opportunity and enforcement. Toxic waste, in the form of e-waste is discussed in more detail in Chapter 9, which looks at the monitoring and investigation of environmental offences. However as White and Heckenberg (2014: 159) identify, chemicals, toxic waste and other pollutants have proliferated over the last 60 years to the extent that while 'normal' (i.e. legal) pollution causes significant environmental harm, illegal pollution represents a significant environmental problem. While it should be noted that Thames Water admitted liability and participated in clean-up and remediation, in some respects the case typifies attitudes towards environmental responsibility and compliance that at their most extreme result in excessive risk taking and non-compliance, as the next section examines.

Corporate Environmental Crime and the Criminal Entrepreneur

The subject of corporate environmental responsibility is dealt with in Chapter 6 as it relates closely to the manner in which corporate actions impact negatively on marginalized and vulnerable communities who often have their environmental rights infringed by the actions of business. However, the activities of transnational corporations can have a significant negative impact on local communities and are problematic in the area of environmental crime.

White (2012d: 15) identifies that 'international systems of production, distribution and consumption generate, reinforce and reward diverse environmental harms and those who perpetrate them'. Referring to production and distribution of unsafe toys, increasing reliance on genetically modified grains and the dumping of hazardous chemicals that are central to production, White identifies that global markets (often legal) are a central factor in environmental harm. Lynch and Stretesky (2014) refer to this as the 'treadmill of production', the increase in production and economic growth that has negative impacts for the environment. This is a significant concern of green criminology; that growth seen as good in the context of increased productivity, profits and consumption results in environmental harm when externalities, such as environmental damage, are not taken into account by markets. In this respect arguably markets do not reflect the true cost of their activities and consumers, who generally want cheaper products and a wide range of choice, are not called upon to pay the true costs of their products. Instead these are often borne by local communities in the source countries, some of whom are exploited by corporations who occupy a position of power in markets and are able to set prices and dominate supply chains and the retail environment. Thus, the legal market is a significant cause of environmental harms that green criminological discourse might well argue should be made or considered to be criminal (Lynch and Stretesky, 2014; Ellefsen et al., 2012; White, 2008) particularly if one is to adopt a victim's perspective on the consequence of corporate operations (Hall, 2013).

However, in addition to the harm caused by legal corporate activities, considerable illegality exists in the area of corporate environmental harm.

Nurse (2014) identifies that corporate environmental responsibility is largely a voluntary concept with corporations choosing which of the various standards for measuring responsibility and environmentally friendly activity they will abide by. Chapter 6 identifies that monitoring of these standards is piecemeal and, in practice, corporations are broadly only required to comply with the strict wording of legislation. Such wording is often inadequate to deal with the reality of corporate activity on the ground. In the case of transnational corporations, corporate abuses of power, the victimization of employees, local public and consumers, and the crimes of the powerful more generally have been relatively free of state, public and academic scrutiny (Pearce and Tombs, 1998). However, Tombs and Whyte (2015) argue that the private, profit-making corporation is a habitual and routine offender that in its present form is permitted, licensed and encouraged to systematically kill, maim and steal for profit. In the case of environmental crime, this freedom is arguably encouraged by weak regulatory systems that fail to deal with corporate criminality or recognize the corporation itself as a criminal entity.

Criminology has dealt with corporate offending primarily via discourse on white-collar crime, which Nelken (1994: 355) describes as being typified by a situation where 'successful business or professional people are apparently caught out in serious offences, quite often for behaviour which they did not expect to be treated as criminal, and for which it is quite difficult to secure a conviction'. Nelken and other scholars have conceptualized white-collar criminals as responsible people whose crimes are possibly an aberration in an otherwise law-abiding lifestyle. White-collar criminals are usually in gainful employment and thus arguably lack the stressors of other offenders. They are not, for example, directly comparable with those street criminals who steal or commit violence out of necessity or as a response to perceived relative deprivation (Lea and Young, 1993). Thus the crimes they commit raise questions that are not posed by other types of criminal behaviour, namely: Why do they do it when they have so much to lose? How likely are they to be caught? What is the true level of crime in their area? However, Merton's (1968) 'anomie' theory, which describes a process whereby the previously accepted rules of a society no longer control the individual, arguably applies to corporate offenders under pressure to increase profits and succeed in an increasingly competitive world. Merton's theory explains the pressures inherent in a capitalist society such as the USA where the goals of society are more important than the means. In other words, individuals continue to feel pressure to acquire money and consumer goods even where the legitimate means to do so are blocked. Merton argued that this caused pressure to commit crime, particularly 'when people experience a level of unfairness in their allocation of resources and turn to individualistic means to attempt to right this condition' (Young, 1994: 108).

However, by applying Merton's strain theory, Lea and Young's relative deprivation theory and masculinities theory (discussed later in this chapter) combined with Friedman's (1970) explanation that business primarily operates on the basis of profit maximization, corporate environmental crime becomes easier to understand.

Corporations are generally not treated as criminals and indeed in some jurisdictions a corporation cannot be prosecuted through the criminal law as a legal offender (Slapper, 2011). Criminality caused by a lawful business operating in an unlawful way is potentially difficult to detect, as they are often subject to business, rather than criminal (law), regulation and their unlawful activities may go largely unnoticed by the public due to the generally closed nature of neoliberal markets (Lynch and Stretesky, 2014). In effect, the criminal justice system expects corporations to self-regulate, to obey the law and to operate according to the rules of their industry regulators. However, there are numerous ways that voluntary compliance and self-regulation can fail, as follows:

- a difference of opinion between stakeholders and the corporation about what is required;
- a difference of opinion between corporations and regulators about what is required;
- a corporate culture that prizes success over compliance;
- the value of profit and minimizing costs over compliance;
- poor enforcement and inadequate penalties for non-compliance.

(Nurse, 2014, 2015b)

McBarnet (2006) uses the term 'creative compliance' to refer to the way in which companies adopt the practice of using the letter of the law to defeat its spirit. She suggests that within white-collar crime, companies develop 'practices that might be illegal, indeed criminal', but which 'if legally structured in one way could be legally repackaged and claimed to be lawful' (2006: 1091). A number of recent high-profile corporate scandals have taken place, involving major corporations such as Enron and WorldCom, where corporations who appeared to be healthy and making major profits were later discovered to have been actively evading regulations while appearing to comply with them.

In discussing Enron, Cavender et al. (2010) suggest that the 'bad apples' explanation was initially used to explain the company's downfall and framed the initial media coverage. This illustrates the general unwillingness of policy-makers and even regulators to accept that corporations may be inherently corrupt (Tombs and Whyte's 2015 claims notwithstanding) but instead to believe that any wrongdoing is conducted by individuals rather than the corporate body. Knottnerus et al. (2006), however, argued that the corporate structure of Enron (and, by implication, WorldCom and others) was such that deviancy had become normalized. In other words, the corporation had developed a way of doing business which, by itself, meant that individual employees behaved in a deviant manner in order to pursue profits for the company. It also led to the corporation developing a culture of creative compliance, which meant that seemingly fraudulent accounting practices were an integral part of the company's business model. In effect, it used legal accounting structures to commit crime. While corporations may publicly claim to be ethically and socially responsible and to take their environmental responsibilities seriously, green criminology has documented the persistent nature of law-breaking in respect of pollution, disposal of toxic waste, and misuse of environmental resources (Pearce and Tombs, 1998). It has also challenged corporate definitions of good environmental practice, and has provided a means through which corporate wrongdoing can frequently be considered as deliberate criminal acts (Lynch and Stretesky, 2003). In addition, Crowther and Aras (2008) argue that corporations do not truly account for the environmental impact of their activities, and externalities are routinely excluded from corporate accounting, with the true costs of corporate damage of the environment being met by communities.

The reality is that society requires corporations, generally seen to do good and provide services of public benefit, to remain in operation thus there is potential conflict between punishing their wrongdoing and allowing business operations to continue. Hawkins (1984) identified the use of criminal prosecution as a means of addressing environmental harms as 'a kind of eminence grise, a shadow entity lurking offstage, often invoked, however discreetly, yet rarely revealed' (i.e. available yet seldom used). Hawkins favoured compliance over policing and criminalization while Gunningham and Sinclair argued that the failure of market-based approaches to compliance necessitates using a range of regulatory measures to address pollution problems (Gunningham and Sinclair, 1999). Such views reflect the need to allow corporations to continue producing products desired by the public, while seeking an effective means to curb the associated environmental damage. Corporations will naturally claim to be operating responsibly and taking account of the needs of communities. However, while companies and their directors have a number of incentives to align their behaviour with accepted standards, numerous cases highlight the failure of corporations to comply with legislation. When found to be operating unlawfully, they often fail to accept responsibility for their actions and remedy the harm they have caused, suggesting the failure of self-regulation and voluntary compliance with ethical standards. While a range of activities that cause harm to the environment are subject to national and international law, there is no single definition of environmental damage for which corporations should be held responsible. Thus a corporate mindset may exist which is inherently environmentally criminal, as Tombs and Whyte (2015) suggest. Situ and Emmons argue that corporate environmental crime is 'a product of motivation and opportunity conditioned by the quality of law enforcement' (2000: 67). While this is not to suggest that all corporations are predisposed towards environmental crime, when the drive for corporate success (in terms of greater profits or lower costs) greatly exceeds the legitimate or profitable means for achieving it, 'the structural groundwork' for motivation is laid. Where this is combined with opportunity and a weak regulatory structure, corporations who see their profits cut and/or their costs increasing may seek to circumvent environmental legislation, even while publicly making pronouncements that the corporation is environmentally responsible. Where corporations may be dealing with multiple environmental performance demands and expectations from stakeholders and investors, the extent to which a corporation sets protection and restoration of the environment as a strategic priority can sometimes result in a conflict between the interests of the corporation and the interests of the environment and the wider community.

However, it can be argued (Nurse, 2015b) that while Baumol identifies a distinction between productive corporate innovation and unproductive activities such as organized crime (1990: 893), within corporate environmental crime discourse, this distinction is not absolute. Corporate compliance with environmental regulations operates along a continuum from absolute compliance to total non-compliance consistent with Hobsbawm's view that private enterprise has a bias only towards profit (1969: 40). Accordingly, non-compliance with environmental regulations and entrepreneurship that actively subverts or minimizes the costly impact of regulatory compliance can represent a form of innovation. Corporations exploit business opportunities cognisant with the goal of maximizing profit. Embracing green credentials, reassuring consumers and governments that they take their social and environmental responsibilities seriously are legitimate means through which corporations demonstrate alertness to opportunity, creativity and respond to consumer demand for ethical corporate practice. Friedman theorized that the main responsibility of the corporate executive is 'to make as much money as possible while conforming to the basic rules of the society' (Friedman, 1970). Crowhurst (2006) identified that while responsible industry usually welcomes certainty in environmental legislation and clarity in Corporate Environmental Responsibility there are corporations that actively seek to avoid 'costly' legislation. Global corporations that produce harmful environmental effects and who have the economic power to do so deliberately, invest in 'pollution havens' (countries with low levels of environmental regulation) so that as standards of environmental liability become stricter in the EU and other Western countries global companies move their investments and harmful environmental activities out of the reach of the tougher regulatory systems. This represents a form of 'criminal' entrepreneurship (Nurse, 2015b).

McBarnet suggests a tension between conflicting responsibilities such that creative compliance becomes 'something to be emulated rather than reviled' (2006: 1092) and is considered clever rather than deviant. McBarnet primarily refers to 'clever and imaginative legal problem solving' (2006: 1096) and the use of legal mechanisms to make potentially unlawful mechanisms and practices lawful (see later discussion on biopiracy, p. 104). However, corporate practices that embed environmental compliance within policies that can be referred to in the event of regulatory investigations but which in practice may not be effective also represent a form of creative compliance. Gallicano refers to active 'greenwashing' where individuals are actively misled about a company's environmental practices (2011:1). In a broader sense, inconsistency between a company's environmental claims and its actual behaviour also represents a form of 'greenwashing'.

Masculinities as a Cause of Environmental Crime

Before leaving the subject of causes of crime it is worth considering the extent to which environmental offenders (including wildlife offenders) share certain characteristics as criminology has historically paid little attention to the specific behaviours of environmental and wildlife offenders. However, understanding the psychology of offenders, the economic pressures that affect them and the sociological and cultural issues that impact on behaviour greatly aids understanding of what needs to be done to address behaviours and conditions that lead to environmental and wildlife crime. Some offences are motivated by purely financial considerations, some by economic or employment constraints (Roberts et al., 2001: 27) and others by predisposition towards some elements of the activity such as collecting, or exercising power over animals. Nurse (2011, 2013a: 69–70) identified five categories of wildlife offender:

1. Traditional profit-driven offenders
2. Economic criminals
3. Masculinities criminals
4. Hobby offenders
5. Stress offenders.

His analysis concluded that certain wildlife offences involve different elements, some incorporating the taking and exploitation of wildlife for profit (wildlife trade) others involving the killing or taking or trapping of wildlife either in connection with employment (bird of prey persecution) or for purposes linked to field sports (hunting with dogs). Environmental offences such as pollution and toxic waste offences are primarily profit-driven offences, undertaken to gain maximum profit for a corporation. However, they also fit the economic offender model, where crimes are committed by those in otherwise lawful employment as a result of economic and employer pressures whether real or imagined (Nurse 2013a: 70).

Sykes and Matza's neutralization theory (1957) is a useful model for identifying the justifications used by offenders that gives them the freedom to act (and a post-act rationalization for doing so) while other theories explain why environmental and wildlife offenders are motivated to commit specific crimes. Nurse (2013a) observes that wildlife offenders exist within communities, although there may not be a community where the crimes take place or neighbours to exert essential controls on wildlife offending. Similarly, corporate environmental offenders exist within a community or corporate subculture of their own that accepts their offences, as many environmental offences are regulatory in nature carrying only fines or lower-level prison terms which reinforces environmental crime as 'minor' offences unworthy of official activity. In addition, Sutherland's (1939) differential association theory helps to explain the situation that occurs when potential corporate offenders learn their activities from others in their community or social group (Sutherland, 1973 [1942]). As McBarnet's (2006) analysis identifies, corporate culture may rationalize an appeal to higher loyalties (profits and shareholders) and that there is no harm in continuing with an activity that represents standard or widespread industry practice. Similarly, in wildlife crime, junior gamekeepers on shooting estates learn techniques of poisoning and trapping from established staff as a means of ensuring healthy populations of game birds for shooting (Nurse, 2013a). Awareness of the illegal nature of their actions leads to the justifications outlined by Sykes and Matza (1957) but the association with other offenders, the economic (and employment related) pressures to commit offences and the personal consequences for them should they fail are strong motivations to commit offences (Merton, 1968).

Past academic debate on crime has generally accepted that crime and criminality are predominantly male concerns (e.g. Groombridge, 1998). This perhaps reflects the role of gender and predominance of male offenders in serious and violent crime and concerns over youth crime; in particular both the propensity towards violence of young males and the extent to which young males might become victims of crime (Norland et al., 1981; Campbell, 1993; Flood-Page et al., 2000; Harland et al., 2005). Some offences are also crimes of masculinities involving cruelty to or power over animals, in some cases linked to sporting or 'hobby' pursuits, perceptions by the offender of their actions being part of their culture where toughness, masculinity and smartness (Wilson, 1985) combine with a love of excitement. In the case of badger-baiting, badger-digging and hare coursing, for example, gambling and association with other like-minded males are factors and provide a strong incentive for new members to join already established networks of offenders. Similarly within a corporate culture of risk-taking, pressure to succeed arguably impacts differently on male employees than female employees such that much corporate environmental offending might reflect Nurse's (2011) notion of the *Masculinities Offender* who is primarily motivated by power and notions of masculinity. In wildlife crime, Nurse (2011, 2013a) observed that masculinities offences are seldom committed by lone individuals as such crimes predominantly motivate via group activity, such as gambling and its associations with organized crime and conflict with law enforcement (Clawson, 2009).

US research on wildlife-oriented crimes of the masculine, including cockfighting and cockfighting gangs, explains that: 'cockfighting can be said to have a mythos centered on the purported behaviour and character of the gamecock itself. Cocks are seen as emblems of bravery and resistance in the face of insurmountable odds' (Hawley, 1993: 2). The fighting involved is 'an affirmation of masculine identity in an increasingly complex and diverse era' (1993: 1) and the fighting spirit of the birds has great symbolic significance to participants, as does the ability of fighting and hunting dogs to take punishment.

However, masculine stereotypes can be reinforced and developed through offending behaviour (Goodey, 1997) and are important factors in addressing other offending behaviour that may sometimes be overlooked (Groombridge, 1998). Research (Nurse, 2013a, 2011) has identified that wildlife offenders in the UK are almost exclusively male and in the case of the more violent forms of wildlife offender exhibit distinctly masculine characteristics. Corporate environmental offenders are also predominantly male, in part because males likely occupy the relevant positions of power that are conducive to the commission of offences thus male employees have the requisite means, motive and opportunity to commit offences and take decisions that might result in environmental offending. The literature on wildlife crime identifies a group of mostly young males involved in crimes of violence (albeit towards animals) that could turn to more serious forms of crime or expand their violent activities beyond animals and towards humans (Ascione, 1993; Flynn, 2002; Clawson, 2009). Offences such as hare coursing, cockfighting and badger digging all involve gambling, with wagers being placed on individual animals, the outcome of a fight and other factors (including the power or strength of an animal). Such offences also point to the existence of criminal subcultures that are arguably replicated within corporate structures where adherence to norms such as non-compliance with regulation may be a necessary survival or success mechanism.

Wildlife crime discourse (Wyatt, 2013; Nurse, 2012) identifies that group relationships within offender communities replicate informal criminal networks. Maguire's (2000) description categorizes some loose criminal networks as being 'like an "old boy network" of ex-public school pupils, individuals would be able to call upon others for collaboration, help or services when they needed them, and would be able to verify their "bona fides" to those they did not know' (Maguire, 2000: 131). There is also a 'secret society' element to such crimes and here the community can actually encourage crime. Such principles can equally be applied to the corporate arena. The male-bonding element identified by Hawley when talking about cockfighting is as significant to the corporate world as is the banding together of men from the margins of society and for whom issues of belonging, male pride and achievement are important. In discussing cockfighting in the USA, Hawley (1993) explains that 'young men are taken under the wing of an older male relative or father, and taught all aspects of chicken care and lore pertaining to the sport'. (Such subcultural arrangements also exist within the dogfighting world (Forsyth and Evans, 1998).) Similarly, socialisation within corporate environments dictates that new employees are shown the ropes and are integrated into corporate culture and expectations. Thus within a corporate culture of non-compliance individuals either become socialised to such normative practices or face the prospect of having to leave their employment should they wish to make a stand for compliance and adherence to wider social values (see for example McBarnet on Enron, 2006). Thus within a corporate structure an appeal to higher loyalties and an attachment to smaller groups (one's immediate team or office) takes precedent over attachment to mainstream societal values in much the same way that Forsyth and Evans (1998) found in researching dog fighting in the USA. Thus wildlife offenders may rationalize on the basis of historical precedent, tradition or pseudo-psychological notions of a victimless crime given that the birds or animals feel no pain (Hawley, 1993). Corporate offenders may also rationalize on the grounds of a corporation's wider good works, the services it provides and the jobs it creates while also arguing that nobody is being harmed because natural resources belong to no one and are there to be exploited (Stallworthy, 2008). They may also 'condemn the condemners' (Sykes and Matza, 1957) arguing that environmental regulation is bad for business, is not a legitimate use of enforcement resources and is unjustified given that generally the market is able to police itself in accordance with Adam Smith's 'invisible hand' theory (Dine, 2007). This bears some resemblance to the aggressive response of field sports enthusiasts towards NGOs such as People for the Ethical Treatment of Animals (PETA) and other advocacy groups whom they demonize as 'effete intellectuals and kooks' lacking understanding of their activity (Hawley, 1993: 5).

In wildlife crime the public policy response to masculinities crimes reflects acceptance of the propensity towards violence of offenders and is similar to that employed for organized crime. Techniques employed by enforcers include infiltration of gangs, surveillance activities and undercover operations. While wildlife masculinities offenders are considered to be more dangerous than other wildlife criminals and are treated accordingly, their less dangerous corporate offending brethren are similarly the subject of infiltration and surveillance techniques, reflecting the closed world of such offending (TCEQ, 2012).

Summary

As Situ and Emmons (2000) identify, environmental crime is primarily caused by weak regulatory structures combined with considerable incentives for offenders to ignore or seek to subvert regulations. This is particularly so in the corporate sphere, where profit-making pressures and entrepreneurial and risk-making cultures may be in conflict with environmental concerns and priorities. Corporations, primarily created to provide products and services within neoliberal markets, may well see environmental regulation as burdensome and inhibiting business innovations. They are perhaps supported in this view by political ideologies that see environmental regulation as not interfering with free market principles and as being subservient to market needs (Lynch and Stretesky, 2014). Thus while various environmental protection measures exist in the form of international conventions and national legislation and regulations, the regulatory approach and criminal justice response to environmental crime is often limited to treating environmental offences as relatively low-level crime, seldom attracting serious penalties.

Lynch and Stretesky argue that 'the societies that tend to be the least willing to respond to environmental problems are those that cause the most environmental damage because of the economic gains involved' (2014: 22). In doing so, they further argue that neoliberal markets and a human-centred view of nature as being a resource for human benefit undermine the willingness of legislators and states to deal with environmental harms while simultaneously identifying how criminology's techniques of neutralization (Sykes and Matza, 1957) are employed as tools to nullify culpability for environmental harm and minimize enforcement actions intended to address these. This chapter has outlined some of the difficulties in taking action over corporate crime. The nature of corporate organization and the financial and political power that the major corporations have means that they are able to influence the regulatory climates in both indirect and direct ways. Corporate regulation and penalties for corporate wrongdoing are therefore generally less than for individual crimes. While most 'ordinary' crime is generally committed against the public or in public, much corporate wrongdoing goes on behind closed doors, making it difficult for law enforcement to obtain information about corporate crimes. In addition, corporate crime is monitored and responded to by a variety of criminal, administrative and regulatory bodies, including financial investigators, environmental protection agencies, health and safety regulators, tax, customs and fair trading offices, alternative dispute resolution services (e.g. Ombudsmen), the police and others. Thus jurisdictional and practical enforcement issues (e.g. cooperation) may impact negatively on effective enforcement.

Self-study Questions

1. Corporate environmental offending illustrates the relationship between the legal and the illegal. To what extent is this a symbiotic relationship?
2. Risk-taking, bending the rules and a flexible approach to complying with legal norms are attributes integral to successful business activity. To what extent do these business behaviours cause corporate crime and criminality?
3. Why are most wildlife offenders male? Consider the differences between the genders in criminal behaviour and criminality as part of your answer.
4. To what extent are masculinities a factor in environmental and wildlife crimes? Consider the links with mainstream criminology and criminological theory in your answer.
5. How should the criminal justice system deal with the distinctly masculine offender and masculinities crimes? Consider the impact of sentencing and relevant criminological theory as part of your answer.
6. Why are there distinctly masculine subcultures within environmental and wildlife offending? Consider corporate offending and relevant theory on corporate culture and criminality as part of your answer.
7. Environmental crime is often not a core policing responsibility, is frequently left to NGOs to monitor or is dealt with via 'lesser' options like environmental tribunals, and is the responsibility of environment departments like DEFRA (UK) and the Department of the Interior (USA) rather than criminal justice ones like the Home Office (UK) and Department of Justice (USA). Why might this be the case?

PART II
ENVIRONMENTAL CRIME
AS GLOBAL CRIME

4

THE FUTURE PROTECTION OF WILDLIFE: RESOLVING WILDLIFE CRIME AND ILLEGAL WILDLIFE TRAFFICKING

By the end of this chapter you should:

- Have a firm understanding of what constitutes wildlife crime and the nature of illegal wildlife trafficking.
- Understand the links between the legal and illegal wildlife trades and the extent to which a symbiotic relationship exists with the legal trade facilitating the illegal trade.
- Understand how and why globalization is a factor in the continuing illegal wildlife trade and how global flows of goods, people and services facilitate the trade.
- Understand public policy perspectives on the protection of wildlife and the ongoing conflict between wildlife conservation and continued exploitation of wildlife for human interests.
- Understand the extent to which wildlife protection laws and wildlife protection are a social construction and have an awareness of the increasing politicization of wildlife protection.

Introduction

This chapter examines the illegal trade in wildlife, one of the largest areas of global crime (Nurse, 2015a; Wyatt, 2013; US Department of State, 2009). It also examines other areas of wildlife crime and the protection of wildlife by justice systems.

As Chapter 1 indicates, species justice discourse considers the responsibility man owes to other species as part of broader ecological concerns (Benton, 1998). The application of criminal justice norms to nonhuman animals is also a core concern of green criminology. Wildlife laws are an integral part of species justice and provide a means through which contemporary criminal justice can extend beyond traditional human ideals of justice as a punitive or rehabilitative ideal, to incorporate shared concepts of reparative and restorative justice between humans and nonhuman animals. Most jurisdictions have wildlife protection laws and create offences in respect of unsustainable exploitation of wildlife. However, animals, particularly wild animals, are often viewed solely in relation to their economic or property value. Thus legal protection for wildlife often exists only so far as wildlife use corresponds with human interests in using animals for food or other forms of commercial exploitation (e.g. trade in skins, parts or derivatives). Such use is also socially constructed and varies according to the cultural use or significance of animals within a society. Thus, some cultures may consider wildlife to be a vital exploitable resource, whereas others may consider that wildlife should be protected for its intrinsic value and safeguarded for future generations.

In practice, wildlife often receives less protection than domestic animals that rely on humans for food and shelter (Nurse, 2013a; Donaldson and Kymlicka, 2011). Wildlife campaigners in the UK, USA and across Europe have consistently argued for stronger wildlife laws (Nurse, 2012, 2003) reflecting the perception that current wildlife laws are generally inadequate to achieve effective animal protection. This also reflects the perception and ideological belief that a more punitive regime is required to deal with the criminality inherent in wildlife crime. However, for the most part, wildlife law remains outside the mainstream of criminal justice and is dealt with as an environmental issue (Nurse, 2012). Thus it is primarily the responsibility of government environment departments, rather than being firmly incorporated into the responsibilities of the relevant justice and policing ministries, despite evidence of the links between wildlife crime and other forms of criminality (Lockwood, 1997; Linzey, 2009).

Currently, levels of wildlife protection in the UK and USA are being reduced either through proposed changes to wildlife legislation (in the UK) or a reduction in the protection afforded to specific species (e.g. reduced protection for wolves in some parts of the USA). Such legislative and policy proposals risk reducing the protection available for wildlife by failing to address specific problems of wildlife criminality and rolling back wildlife protection to serve other interests. Continued wildlife exploitation may well be in a state's interest. Particularly in those states reliant on hunting and wildlife sport tourism revenue, legal protection for wildlife may be at odds with economic or cultural priorities. In the specific context of human–animal relationships and species justice, green criminology is uniquely placed to promote news ways of thinking about our attitudes towards and exploitation of animals as an integral part of mainstream criminal justice. White's (2008) green criminology notion of animal rights and species justice deals with animal abuse and suffering, and a criminological perspective that sees a comprehensive justice system as including both humans and nonhuman animals. Increased levels of wildlife protection over the last 30 years or so reflect a growing environmental awareness and the efforts of a variety of NGOs to influence the policy agenda in respect of wildlife crime and wildlife protection.

Defining Wildlife Crime

Although difficult to monitor, wildlife trafficking is thought to be the second or third most valuable illicit commerce in the world after drugs and weapons (Webster, 1997), and is worth an estimated US$10 billion a year, according to the US Department of State (2009) while other estimates place it at between $10 and $20 billion annually (South and Wyatt, 2011). Difficulties naturally exist in any attempt to identify the scale of an illegal trade, much of which takes place outside of the sphere of the legitimate monitoring bodies and which, like much environmental crime and ecological or animal harm, is subject to variations in the way the activity is measured. But estimates based on CITES and NGO data and extrapolated from seizures by enforcement bodies consistently reinforce the perception of a large-scale trade with a minimum value of $10 billion and which is consistently considered to be second only to the drugs trade. Birds are the most common contraband, with the US Department of State (2009) estimating that between 2 million and 5 million wild birds, from hummingbirds to parrots to harpy eagles, are traded illegally worldwide every year. The trade is influenced by the ease with which wild birds can be caught, traded and sold and the difficulties that sometimes exist in distinguishing between legal specimens and those prohibited from trade by CITES. Many rare parrots, for example, are similar in appearance to less threatened species requiring expert identification to distinguish between species listed in CITES Appendix I or II and which are subject to trade controls, and those which can be freely traded and breed easily in captivity. However, millions of turtles, crocodiles, mammals, insects, snakes and other reptiles are also trafficked.

Wyatt proposed 'processed commodities, collector's items, traditional medicines, and food' (2011: 1) as the main four categories of wildlife trafficking, while Cook et al. (2002: 4) suggested that the illegal wildlife trade broadly consists of the following five areas of activity:

- specimen collecting;
- skins, furs and traditional Asian medicines (e.g. use of bones);
- activities associated with drug trafficking;
- caviar trafficking;
- illegal timber trade.

Both Wyatt's and Cook et al.'s categories, except for the illegal timber trade, are sometimes classified as animal crime as they will frequently involve *direct* harm to animals that are the target of the trade, whereas this is not always the case with the timber trade. However, the timber trade has an indirect effect on animals where the removal of timber from forests results in the loss of habitats. Deforestation can also result in the destruction of active wildlife habitats causing *direct* harm to animals in the process and has been cited by some NGOs as either causing the extinction of certain species or severely impacting on their populations (de Bohan et al., 1996). Illegal logging and the timber trade are an aspect of wildlife trafficking where the failure of timber traders to consider the impact of their activities in the pursuit of profits has the potential to cause significant environmental and animal harm.

The sheer scale of the legal wildlife trade facilitates an illegal trade that often exists alongside its legal counterpart but also illustrates the profits to be made by trading in wildlife. The CITES Secretariat's most recent data indicates that the current trend of CITES transactions is generally upwards 'and averages 850,000 permits a year nowadays' (CITES, 2010: 4). With many species of wildlife selling for several thousands of pounds per specimen this is a significant level of ostensibly legal trade although determining legality is problematic. This fact is readily exploited by traders wishing to disguise illegal transactions as legal ones in order to meet 'unchecked demand for exotic pets, rare foods, trophies and traditional medicines' (US Department of State, 2009). Cook et al. report that each category of (illegal) wildlife trade has particular 'methods, markets, routes and "tricks of the trade", which include concealment, mis-declaration, permit fraud and the laundering of illegal wildlife products through the complexities of re-exports' (2002: 4). Thus considerable criminal ingenuity is applied to frustrating law enforcement and monitoring efforts in order to ensure that illicit trading efforts are successful. According to Schneider, the trade's basis is simple in that

> going beyond the simple notion that thieves steal to make money, preliminary market-level analyses reveal that thieves steal because they know there are ways for them to sell the goods they steal. In other words, the crime of handling is supported by a structure that allows thieves the opportunity to sell stolen property either to people who use the items themselves or to those who sell it on to others. (2008: 276)

Thus wildlife traders seek both to obtain wildlife and sell to an end consumer, or to a dealer or other middleman who has consumers ready to purchase wildlife products. However, the transnational illegal trade is complicated by the participation of a range of criminal actors. These include low-level thieves, poachers and handlers through to sophisticated sellers and large-scale commercial operators, involved at various stages. Thus identifying wildlife traffickers is problematic as these criminal actors operate from capture through to eventual sale given that at each stage, money can be made without necessarily relying on the eventual sale of an animal (except in the sense that this is necessary for the trade to continue).

This provides a simple motivation for much of the trade: profit. At the upper end of the scale, profits can be in the tens of thousands of pounds or dollars, sometimes for a relatively small operation in terms of numbers of species sold and, as the CITES data shows, the trade is now global, highly organized and employing sophisticated methods to achieve its profits. As strain theory (Merton, 1968) illustrates, when legitimate opportunities to achieve success are blocked people will sometimes turn to illegitimate means to pursue their goals. Zimmerman argues that whereas exotic animal traders 'were once viewed as small-time criminals' who sold birds in fairs, the international community must now recognize 'the extensive, powerful involvement of organized criminal rings in the illegal wildlife trade' (2003: 1659).

However, it should be noted that wildlife trade is not the only form of wildlife crime. Wildlife is killed on shooting estates, for example, because predator species are seen as being in conflict with legitimate game species and require control. Some wildlife are simply seen as pests and are subject to animal control measures, others are seen as animals to be exploited for participation for sport or are a commodity to be shot and hunted for sport and trophy hunting. For example, Lindsey et al. (2006) identify 23 African countries as having hunting industries, noting that South Africa, the largest industry, generated revenues (paid to operators and taxidermists) of US$100 million a year with industries in Namibia and Botswana each generating annual revenues in excess of US$20 million. In some rural areas, animals are also seen as a vital source of food and may be killed or taken illegally to meet subsistence needs. Thus, a wide range of wildlife crime is possible where a range of activities might breach animal and wildlife protection laws (Nurse, 2015a; Schaffner, 2011).

The Politicization of Wildlife Laws

While in principle wildlife laws are about protection and effective management of wildlife, political concerns increasingly influence the manner and extent to which wildlife is protected by law. Organ et al. (2012) identify that the increasing politicization of wildlife management threatens the existence of the North American Wildlife Management model, which argues that: wildlife should only be killed for a legitimate purpose; that science is the proper tool to discharge wildlife policy; allocation of wildlife is the responsibility of law; and wildlife should be considered an international resource. Species justice discourse would broadly agree with these principles and it is not too dissimilar from the model adopted in the UK (although it should be noted that some animal rights discourse promotes an absolute prohibition on animal use and killing).

However, current wildlife law policy in the UK and USA, which has relaxed protection for some species such as wolves and allowed the killing of others such as badgers, indicates that wildlife law is less about achieving effective species justice and more about perpetuating the use of wildlife and its regulation within an environmental rather than criminal justice context. At time of writing, the UK is currently in the process of reviewing its wildlife law by way of proposals from the Law Commission which seek to abolish the majority of existing law and introduce a single wildlife management Act. This is to replace the current confusing regime of different legislation for different species with different levels of wildlife protection (Law Commission, 2012). In the USA, NGOs have recently fought against efforts by anti-bison ranchers to remove the last genetically pure bison from Montana and also fought against the US Fish and Wildlife Service's decision to remove federal protection from grey wolves by making amendments to species listings under the Endangered Species Act 1973. The effect of changes to the grey wolf listing is that, paradoxically, the grey wolf is 'endangered' and fully protected in some areas of the USA but can legally be killed in other areas.

These law reform initiatives highlight the political nature of wildlife law and the difficulties of achieving effective species justice. In the UK, particularly with the return of a Conservative majority government in the May 2015 general election, wildlife and environmental regulation is seen by government as imposing an excessive regulatory regime on business (Cabinet Office, 2011). Thus UK wildlife law reform proposals take an approach consistent with the view held by the (2010–15) UK coalition government and the 2015 Conservative administration that regulation and criminalization should be a last resort when dealing with business offending. This view is consistent with liberalist, free trade ideology generally adopted by conservative governments. It is also notable that the Hunting Act 2004, which prohibits hunting wild animals with dogs in the UK, is excluded from current wildlife law reforms in part because of political sensibilities around the issue. Indeed, July 2015 attempts by the Conservative administration to amend the Hunting Act 2004 via the use of secondary legislation rather than a full legislative change drew considerable public and political criticism. The measure failed, in part, due to the arithmetic of parliamentary opposition which forced the Government to abandon its plans (Mason, 2015). In the USA, the conflict between ranching and farming, and environmental protection interests is a factor in some endangered species listings and decisions to allow wolf killing. Thus problem species or at least those perceived as causing an economic problem to countryside interests, risk having their protection removed or at least temporarily reduced.

Arguably, these approaches to wildlife law reform, while reflecting the conflict between socio-economic interests and natural resource protection, risk ignoring the individualistic nature of much wildlife offending (Nurse, 2011) that requires an effective criminal justice approach to resolve. The UK's approach takes, as its starting point, a presumption that a suitable regime already exists and simply requires amendment (Law Commission, 2012). Similarly, review of wildlife protection in the USA is primarily based around amendments to existing law and a belief in the existing system as broadly controlling wildlife crime problems. However, despite the existence of federal enforcement in the shape of the US Fish and Wildlife Service, NGOs such as Earthjustice and Defenders of Wildlife have raised concerns about the continued illegal persecution of species such as wolves, bears and bison. They also raise concerns about the political motivations and vested interest pressures perceived to influence decisions to remove legal protection from certain species via Endangered Species Act 1973 listings. In 2011, Defenders of Wildlife identified that the (then) US Congress had 'introduced more than a dozen bills or legislative proposals to undermine the Endangered Species Act' (2011: 3), arguing that such legislative moves either chipped away at the foundation of the Act or singled out species no longer deemed worthy of protection. Economic considerations and the demands of neoliberal markets and business interests are perceived as providing the basis of such legislative change. Environmental law experts and green criminologists (Lynch and Stretesky, 2014; Stallworthy, 2008) identify how natural resource and wildlife protection and their associated legislative compliance could potentially be a costly issue for business, and government, keen to reduce the regulatory burden on business, has sought to streamline or reduce wildlife protection.

Problems of Wildlife Law Enforcement

Considerable research evidence indicates that existing wildlife law regimes do not work in their implementation rather than in their basic legislative provisions albeit critiques of legislation dominant policy discourse (Nurse, 2012; Wilson et al., 2007). Practical enforcement problems are endemic to the UK's wildlife law system as identified by Nurse (2003, 2009, 2011, 2012) and Wellsmith (2011) in their respective analyses of the UK's wildlife law enforcement regime, which identified a regime consisting of legislation inadequate to the task of wildlife protection, subject to an equally inconsistent enforcement regime (albeit one where individual police officers and NGOs contribute significant amounts of time and effort within the confines of their specific jurisdiction) and one that fails to address the specific nature of wildlife offending.

Wildlife law is often a fringe area of policing whose public policy response is significantly influenced by NGOs (Nurse 2012) and which continues to rely on NGOs as an integral part of the enforcement regime. White (2012b) identifies that third parties such as NGOs often play a significant role in investigating and exposing environmental harm and offending and have become a necessity for effective environmental law enforcement. In wildlife protection, NGOs are an essential part not only of practical enforcement regimes, but also the development of effective policy. NGOs act as policy advisors, researchers, field investigators, expert witnesses at court, scientific advisors, casework managers, and, in the case of a small number of UK and US organizations, prosecutors playing a significant practical role in policy development and law enforcement.

One difficulty with wildlife legislation is its intended use as conservation or wildlife management legislation rather than as species protection and/or criminal justice legislation. For several years, academics, investigators, NGOs and wildlife protection advocates have voiced concerns about the perceived inadequacy of US and UK enforcement regimes (Defenders of Wildlife, 2011; Wilson et al., 2007; Nurse, 2003). NGOs have highlighted inadequacies in individual legislation such that legislation intended to protect wildlife often fails to do so and ambiguous or inadequate wording actually allows animal killing or fails to provide adequate protection for effective animal welfare (Parsons et al., 2010). Such confusion also causes problems in the investigation of wildlife crime, with investigators and prosecutors needing to understand a complex range of legislation, powers of arrest and sanctions.

Wildlife crime is currently enforced reactively, in the UK this means relying on charities to do the bulk of the investigative work into wildlife crime and to receive the majority of crime notifications. While the UK has an excellent network of Police Wildlife Crime Officers (PWCOs), many of these officers carry out their duties in addition to their 'main' duties (Roberts et al., 2001; Kirkwood, 1994) and both public and seemingly governmental perception is that charity support is an integral part of the enforcement system. But although the USA has the federal and dedicated enforcement body that many UK NGOs desire – in the form of the Fish and Wildlife Service – US NGOs have expressed dissatisfaction with their system ranging from issues with poor wildlife management through to bad legislation (including delisting of endangered species). Concerns have also been raised about cuts to the Fish and Wildlife Service's budget and its possible effect on wildlife law enforcement. In addition, wildlife law enforcement is primarily based upon a socio-legal model which relies on use of existing law and an investigation, detection and punishment model rather than the use of target-hardening or other forms of preventative action (Wellsmith, 2010). Thus the policy approach adopted in wildlife law and its enforcement is primarily one of dealing with wildlife crime after it has happened, albeit through an under-resourced regime which often fails to recognize the varied criminality that exists in wildlife crime (Nurse, 2011) or which does not adequately reflect the nature and impact of this area of crime in its sentencing and remediation provisions (Lowther et al., 2002).

Enforcement Options and Regulatory Approach

The failures of existing regimes raise the question of how wildlife laws should be enforced. What is needed is to take what is good in existing wildlife protection regimes and to develop proper effective legislation and an effective enforcement regime that recognizes wildlife crime as part of mainstream criminal justice, and does not continue to see it solely as an environmental problem.

The UK Law Commission's enforcement approach for its proposed new regime is based on a mixture of criminal and civil sanctions suggesting that 'criminalising regulatory transgressions may not always be the appropriate way of ensuring beneficial outcomes. It may be better to provide the non-compliant individual or organisation with advice or guidance' (Law Commission, 2012). This is consistent with the (2010–15) UK coalition government's belief in 'risk-based regulation' in accordance with the Hampton Principles (Hampton, 2005) and which suggests that regimes for achieving compliance with business regulations through regulatory inspections and enforcement are generally complex and ineffective. The Commission identifies that the government's approach is generally that regulation should only be resorted to where 'satisfactory outcomes cannot be achieved by alternative, self-regulatory, or non-regulatory approaches' (Law Commission, 2012).

However, while the risk-based, prosecution-as-last-resort regulatory approach is consistent with liberalist government policy and its approach to 'light touch' regulation there are potential flaws with this approach, not least the possibility that offenders could engage in repeat offending before any use of criminal sanctions is considered or begins to bite. Given academic and policy research on the nature of criminality in wildlife law violations the advice and guidance/ decriminalization approach proposed within the UK wildlife law reform proposals raises species justice concerns. While in principle the Hampton risk-based regulation approach may be an appropriate model to deal with (business-based) regulatory crime, in practice the implementation of these principles is problematic in the face of the persistent law breaking that characterizes much wildlife crime.

Academic research on the use of civil sanctions as an approach to consumer problems conducted on behalf of the (then) Department for Business Enterprise and Regulatory Reform (BERR) in 2008 noted both a lack of willingness on the part of enforcers to use civil sanctions and the increased resources required for this approach to be effective where criminality was an inherent problem that needed to be addressed (Peysner and Nurse, 2008). Thus doubt was cast on the effectiveness of civil sanctions in certain circumstances. In addition, while the UK's Law Commission refers to the US Environmental Protection Agency's (EPA) use of administrative penalties, these have often been ineffective as a solution to wildlife crime and environmental non-compliance, resulting in US NGOs challenging the ineffectiveness of EPA enforcement activity which has persistently failed to address problems and allowed ongoing non-compliance. Thus while civil sanctions may be attractive politically as a way of reducing the regulatory burden and decriminalizing legitimate business activity they are often ineffective in dealing with environmental and wildlife criminality. The UK wildlife law reform consultation documents suggest that the current wildlife law regime is too reliant on criminalization. But a different view emerges from research evidence suggesting instead that a weak enforcement regime allows a wider range of criminality and transfer of criminality from mainstream crime into wildlife crime. The evidence of organized crime as active participants in wildlife crime (South and Wyatt, 2011; Nurse, 2013a) also requires consideration of wildlife crime as serious crime rather than it being a regulatory problem.

The Future Protection of Wildlife

Despite improvements in law and high-profile publicity for wildlife crime it is still not seen as serious crime within the context of mainstream criminal justice. This allows offenders such as gamekeepers or ranchers caught poisoning, shooting or trapping protected wildlife to deny that they are criminals, although they can easily admit and identify criminality in others, such as poachers. They may deny that their actions are a crime, explaining them as legitimate predator control or a necessary part of their employment or may accept that they have committed an 'error of judgement' but not a criminal act. Matza's (1964) drift theory applies to these offenders who drift in and out of delinquency, fluctuating between total freedom and total restraint, drifting from one extreme of behaviour to another. Although they may accept the norms of society they develop a special set of justifications for their behaviour which allows them to justify behaviour that violates social norms. These techniques of neutralization (Sykes and Matza, 1957) allow them to express guilt over their illegal acts but also to rationalize between those whom they can victimize (e.g. animals) and those they cannot (other humans), rationalizing when and where they should conform and when it may be acceptable to break the law. As an example, for those offenders whose activities have only recently been the subject of legislation, the legitimacy of the law itself may be questioned allowing for unlawful activities to be justified. Many fox hunting enthusiasts, for example, strongly opposed the UK's Hunting Act 2004, which effectively criminalized their activity of hunting with dogs, as being an illegitimate and unnecessary interference with their existing activity. Thus, their continued hunting with dogs is seen as legitimate protest against an unjust law, bolstered by government rhetoric that the law should be repealed, and is denied as being criminal (Pardo and Prato, 2005). In other contexts, non-compliance with anti-hunting laws can be seen as a form of resistance (von Essen et al., 2014) as can challenges to the legitimacy of such laws, which sometimes translate into campaigns to overturn them.

Effective enforcement of wildlife crime and the illegal wildlife trade needs to directly address the criminality involved as part of mainstream crime rather than solely examining it as an environmental or conservation problem. In reality, however, effective enforcement is sadly lacking with little attention paid to consumers or the causes of the trade.

While options for prison sentences exist in some wildlife legislation; a *potential* effect of the UK Law Commission's proposals and of the US Fish and Wildlife Service's delisting approach to certain species is to allow for an increased ability to exploit wildlife through a relaxation of the regulatory regime and reduced scrutiny of 'authorized' animal killing. Wildlife laws are often broadly adequate to their purpose as conservation or species management legislation but are inadequate to fulfil their role as effective criminal justice legislation due to their reliance on a reactive enforcement regime that in practice is often ineffective and lacking resources.

The future protection of wildlife requires not only robust legislation that actually *protects* wildlife but also an effective enforcement regime that contains mechanisms for dealing with wildlife criminality and reduces repeat wildlife crimes. Thus reviewing wildlife laws requires providing a coherent system of protection for all wildlife as part of mainstream criminal justice systems, rather than relying on the expertise of environmental enthusiasts, charities and volunteers.

Summary

Despite common acceptance of the scale of the illegal trade in wildlife it remains an area of law enforcement that is significantly under-resourced and remains on the fringes of criminology. White (2008) and others have highlighted that the problem of transnational environmental crime and the illegal trade in wildlife is an area of global significance in respect of the harm it can do. White identifies that a central dilemma for green criminologists is 'how to sensibly move the debate beyond standard approaches to environmental crime, and how to shift policy and practice in ways that are more effective than conventional forms of environmental regulation' (2008: 46). The policy and law enforcement response to the illegal wildlife trade illustrates this dilemma perfectly. A common theme running through most analyses of the illegal wildlife trade is the claim of environmental harm, depletion of stocks of protected wildlife and the resultant damage to biodiversity and loss of some of the world's rarest animals. Yet enforcement remains routed in the 'search and seizure' doctrine where enforcement action is primarily taken after the event and arguably amounts to little more than containment; taking action against low-level dealers or those at the public end of the supply chain rather than dealing with source or demand problems.

Other aspects of wildlife crime illustrate the conflict between sustainable wildlife use and the needs of wildlife protection. As this chapter discusses, wildlife protection has become increasingly politicized where wildlife and human interests conflict. While in principle strong wildlife protection exists on paper, in practice its enforcement is determined by the extent to which laws are enforced. This is both a political consideration and a practical policing one. Green criminologists argue that the resources allocated to policing wildlife crime are often inadequate to the task (Schneider, 2008; Wyatt, 2013; Nurse, 2013a) reflecting the political reality that interpersonal violence and property crimes remain the dominant policing priorities. Effective investigation and enforcement of environmental crimes requires developing a policing and justice approach that recognizes the importance and specific characteristics of contemporary environmental problems. The following chapters examine these issues.

Self-study Questions

1. Why do we criminalize some activities and not others (e.g. wildlife trafficking versus wildlife tourism, illegal drugs versus precursors for illegal drugs production, alcohol versus marijuana)?
2. How is legitimate wildlife trade related to illegal trafficking (of pets, endangered species and even wildlife parts and derivatives as 'commodities')? Who benefits from illegal flows of goods and wildlife?
3. Is trafficking the main problem of the global illegal trade in wildlife? Or is it only a small part of a bigger problem?
4. Given its recognition by Interpol and international law as a serious issue how can mainstream criminal justice techniques be applied to wildlife crime and, in particular, the illegal trade in wildlife?

5

REGULATING ENVIRONMENTAL HARM: ENVIRONMENTAL CRIME AND GOVERNANCE

By the end of this chapter you should:

- Understand the key international environmental (including wildlife) protection laws that provide for contemporary environmental protection.
- Understand the key regulatory schemes that provide for contemporary environmental protection and inhibit environmental harms.
- Have a firm understanding of the key obligations on states to provide for environmental protection.
- Understand the key problems inherent in developing and maintaining an international environmental protection regime.

Introduction

As previous chapters have indicated, international environmental law provides a framework setting out the obligations on states in respect of legal standards for environmental protection. Chapter 3 outlined core international instruments such as the World Charter for Nature (1982), which identifies the principle that nature should be protected and that human exploitation of the environment should not interfere with ecosystems to the extent that nature and species living within it become extinct. Stallworthy (2008: 4) identifies environmental law as being a 'conceptual hybrid' a form of law that borrows from lots of other areas such as the criminal law, tort (civil wrong and implementing principles of rights and obligations) and even the law of contract. From a green criminological perspective, particularly a harm-based perspective (Lynch and Stretesky, 2014) this may seem unnecessarily complex. However, Stallworthy's analysis is useful in identifying that environmental law is concerned with the idea of rights, responsibilities and obligations. Thus when environmental damage occurs the public policy and law enforcement response is concerned with who is responsible for that damage, whose rights may have been infringed and which obligations have been breached.

As earlier chapters have identified, enforcement of green laws requires considering more than just who should be punished when environmental offences occur. Effective environmental justice needs to provide a framework for environmental protection, a mechanism for enforcing that framework and dealing with environmental wrongdoing and a means of resolving environmental harms when damage occurs. While the broad framework exists at international level, the detail of environmental justice systems is often a state issue placed in the hands of a range of environmental regulators, enforcers, investigators and prosecutors (see also Chapter 9). This chapter considers how law and governance structures both impose obligations on states to provide environmental protection and deal with state failures in environmental protection. Its starting point is that environmental crime and environmental enforcement often falls outside of the remit of mainstream criminal justice.

This chapter explores the extent to which law and governance contribute to the protection of the environment and introduces the interlinked concepts of environmental governance and environmental law. It identifies that regulating environmental offending and harm is complex and involves a range of institutional, economic and social frameworks within which environmental management and governance takes place. This chapter aims to provide an overview of the role of environmental law, which theoretically has considerable weight in prevention and protection of the environment and establishes the framework for clean up, compensation and other remediation of environmental damage.

Arguably state failure to effectively protect the environment is or should be criminal (Lasslett, 2014; Nurse, 2015a). A wide range of environmental obligations is imposed on states under international law and is also implicit on states as part of customary international law, which sets out expected levels of state action in various areas (Bodansky, 1995). Thus a failure to provide for effective environmental protection arguably represents a state crime. National justice systems are primarily concerned with individual offenders and, as this chapter explores, are rarely adequate to deal with state failures, thus an international justice system has been created. However, the extent to which that system effectively deals with state failures is questionable given that it often relies on other states to be affected and on their willingness to bring an action at an international level.

Key Aspects of Environmental Law

International law is of significance in respect of identifying shared values between states; particularly the basic idea that the environment should be protected and that excessive environmental damage should be subject to some form of punishment. With this in mind, environmental law, particularly in the form of treaties, sets out general expectations as well as specific commitments by which states are required to abide. Nurse (2015a) identifies that a range of international environmental law measures seek to achieve everything from preventing the international transfer of toxic waste through to protecting migratory wildlife and requiring states to take measures to ensure such species' survival. However, Stallworthy (2008: 8) argues that 'environmental commitments under international law are typically in the form of "soft" law, which has no binding effect and lacks both specificity and enforceability.' In this respect, Stallworthy suggests international environmental law is primarily aspirational; setting out principles that might develop into specific laws and allowing national sovereignty to be retained.

National sovereignty is an important concept given that states are often required to implement international law through their own domestic legislation that can take into account cultural and social sensibilities. Thus, laws on pollution may well differ between countries, but so too may their enforcement (see, for example Chapter 3; discussion of different approaches in the UK and USA to clean air legislation). Environmental enforcement might also consist of a mixed (civil and criminal) approach in one country or a strict criminal approach in another; dependent on the perceived level of the problem, influence of lobby and political groups and nature of the justice system itself.

At the core of environmental obligations is the need for environmental justice systems to provide for some form of regulation and governance. However, White and Heckenberg (2014: 197) identify that the approach of the state has generally been 'to emphasize efficiency and facilitation, rather than control' reflecting the conflict between continued use of natural resources and sustainability principles. Although Wood (2009: 55) goes further in criticizing state environmental enforcement:

> The modern environmental administrative state is geared almost entirely to the legalization of natural resource damage. In nearly every statutory scheme, the implementing agency has the authority – or discretion – to permit the very pollution or land destruction that the statutes were designed to prevent. Rather than using their delegated authority to protect crucial resources, nearly all agencies use their statutes as tools to affirmatively sanction destruction of resources by private interests.

Wood's critique identifies that the central problem of natural resource law is its implementation as management rather than protective law and that it is often characterized by an overly complex layered system which is based on permitting natural resource exploitation. This is often carried out in a manner that Wood describes as being 'a colossal failure, despite the good intentions and the hard work of many citizens, lawyers, and government officials' (2009: 43). Similarly, environmental protection laws and environmental enforcement are being potentially skewed towards the needs of business rather than pure environmental concerns (Nurse, 2015b). This idea is contextualized within Ruhl's (1997) suggestion that environmental law discourse is dominated by the following six principles:

- libertarianism (freedom of contract and markets);
- limited acceptance of regulatory restraint;
- a regulatory approach that balances (market) interests with minimizing environmental harm;
- substantive environmental law through the use of sustainability and precautionary principles;
- environmental justice and the sharing of costs and benefits among citizens;
- a deep green perspective prioritizing ecological over human interests.

Ruhl's principles indicate the conflict between market interests (i.e. economically based natural resource exploitation) and conservation and protectionist principles. Both are functions of the state, setting up a potential conflict between the need to promote free trade and maximize economic gain from natural resource exploitation versus the obligation to promote sustainable use and otherwise protect natural resources. This conflict is enshrined in the Convention on Biological Diversity (the Rio Declaration), signed by 150 world leaders at the 1992 Rio Earth Summit (currently [mid 2015] more than 187 countries have ratified the Convention). The Convention is an international agreement aimed at promoting sustainable use of biological diversity and protecting ecosystems via the following three core objectives:

- the conservation of biodiversity;
- sustainable use of the components of biodiversity;
- sharing the benefits arising from the commercial and other utilization of genetic resources in a fair and equitable way.

Principle 7 of the Rio Declaration on Environment and Development 1992 also specifies:

> States shall cooperate in a spirit of global partnership to conserve, protect and restore the health and integrity of the Earth's ecosystem. In view of the different contributions to global environmental degradation, States have Common but differentiated responsibilities. The developed countries acknowledge the responsibility that they bear in the international pursuit of sustainable development in view of the pressures their societies place on the global environment and of the technologies and financial resources they command.

In requiring governmental action to protect biodiversity, the Convention's provisions include:

- Measures and incentives for the conservation and sustainable use of biological diversity.
- Regulated access to genetic resources.
- Access to and transfer of technology, including biotechnology.
- Technical and scientific cooperation.
- Impact assessment.
- Education and public awareness.
- Provision of financial resources.
- National reporting on efforts to implement treaty commitments.

(Convention on Biological Diversity, 2014)

Implicit in these goals is continued exploitation of natural resources for human benefit. However, the Convention as part of international environmental law provides official recognition of biological diversity as 'a common concern of humankind' requiring protection through international law. The agreement between countries enshrined in the Convention covers all ecosystems, species and genetic resources. Legal instruments such as treaties are rarely sufficient on their own (Pirjatanniemi, 2009) requiring implementation through national legislation before they become effective. Stallworthy notes that the Convention retains an emphasis on national sovereignty arguing that 'many aspects regarding conservation are premised upon what amounts to encouragement of appropriate protection measures' (2008: 11). As a result, arguably states comply with international environmental law only to the extent to which doing so serves national interests and local governance needs.

Flexibility exists in how states approach their international environmental law obligations and the manner in which they implement the requirements of law commensurate with the idea that states have autonomy and discretion over how best to exploit national resources (Nurse, 2015a; Stallworthy, 2008). This is especially true in respect of 'soft' international law that is not directly enforceable but which sets out shared standards or aspirations for states, albeit these may be subject to varied interpretations commensurate with state interests. International environmental law is primarily concerned with 'managing' rather than entirely preventing negative human impact on the environment. For example, White and Heckenberg (2014) identify that in relation to wildlife trade, the function of law is to define legal notions of harm and criminality and not to provide for the health and wellbeing of animals. In this regard, the logic of international wildlife law 'is not simply to protect endangered species because they are endangered; it is to manage these "natural resources" for human use in the most equitable and least damaging manner'

(White and Heckenberg, 2014: 133). Thus exploitation of natural resources is generally legal; offences occur primarily when such exploitation exceeds the limits set by laws and regulations or fails to comply with the specific requirements of governance systems, often dominated by licensing and permit systems.

A diverse range of functions and motivations exist for international environmental regulation. Measures identified by various scholars (White and Heckenberg, 2014; Stallworthy, 2008; Situ and Emmons, 2000; Connelly and Smith, 1999) arguably suggest that environmental regulation serves the following broad purposes:

- addressing damage to human and nonhuman physical and mental health;
- addressing known threats such as global warming, ozone depletion, acid rain and biodiversity loss;
- controlling the use of transport and dumping of hazardous chemicals;
- creating offences in respect of 'serious' environmental harm;
- preserving air and water quality;
- preventing and punishing deforestation and desertification;
- preventing and punishing unsustainable business practices that harm the environment;
- protection of the natural environment, ecosystems and wildlife;
- promoting marine ecosystem health;
- protecting the value of natural resources;
- protection of migratory and endangered species;
- regulating sustainable use of natural resources;
- safeguarding the environment for future generations.

Although this is not an exhaustive list, it provides a broad framework through which various laws have been created such as the Convention on the Conservation of Migratory Species of Wild Animals (1979) (also known as the Bonn Convention); the UN Convention on the Law of the Sea (dealing with marine pollution threats); the 1998 Protocol on Persistent Organic Pollutants; and the EU's Wildlife Trade Regulations and Environmental Liability Directive. All of these measures are protective in nature and through various means attempt to regulate the use of natural resources in line with sustainability principles and to define the limits on natural resource exploitation by specifying unacceptable practices.

Space does not allow for detailed discussion of these individual mechanisms, or of the full remit of existing international environmental law. However, considering international environmental law as part of international justice systems requires some understanding of those justice systems available to address state environmental protection failures. The existence of international environmental treaties and conventions reflects the view that these are matters considered to be of such importance that only a consensus between states can deal with the subject matter (Skjærseth, 2010). International criminal law (ICL) provides a legal framework for international crimes via international rather than domestic law (Akande, 2003). International crimes are those seen as seriously violating rights of the individual and threatening international peace and security by threatening 'customary rules' of international law, and are broadly defined within the Rome Statute that created an International Criminal Court (ICC) as being 'the most serious crimes of concern to the International community' (Preamble and Article 5 of the 1998 Rome Statute of the ICC). These are broadly defined as war crimes, crimes against humanity, genocide, aggression and torture. The list of crimes contextualizes international crime as being those crimes seen as seriously violating rights of the individual and threatening international peace and security by threatening 'rules' of international law and international security and state sovereignty. Notably, ICL exists where there is a need for perpetrators to be punished according to the rule of law but domestic criminal law is considered inadequate to deal with such cross-border/multi-state crime.

Notably absent from the list of international crimes is mass environmental damage, despite green criminologists' views that significant environmental damage is one of the greatest threats to human security (Lynch and Stretesky, 2014; Ellefsen et al., 2012). Chapter 7 discusses the proposed crime of 'ecocide'; attempts have been made to have this added to the ICC's jurisdiction, largely via a fully developed law proposal presented to the United Nations by Polly Higgins in 2010 (Higgins, 2015; 2010). This proposal defined ecocide as 'the extensive damage to, destruction of or loss of ecosystem(s) of a given territory, whether by human agency or by other causes, to such an extent that peaceful enjoyment by the inhabitants of that territory has been or will be severely diminished.' However, while the ICC does not currently hear cases relating to ecocide, and there are difficulties in pursuing environmental cases under the other existing international crime definitions, other international courts are able to consider certain environmental matters.

Nurse (2014) identifies that where harm has crossed state borders such that a country has cause to take action against a violating state, the International Court of Justice (ICJ) has been active in examining environmental matters (Viñuales, 2008; Nurse, 2014). This is primarily in relation to its core jurisdiction of resolving disputes between states that cannot be resolved through domestic means or negotiation. While in practice countries have to consent to the court's jurisdiction, thus preserving their sovereignty, the ICJ provides one means through which international environmental law can be enforced where there has been a failure at a state level. The remedy has been underused; the ICJ, in fact created a special Chamber for Environmental Matters in 1993, which was periodically reconstituted until 2006. However, in the 13 years of this Chamber's existence no state ever requested that a case be dealt with by it, thus in 2006 the ICJ retired its environmental chamber by deciding not to hold elections for a Bench for the Chamber. Despite this, Nurse (2014, 2015) reports that the issue of Japan's alleged breach of the moratorium on commercial whaling (see Chapter 8) was considered by the ICJ in an action brought in 2010 by Australia (later joined by New Zealand). In 2014 the ICJ delivered a ruling banning Japanese Southern Antarctic whaling that, at time of writing, Japan has agreed to abide by. This case demonstrates that effective international justice arguably exists in some form, although it should be noted that in 2015 Japan has developed proposals that, if accepted, would allow it to resume Southern Antarctic whaling and which purport to address the issues raised in the ICJ case.

However, beyond international mechanisms, much environmental regulation takes place at a state level within governance systems that are primarily regulatory in nature rather than based within criminal law. But environmental governance systems still define offences against the environment and state environmental standards and may well resort to the criminal law when other means of dealing with offending and non-compliance fail.

Governance and Regulatory Compliance

White and Heckenberg (2014: 200–2) identify environmental regulation as broadly operating along a continuum from direct command and control from the state through to voluntary regulation by business. Failures in environmental governance are discussed in more detail in Chapter 6. However, the basics of environmental governance frameworks are summed up by Potoski and Prakash (2004: 152) as follows:

> Across the United States and around the world, businesses have joined voluntary governmental and nongovernmental environmental regulations. Such codes often require firms to establish internal environmental management systems to improve their environmental performance and regulatory compliance. Meanwhile, governments have been offering incentives to businesses that self-police their regulatory compliance and promptly report and correct violations.

As this indicates, the central issue of environmental governance is state regulatory (rather than criminal justice) control, allied to a self-policing structure intended to promote and encourage voluntary corporate environmental responsibility rather than to directly compel it. However, the central problem in assessing appropriate standards of Corporate Environmental Responsibility (CER) is that a range of approaches to CER exist within the broad Corporate Social Responsibility (CSR) framework in which corporations audit and report on the impact of their activities on environments and local communities (Jamison et al., 2005). But the largely voluntary nature of CSR frameworks means they have considerable discretion in how they do this, including which methods to adopt and the manner in which the information is made available to the public (Spence, 2011). Thus the effectiveness of CER and the extent to which it is enshrined in corporate practices is a core concern of governance systems. Potoski and Prakash (2004: 152) indicate that one trend in CER and environmental governance is the proliferation of voluntary compliance mechanisms such as ISO 14001 and the UN's Global Compact; measures outlining indicative standards of behaviour and environmental compliance and expectations on business and states. The second is government and enforcer experimentation with regulatory relief (or compliance incentive) programmes where environmental protection agencies and regulators 'offer businesses incentives for complying with regulations, including greater flexibility in how they meet regulations, technical assistance, and sometimes even forgiving violations and eschewing punishments and sanctions' (Potoski and Prakash, 2004: 152). Such mechanisms reflect the perception of business as being legitimate actors for whom state agencies may consider criminalization is undesirable (as indicated in Chapter 3). But while Potoski and Prakash identify that such programmes have an appealing rationale by encouraging business to work towards compliance, they also offer business immunity (both civil and criminal) for self-reported and corrected violations thus tacitly endorsing criminality and corporate wrongdoing if reported after the event within a culture of negotiated compliance.

Such measures are seldom in place elsewhere in justice systems where offenders are generally subject to a punitive criminal justice system, albeit reduced sentences are sometimes offered in the case of pleas in mitigation or prompt admissions of guilt. However, they do raise questions concerning the sincerity of CER policies and compliance, which Harris indicates may be adopted for a variety of reasons, namely:

1. Acting ethically is the right way for the company to behave.
2. Doing what is right and fair is expected of an organization.
3. Acting ethically is in the organisation's best interests.

(Harris, 2011: 39)

The priority applied to these reasons varies according to corporate circumstances and motivation, including the threat of regulatory or enforcement activity or adverse publicity. This potentially impacts on the extent to which CER is adopted as part of operational practices ensuring that the corporation considers the impact and wider implications of its activities, or whether CER becomes solely an aspect of marketing and brand management, a PR tool or an enforcement mitigation strategy. The need to combat negative publicity or perceptions of a corporation and its valuable brand may, for example, lead to the adoption of CER purely to obtain benefits for a Multinational Enterprise's (MNE) public image. Similarly, knowledge of the compliance concessions and negotiated compliance potential allowed by voluntary regulator schemes can be a powerful motivator behind joining a scheme and admitting to offences within its confines.

There may even be inconsistency within a MNE about the extent to which CER should be observed or apply to its operations, especially where there is no clear chain of CER ownership at board (strategic) level and CSR reporting is outside of core corporate governance, external scrutiny or stakeholder audit.

Thus while some MNEs may engage with CER as an integral part of their corporate practices and governance, others may only superficially engage with CER. An organization's reporting of environmental compliance and its adoption of CER strategies are immaterial if the strategies are not adhered to in practice and make no impact on decision-making. Voluntarism thus fails in part because CER might be adopted to suit the needs of a corporation's stakeholders or the development and protection of its brand, rather than being adopted as part of an ethical operating strategy that minimizes the impact on communities affected by their actions. But it may also fail because of the lack of an enforceable, independently verified CER standard against which an organization's performance and the accuracy of its reporting can be assessed. Thus CER voluntarism by itself may be inadequate and legal controls may be required to enforce CER although this can itself be problematic.

Enforcing CER and Ethical Governance

As outlined in earlier chapters, corporations who break environmental laws and accepted standards of behaviour are not always prosecuted via the criminal law but are sometimes subject only to civil or administrative sanctions. In many cases this is the role of environmental regulators such as the EPA in the USA and The Environment Agency in the UK rather than statutory policing or criminal justice agencies (discussed further in Chapters 8 and 9). Potoski and Prakash (2004) argue that voluntary compliance and regulatory relief programmes represent a win—win where they achieve superior compliance via cooperation with business. However, they acknowledge that where they fail 'regulatory enforcement will result in lose–lose conflicts that are all too common in environmental governance' (2004: 153). Such conflicts have the dual negative consequence of having allowed a corporation to perhaps continue with offending for longer than was necessary, while also leaving affected communities without a remedy when enforcers and regulators resort to criminal prosecution where this is the default or backup option behind a voluntary compliance scheme. Ayres and Braithwaite (1992) refer to this as enforced regulation where the initial light-touch, voluntary regulation scheme may give way to 'command regulation with non-discretionary punishment' (White and Heckenberg, 2014: 203).

The risk with such mechanisms is that they often fail to provide redress for victims of environmental damage whose victimization may not be redressed through criminal enforcement that comes only after a prolonged period of offending. Nor are they directly addressed where regulatory measures pursue negotiated compliance that effectively allows offending to go unpunished. Slapper (2011) identifies that there have been modest developments in the use of the civil law to address corporate abuses (2011: 95) and that 'apart from a growth in domestic criminal liability of corporations' there has been an increase both in civil litigation against companies 'but also the advent of domestic liability for corporate torts that are committed abroad' (2011: 95). Thus, while international law may not yet have caught up with corporate abuses, domestic law might, in some cases, provide a civil remedy for environmental wrongdoing.

Slapper's point is illustrated by US civil law in the form of the Alien Tort Claims Act 1789, which allows action to be taken against companies for their actions overseas (Slapper, 2011: 95). The Act confers on US federal courts jurisdiction over 'any civil action by an alien for a tort only, committed in violation of the law of nations or a treaty of the United States'. Thus where corporate acts that are the subject of litigation raise international concerns and constitute crime against humanity, a remedy potentially exists for victims of corporate abuses able to bring a case in US courts (Berman, 2012). Cases can also be brought in the European Union (EU) against a parent company resident in the EU where it can be shown that the relevant management decisions (i.e. those which influenced or caused the local incident) were made at parent company level. Fagan and Thompson identify class actions as being the primary legal mechanism feared by US corporations, which Hodges (2008) identifies as being based on a model where 'one individual claim is asserted to represent a class of others, whose owners are bound by the result of the single claim unless they opt-out of the class and procedure' (2008: 2). The class action procedure allows for punitive damages and requires parties to meet their own costs (Fagan and Thompson, 2009: 56–7).

The existence of CSR policies can also be a factor in litigation. The International Council on Human Rights Policy notes that while many company CSR codes are little more than public relations exercises, where worded with sufficient clarity 'they can also have legal significance because they set out the values, ethical standards, and expectations of the company concerned, and might be used as evidence in legal proceedings with suppliers, employees or consumers' (2002: 70). Fagan and Thompson (2009: 55) identify that litigation has already been brought against companies such as Wal-Mart and Nike for publishing allegedly misleading CSR materials. Nike was the subject of litigation after having allegedly lied in PR materials about the mistreatment of workers in its supply chain, while Wal-Mart was sued for a failure to enforce its supplier standards. Thus while international human rights norms might be difficult to enforce against companies, CSR materials can, in the USA at least, be used as evidence of the standards that a corporation claims to meet and Fagan and Thompson argue that consumers might be able to bring misrepresentation claims against corporations if they can demonstrate that they have suffered recoverable loss as a result of the claims made (2009: 55). The threat of such litigation might encourage a change in corporate behaviour and when combined with criminal action such as that employed in the US Foreign Corrupt Practices Act (and also within UK legislation) of providing incentives for corporations to work with enforcers in order to avoid criminal prosecution and to settle cases through civil mechanisms (Hatchard, 2011: 153–5) can provide a remedy.

Environmental Offences and Human Rights

Environmental regulation also extends to the interface between environmental rights and human rights. Chapter 6 explores the criminal exploitation of natural resources, particularly in the oil, gas and timber trades where the rights of local communities are sometimes infringed by transnational corporations. Within mainstream criminal justice, the dictates of human rights law sometimes requires states to act positively to uphold citizens rights, even where doing so may arguably inhibit the effective operation of criminal justice (Stone, 2010; Fenwick, 2007). Smith (2010: 369) also identifies that the United Nations Global Compact, which contains measures aimed at encouraging business to respect human rights, also contains principles relating to the environment as follows:

- **Principle 7** – Businesses should support a precautionary principle to environmental challenges;
- **Principle 8** – states should undertake initiatives to promote greater environmental responsibility; and
- **Principle 9** – encourage the development and diffusion of environmentally friendly technologies.

The Compact recognizes the importance of environmental rights and that interference with them produces serious negative effects for communities. Although often not specifically enshrined in the criminal law, rights relating to the environment are spread across a number of instruments including: the Universal Declaration on Human Rights; the International Covenant on Economic Social and Cultural Rights; the International Covenant on Economic Social and Cultural Rights; the Convention on the Rights of the Child; and within various case law and national legislation. These and other instruments contain the following broad environmental rights:

- Right to ecologically sustainable development.
- Right to an adequate standard of living including access to safe food and water.

- Rights of children to live in an environment suitable for physical and mental development.
- Right to participation in environmental decision making.
- Right of access to education and information including information on the links between health and the environment.

In particular, the UN 1972 Declaration on the Environment contains the following:

- **Principle 1** – Man has the fundamental right to freedom, equality and adequate conditions of life, in an environment of a quality that permits a life of dignity and well-being, and he bears a solemn responsibility to protect and improve the environment for present and future generations.
- **Principle 2** – The natural resources of the earth, including the air, water, land, flora and fauna and especially representative samples of natural ecosystems, must be safeguarded for the benefit of present and future generations through careful planning or management, as appropriate.

Such provisions set out a basic framework linking man's fundamental rights and freedoms with the quality of the environment, which is expanded upon by the Universal Declaration on Human Rights which specifies that:

- **Article 22** – Everyone has the right to social security and is entitled to realization of the economic, social and cultural rights indispensable for his dignity and the free development of his personality.
- **Article 25** – Everyone has the right to a standard of living adequate for the health and well-being of himself and of his family, including food, clothing, housing and medical care and necessary social services.
- **Article 27** – Everyone has the right freely to participate in the cultural life of the community, to enjoy the arts and to share in scientific advancement and its benefits.

Although the environment is not mentioned as a specific right within the Universal Declaration on Human Rights, the Declaration has been interpreted positively to consider how standards of living and right to access the benefits of society are inextricably linked, as the following quote illustrates:

> If you deliberately dump toxic waste in someone's community or disproportionately exploit their natural resources without adequate consultation and compensation, clearly you are abusing their rights ... changes in the environment can have a significant impact on our ability to enjoy our human rights. In no other area is it so clear that the actions of nations, communities, businesses and individuals can so dramatically affect the rights of others——because damaging the environment can damage the rights of people, near and far, to a secure and healthy life.
>
> (Office of the UN High Commissioner for Human Rights, 2015)

Thus a conception that environmental crime impacts negatively on environmental rights exists, so too does disproportionate exploitation of natural resources. Generally under human rights Conventions, states are required to take action to positively uphold rights or to ensure that they are interfered with only so far as is necessary. Thus, human rights Conventions and national human rights law potentially provide additional weapons in the environmental protection toolkit. The European Convention on Human Rights (ECHR), for example, does not specifically provide for a right to live in a healthy environment but manages to achieve this goal by engaging several of its individual rights. Article 2 (right to life) Article 8 (respect for privacy and family life) Protocol 1, Article 1 (the right to peaceful enjoyment of possessions and property) and even Article 6 (the right to a fair hearing) have all been used in cases before the European Court of Human Rights (ECtHR) to develop the idea of a right to a healthy environment that public authorities (e.g. the state and local government) are required to uphold.

The following section provides a brief overview of some relevant cases:

Article 2 The Right to Life

In *Oneryildiz v. Turkey*, 48939/99 [2004] ECHR 657 (30 November 2004), the first ECtHR case involving loss of life, the right to life linked to a healthy environment was explicitly considered. In 1993 a foreseeable methane explosion killed nine members of the applicant's family. No measures had been taken to prevent this from occurring despite the existence of an expert report dating back to 1991 and identifying no measures had been taken to prevent a possible explosion of methane gas from a rubbish tip near where the applicant lived. A complaint made under Article 2 of the ECHR (the right to life) that the accident had occurred as a result of negligence on the part of the relevant authorities was upheld. The ECtHR concluded that as the Turkish authorities knew or should have known about the risk to the lives of people living near the tip they had an obligation to take measures to protect the residents. Accordingly, there had been a violation of right to protection of life enshrined in Article 2 in its procedural aspect; violation of the right to peaceful enjoyment of possessions as protected by Article 1 of the Protocol No. 1; and violation of the right to a domestic remedy.

Budayeva and Others v. Russia, Application, 15339/02, 21166/02, 20058/02, 11673/02 and 15343/02 [2008] (20 March 2008) involved a claim that the Russian government had failed to fulfil its obligations under Article 2 of the ECHR to protect the right to life. A mudslide that caused eight deaths was considered to be a breach of Article 2 ECHR, because the authorities failed to implement land-planning and emergency-relief policies despite the fact that the area of Tyrnauz where the incident occurred was known to be vulnerable to mudslides. Failure by local authorities to take action exposed residents to known 'mortal risk', which raised an obligation to take action to prevent loss of life. Failure to take such action was considered to be an infringement of the Article 2 right to life while the lack of any state investigation or examination of the accident was considered by the ECtHR to also constitute a violation of Article 2 ECHR.

Article 8 ECHR

Lopez Ostra v. Spain (Application no. 16798/90) – In this case, state failure to control industrial pollution was considered to be a violation of Article 8 where there was sufficient serious interference with the applicant's enjoyment of their home. Similarly in *Guerra v. Italy* (116/1996/735/932) a state failure to deal with toxic emissions (severe environmental pollution) affected individuals' well-being and prevented them from enjoying their homes in such a way as to affect their private and family life adversely. The ECtHR noted that regard has to be given to the fair balance between the competing interests of the individual and community as a whole (paragraphs 1 and 2 of Article 8). The economic interests of the state (which is regarded as the interest of the community as a whole) can, in some circumstances, override the interest of the individual, thus it is not unreasonable for a state to prioritize economic development and the wider interest of providing jobs and economic growth against the interests of individual citizens. However, in both *Lopez Ostra v. Spain* and *Guerra v. Italy* the ECtHR concluded that where a polluting activity violates national law, the state's overriding economic interest in its continued illegal operation is difficult to assert. The violation, arguably constituting an environmental crime, effectively invalidates any interest the state might claim and the principle that interference with an individual's rights should generally only take place where it is done in accordance with the law, is necessary and is proportionate. The state also has a duty to take positive measures to secure the enjoyment of individual rights to life and property, thus failure to enforce existing law can engage Article 8.

Article 6 Fair Hearing

Although Article 6 is not used as widely as Article 2 or Article 8, in *Kyrtatos v. Greece*, 41666/98 [2003] ECHR 242 the refusal of domestic

(Continued)

(Continued)

authorities to comply with binding decisions of courts and the delays in proceedings engaged this right in conjunction with an Article 8 issue. The applicant's complaint under Article 8 related to the effect of tourist development on an important wildlife refuge adjacent to property owned by one of the applicants. In 1993 the applicants sought judicial review of a decision to allow buildings to be erected near their land, which was considered an important natural habitat for several protected species, arguing that constitutional protection for the environment made the buildings illegal. Their application was successful, but in 1997 it was discovered that the authorities had not enforced these judgments and not only had they failed to demolish the buildings, they had continued to issue permits for building in the area. The ECtHR held that there had been a violation of Article 6 of the Convention due to the non-compliance with earlier judgments pronounced, and as regards the length of the two sets of proceedings; in relation to Article 8 the Court held that there had been no violation.

Okyay and others v. Turkey, 36220/97 [2005] ECHR 476) – failure by the Turkish national authorities to implement a (domestic) courtruling, closing down three thermal-power plants that were polluting the environment. This was a complaint under Article 6 that the right to a fair hearing had been breached by the administrative authorities' failure to enforce the administrative courts' decisions and orders to halt the operations of the thermal-power plants. Failure to comply in practice and within a reasonable time with judgments (1996 for the Administrative Court and upheld by the Supreme Administrative Court on 3 and 6 June 1998) had the effect of depriving Article 6-1 of any useful effect.

These cases illustrate that the right to a healthy environment is often interlinked with other human rights mechanisms and need not be explicitly written into environmental laws or a country's constitution in order to be enforced. It should be noted, however, that certain states have done so, effectively making the right to a healthy environment a public law matter that may be directly enforceable (Fenwick, 2007; Smith, 2010). As Chapter 1 indicates, the Aarhus Convention also provides a conception of environmental justice and regulatory control based around providing distinct access to information about the environment and mechanisms to challenge public decisions that have negative environmental consequences. The Aarhus Convention is based on three core pillars:

- the right to know
- the right to participate
- the right of access to environmental justice.

As Aarhus explicitly recognizes every person's right to live in a healthy environment, the Convention provides a framework for the enforcement of a distinct environmental right and an obligation on states to monitor threats to that right. Within Aarhus, the public must be informed of activity or specific projects that could adversely affect the environment (the right to know) in order that they might exercise rights to question or challenge an activity. The Convention recognizes the role of NGOs as having a role in allowing the public to access environmental justice and by ensuring that the public has recourse to the law also requires that there must be some form of remedy mechanism available to those affected by decisions and projects that could adversely affect the environment. Judicial Review is frequently the mechanism through which NGOs will fulfil this role; the UK, for example, has chosen its judicial review procedure as its mechanism for providing the public with the scrutiny and redress tools required by Aarhus. This provides a means for a person with sufficient 'standing' (in this case those affected by an environmentally harmful decision) to take action through the courts to question the legality of that decision and whether the correct decision-making process has been followed. While there is some complexity, and considerable case law, concerning who has standing, the Judicial Review process has been successfully used by NGOs such as Greenpeace to challenge public authority decisions that have negative environmental consequences.

Summary

This chapter highlights the complexity of environmental law and governance and the basic framework of environmental obligations on states and the manner in which these work in practice. There is considerably more that could be said about this topic and a number of journals devote space to exploring this in depth (see Further Reading section later in this book) but essentially you should understand that international environmental law requires states to protect the environment, to have some form of regulatory or enforcement mechanism to deal with environmental offending and legislative breaches and to give citizens access to environmental information and, in Europe at least, a right of redress where improper decisions are taken that negatively impact on the environment.

The challenges of environmental law and governance are in how best to deal with a system that is dominated by corporate offending. Arguably an inherent conflict exists between the legitimate interests of business and states in exploiting natural resources for human benefit and a green criminological or environmentalist perspective, which argues that environmental exploitation must be significantly reduced or stopped altogether. CER is embraced by business but the question remains to what extent is this just business proclaiming what people expect it to do while at the same time continuing to act either illegally or to challenge enforcement action aimed at environmental harm caused by business practices? As this chapter illustrates, voluntary compliance and self-regulation are core features of environmental governance. But criminologists have previously identified that many transnational corporations have good CER policies on paper but continue to commit criminal or environmentally damaging acts within a weak regulatory system that fails to address environmental deviance (Situ and Emmons, 2000; Doyon, 2014; Nurse, 2014). Thus the issue for green criminology and environmental governance systems to consider is how should good standards of CER be enforced and should this solely require defining what is legal or illegal? Arguably enshrining CER and superior compliance within environmental governance systems requires going further to include standards of behaviour and expectations of corporate behaviour that the public will accept as ethical compliance.

This chapter also identifies that the concept of a right to a healthy environment is a complex one that is officially recognized juridically in three ways:

- As being derived from other rights – primarily rights to life, health and respect for private and family life – but occasionally other rights, e.g. culture, dignity, equality and nondiscrimination.
- As an autonomous entitlement expressly written into environmental and constitutional laws.
- As 'procedural environmental rights' – e.g. the Aarhus Convention rights – right to prior knowledge; right to participate in decision-making; and right to redress.

Human rights instruments provide a means through which these rights are being enforced by environmental victims, where state failure to ensure a healthy environment results in negative consequences including loss of home and/or death. Accordingly when looking at environmental governance and regulation it becomes necessary to examine a range of instruments on the governance spectrum, ranging from coercive legislative instruments to governance approaches that engage the agency and knowledge of resource users and require states to positively implement different forms of environmental protection.

Self-study Questions

1. To what extent is there an obligation on states to provide for effective environmental protection?
2. Why is environmental protection not a core policing responsibility?
3. What problems exist in providing an international enforcement regime for environmental protection that deals with state failures?
4. On what grounds can it be argued that environmental rights exist for human individuals?
5. On what normative grounds can it be argued that people ought to have a claim to specific environmental rights?

6

THE CRIMINAL EXPLOITATION OF NATURAL RESOURCES

By the end of this chapter you should:

- Have a firm understanding of the factors involved in the criminal exploitation of natural resources.
- Understand the links between the legal and illegal oil and gas extraction industries and why there are criminological concerns about industry practices.
- Understand how and why globalization is a factor in the continuing illegal exploitation of natural resources such as oil, gas and timber and why corruption is considered to be endemic in these industries.
- Understand the concept of biopiracy and why this constitutes a crime of the powerful that impacts negatively on the rights of indigenous communities and those living in the Global South.
- Understand the extent to which consumer demand combined with weak regulation and enforcement allows illegal exploitation of natural resources to continue.

Introduction

This chapter follows on from Chapter 5's discussion of environmental governance and regulation, to explore the exploitation of natural resources. While the chapter title refers to 'criminal' exploitation, it continues the theme of legal actors committing offences and the general failure of justice systems to prevent or effectively punish these acts. Thus, the theme of the legal facilitating the illegal is a core concern of this chapter, particularly in respect of (mostly Western) transnational corporations who dominate the oil and gas extraction industries and are able to exert considerable economic power in developing world countries where they operate.

The global operations of multinational (business) enterprises (MNEs) can have significant negative consequences for the communities in which they operate and the wider environment (Nurse, 2015b). Globalization's increased flows of people, products and profits allow multinational corporations (MNCs) to operate freely in developing countries where regulatory controls may be weaker than in the developed world and where public institutions (including government bureaucracy and the judiciary) may be weak and susceptible to economic pressure (Cox, in McGrew, 1997: 51). As Chapter 5 illustrates, while businesses may in principle embrace the concept of ethical operations and human rights compliance claiming to implement these in their CSR or CER policies, the extent to which they do so, the content of these policies and their applicability to the concepts of environmental compliance varies considerably. As this book illustrates, much corporate environmental offending is not, strictly speaking, 'criminal' but relates to regulatory breaches and deviation from permitted exploitation of natural resources, non-compliance with legislation or governance processes and infringements of the environmental rights of communities. While there has been widespread adoption of CSR policies by businesses in developed countries in the last 20 years or so, business activities are often not subject to international law or human rights norms. Harvard Professor John Ruggie, the Special Representative to the UN Human Rights Council, identified that 'the failure to enforce existing laws that directly or indirectly regulate business respect for human rights is often a significant legal gap in State practice' (United Nations Human Rights Council, 2011: 5). Thus not only is judging appropriate standards of corporate behaviour problematic but so too is enforcing such standards and remedying environmental/human rights problems caused by corporations. As Chapter 5 indicates, business activity that harms or impacts on the environmental rights of communities and which is not prohibited by clear criminal laws is subject to a mixture of voluntary compliance, regulatory activity and victim litigation primarily driven by national legislation.

Chapter 5 exposed the reality that while there is no single accepted and binding CER standard a range of voluntary measures is in place. Arguably corporate directors already have a number of incentives to align their behaviour with accepted standards and routinely claim to be operating responsibly, taking account of the needs of communities (Alcock and Conde, 2005). However, CER deals not just with *actual* illegal activity on the part of corporations but also with harm caused by their activities even where legal; a core concern of green criminology (Lynch and Stretesky, 2014). Lawful activities such as oil and gas extraction may result in harmful consequences for ecosystems that may fall outside the strict legalistic definition of crimes (Situ and Emmons, 2000) where these are unintended or accidental consequences of a lawful activity. Arguably, neoliberal markets encourage such activities by valuing profit and ignoring or minimizing externalities, particularly the wide range of environmental harms that arise from ostensibly lawful activities which may result in pollution incidents such as oil spills (Lynch and Stretesky, 2014: 8–10). Alcock and Conde (2005) argue that given the 'natural' controls that already exist, further legislation is unnecessary to enforce CER but numerous cases highlight the failure of corporations to remedy the environmental harm they have caused suggesting the failure of self-regulation and voluntary compliance with ethical standards (see also Chapter 5).

By examining the activities of the oil and gas extraction industries and the emerging area of biopiracy, this chapter examines how legal corporate actors become involved in actions that green scholars (Ellefsen et al., 2012; White and Heckenberg, 2014; Lynch and Stretesky, 2014) would define as criminal. However, although such activities may not be always *directly* addressed through criminal law mechanisms, their processes (bribery and corruption) and consequences (in some cases as extreme as loss of life) can bring industry practice under the scrutiny of criminal justice systems. Thus this chapter argues that the exploitation of natural resources is a significant issue for both mainstream and green criminology.

The Oil and Gas Extraction Industries

White (2007) identifies inequality as a significant aspect of environmental justice, particularly the manner in which ethnic minority and indigenous communities suffer at the hands of Western forces. Rachman (2009) identifies energy derived from oil as significant for the world's largest economies (the EU, USA, China and Russia) none of which are entirely self-sufficient in oil thus relying on sources other than their own to meet energy needs. Considerable incentive, and economic benefit, thus exists for MNCs operating in the oil and gas industries to continue their operations. This also gives major oil companies such as BP, Shell and Exxon (arguably the larger players in the industry together with Saudi Aramco according to Forbes' listings) considerable power when negotiating with governments, particularly within developing nations in Africa where oil resources are integral to a country's economy. Some oil companies wield considerably more economic power than developing world governments. This is particularly the case in African countries where 'administrative neglect, crumbling social infrastructure and services, high unemployment, social deprivation, abject poverty, filth and squalor, and endemic conflict' present enduring problems (Amnesty International, 2009: 9) despite the natural resource wealth and income that might be derived from oil and gas reserves.

Decades of oil exploration in the Niger Delta have resulted in pollution of much of the region's vegetation, fishponds and drinking water, directly impacting on indigenous communities. Steiner (2010: 4) identifies that over the course of 50 years of oil production in the Niger Delta the region has suffered 'extensive habitat degradation, forest clearing, toxic discharges, dredging and filling, and significant alteration by extensive road and pipeline construction from the petroleum industry'. Yet the major oil companies operating in Nigeria generally embrace the concepts of ethical operations and human rights compliance often doing so by claiming to implement these in their CSR.

Oil extraction in Africa and MNCs' behaviour typifies a number of elements common to corporate crime discourse and the green criminological perspective on environmental harm. Amao (2011: 1993) identifies that Nigeria's oil and gas revenues account for 95% of the country's export earnings, over 40% of its GDP and around 80% of government revenue. Oil is thus integral to Nigeria's economy and the lives of its citizens, and the actions of MNCs involved in the oil industry have the potential to impact not just on the environment but also on the human rights of Nigerian citizens. Amnesty International and CEHRD (2011: 33) identify that Nigeria's oil regulation system contains laws and regulations that prohibit the pollution of land and water and which also require oil companies to promote good oil field practice and comply with international standards. However, enforcement of these regulations is considered to be ineffective. Baumüller et al. (2011: 1) noted that 'negative impacts of the oil industry are a major concern in sub-Saharan Africa (SSA), threatening not only the health of local communities, but also the livelihoods they depend on'. They outline that 'consequences attributed to oil spills and gas flaring include the collapse of local fishing and farming, the loss of habitat and biodiversity, acid rain damage and health impacts of air, noise and light pollution' (Baumüller et al., 2011: 17).

Amnesty International (2009: 57) argues that international standards exist for oil industries that MNCs operating in the Niger Delta should be well aware of. Most oil companies operating in Nigeria have in place policies that commit them to good practice in terms of environmental and social impacts. However, Amnesty's research concluded that serious failures existed in some companies' actions when it came to identifying and preventing pollution and environmental harm that leads to human rights abuses. The reasons given included failings because of: 'a significant gap between policy and practice; lack of effective oversight; or through under-funding' (Amnesty International, 2009: 57). Controversially, Amnesty (2009: 57) concluded that the practice of some companies 'went beyond failure to ensure that their operations do not harm the environment, and could not be viewed as anything other than acts of negligence'.

The reality is that the cumulative effect of oil exploration in the Niger Delta is high levels of pollution that in some cases have lowered the life expectancy of citizens in some parts of the region. The United Nations Environment programme's (UNEP, 2011: 167) assessment concluded that 'oil spills are frequent events in Ogoniland'. Oil spills negatively impact on Niger Delta communities destroying livelihoods and endangering the health of local populations to the extent that 'oil contamination in Ogoniland is widespread and severely impacting many components of the environment' (UNEP, 2011: 204). Concluding that the effects of oil pollution are felt by the Ogoni people 365 days of the year, UNEP (2011: 204) also commented that given the low average life expectancy of under 50 years in Nigeria 'it is a fair assumption that most members of the current Ogoniland community have lived with chronic oil pollution throughout their lives'.

White (2012d: 15) identifies that 'much environmental harm is intrinsically transnational' and is by its very nature mobile and easily subject to transference. The global reach of MNCs is situated within international markets and systems of production, requiring a system of understanding and addressing environmental harm that incorporates appreciation of its international dimensions (Beirne and South, 2007). In this respect, where oil companies cause environmental harms in developing world countries, their activities may be viewed as a crime of the powerful (Brockington et al., 2008; Tombs and Whyte, 2003) irrespective of whether formally recognized as such by the criminal law or whether civil law action is required to address the harm. Nieuwoudt (2007) has suggested that bribery by MNCs in seeking to win exclusive drilling and processing or prospecting licences has resulted in payments to the overseas accounts of government ministers or payment of such things as their children's private school fees. NGO Transparency International (2015) also alleges corrupt payments, unchecked bribery and embezzlement and inadequate financial statements as endemic within the oil and gas industry. For example in respect of Brazil's state-owned Petrobas oil company they allege that 34 sitting MPs and 18 companies are involved in corruption where 'companies that won contracts with some Petrobras divisions diverted 3% of their value into slush funds for political parties' (The Economist, 2015). Accounting practices that protect the identities of equity holders and subsidiary companies allow stolen funds to be subsumed within accounting. Ernst and Young (2014: 19) suggest that 'as business in emerging markets continues to grow for the oil and gas sector, companies will become increasingly challenged by bribery and corruption risks' where facilitated payments are a culturally accepted industry practice and the need to engage local contractors with government contacts carries with it the potential to increase corruption and bribery risks.

Thus, the oil and gas extraction industries raise a number of white collar and corporate crime concerns. From a green criminological perspective these industries illustrate environmental justice and associated issues of social inequality and the marginalization of indigenous communities (White, 2007). In the context of green criminology's focus on environmental harms rather than crimes, the demand and wealth of Western oil consumers provide a strong driver for maximizing profits by minimizing regulatory compliance and the integration of local people into the profits of natural resources. They also illustrate corporate crime in the form of active non-compliance and attempts to subvert regulation as a means of doing business and maximizing profits. This is not confined to the activities of oil and gas MNCs in Africa, albeit a considerable amount of academic scholarship has examined this issue, particularly in respect of non-compliance with the human and environmental rights norms outlined in Chapter 5.

Concerns might also be expressed about the manner in which direct harms caused by oil and gas industries are addressed as a criminological issue. Contrast the response to persistent oil spills and localized harm in African countries with the response to the Gulf Oil Spill in 2010 which blew up killing 11 workers and creating significant damage to the local ecosystem. In the Deepwater Horizon, Gulf Oil spill, BP was actively and almost immediately involved in a clean-up operation and cooperated with federal authorities. Shortly after the incident, US attorney general Eric Holder was reported to have said that 'nothing was off the table' in respect of possible charges for illegal behaviour and claimed that US authorities would be forceful in their response (Webb and Pilkington, 2010). While Partlett and Weaver (2011) argued that the law has failed to find a 'proper' response to the disaster, subsequently, considerable activity by enforcers and by BP and its contractors resulted in a $90 million dollar civil settlement, criminal plea agreements in excess of $4 billion in which the US government waived criminal prosecution in return for payment of criminal recovery costs, criminal fines and agreements by some of the involved parties to be placed on probation. The US Courts Service has also set up a dedicated website providing information on the various settlements judgments and compensation schemes (online at: http://www.laed.uscourts.gov/OilSpill/OilSpill.htm) and a section of the EPA's website is also devoted to its enforcement activity. By contrast, oil spills in the Niger Delta are often characterized by denial on the part of oil companies and considerable difficulties exist in bringing cases to court such that the involvement of NGOs and private lawyers may be required to pursue civil claims in the absence of effective criminal prosecution (Ladan, 2011).

From a criminological perspective, the corporate response to problems within the oil and gas extraction industries indicates Sykes and Matza's (1957) neutralization techniques in operation. Given the continued legality of oil extraction and natural resource exploitation and sustainable use, MNCs engaged in lawful activity that is then linked to perceived wrongdoing in a way that arguably challenges their status as legitimate actors by labelling certain actions as 'criminal', requires a response. One consequence of this is that the MNCs respond to the labelling either in an increasingly deviant manner (Sykes and Matza, 1957; McBarnet, 2006) or via the use of neutralization techniques that assert their core values and the underlying legitimacy of their actions while challenging the enforcement or regulatory regime. Thus techniques such as denial of responsibility, claim of entitlement, denial of the necessity of the law, defence of necessity and condemnation of the condemners are all present, reflecting the research of Sykes and Matza (1957) which identified that individuals involved in crime use these techniques both before and after engaging in illegal activity.

The Illegal Timber Trade

Similar problems occur in respect of the illegal timber trade. Myburg (cited in Haken, 2011) suggests that the illegal timber trade is worth as much as US$7 billion per year, (unreported and unregulated) fisheries trade alone was valued at between US$4.2 billion and US$9.5 billion per year. Figures reported by the United Nations Office on Drugs and Crime (UNODC) put the trade in illegal timber from South-East Asia to the European Union and Asia as worth an estimated $3.5 billion in 2010.

Economic considerations drive much (albeit not all) environmental crime; particularly profit-driven crimes fuelled by demand for forest products or where wildlife has negative economic impact on producers such that its destruction or removal and destruction of habitats becomes desirable to achieve or maintain economic benefit (White, 2008). Timber markets, for example, demonstrate the relatively simple mechanics of supply and demand and the symbiotic relationship between producers and consumers. Where demand for such products is high and lawful supply is limited, illegal logging is likely to occur particularly to fuel the demand of an international market where end consumers and participants in the trade may be 'flexible' concerning the source of products and where historically weak trade rules have allowed the trade to continue (Smith et al., 2003). The illegal timber trade leads to deforestation and threatens critical habitat while also fuelling underground crime and affecting jobs in the legitimate timber industry (EIA, 2013). Rhodes et al. (2006) identify problems of illegal logging as primarily being based in economic concerns where loggers with uninhibited access to source woods are able to supply the market irrespective of the wider costs (and externalities) of any illegal activity they conduct. EIA (2013) identified the illegal timber trade in Russia as being one in which corruption is endemic with hardwoods being illegally harvested in Russia, smuggled over the border to China and then passed through factories and warehouses to showrooms where consumers purchase products likely unaware of their illegal origins and the negative impact on the environment, local people and ecosystems.

Kishor and Lescuyer (2012) in their discussion of illegal logging argued that 'little has been done so far to specifically fight illegal logging in the domestic markets of the tropical countries' (2012: 8), less has been done in consumer countries albeit consumer-based social crime prevention is emerging as a potential solution to illegal timber trafficking and endangered species trade. Bisschop (2012) identifies that the social organization of transnational environmental crime is shaped by the global context of the places of origin, transit and destination, where an almost symbiotic relationship exists between the legal and the illegal. Solinge (2008) and Nurse (2015a) note that links have been made between illegal timber, arms trading, armed militias and terror groups, noting that in some cases illegal timber is logged and exported with the authorization of governmental authorities despite its unlawful origins. Thus, corruption between state and other authorities and corporations and organized crime groups is a part of the trade. This illustrates both the value of timber as a tradeable commodity and the links between the legal and illegal trades.

The demand and wealth of (urban) consumers of forest products (including exotic woods) can be a strong driver of illegal wildlife and forest activities where enforcement action is largely targeted at suppliers. Schneider (2008) suggests a market reduction approach to such trafficking, reflecting the importance of users in facilitating continued illegal trade. Besides users on the supply side, such as local subsistence users, commercial hunters and forest concessionaires, a diverse group of users exists on the demand side. These include consumptive end-users in markets and restaurants, and non-consumptive users, such as tourists. Schneider's market reduction approach consists of identifying 'hot' products and market-based analysis of these products to identify who is involved in their criminal exploitation and subsequent analysis of the reasons for their involvement. Schneider identifies ivory, rhino horns, and animal skins and parts as status symbols prized by wealthy customers around the world who are not traditionally the subject of law enforcement attention (2008). Wildlife resources are also allegedly used to fund other activities such as conflict (terror) groups and militias. However, demand for oil, gas and other natural resources is a significant factor in the exploitation of these resources where legal entities operate alongside illegal ones.

Thus market-based approaches address the demand for and supply of wildlife products targeting prices and markets for wildlife products and substitutes such as sustainable harvested resources. Common, market-based strategies to prevent illegal trade in wildlife products include the following tactics:

- imposing taxes or other levies to raise consumer prices or reduce producer profitability;
- lowering tax rates on (sustainable) substitute products; and
- increasing the profitability of sustainable-harvested production through subsidies, value adding, certification and labelling.

(UNODC, 2012: 346)

However, market-based instruments rely on clearly established property rights, a contested issue in many source countries for wildlife and timber products and the cooperation of governments to apply financial and economic instruments to the wildlife and timber trades. Thus, certification measures and trade regulations (both international and domestic) provide a means through which social crime prevention might be attempted by addressing consumer and retailer behaviour, although they are significantly under-utilized. The EU seeks to achieve this via its timber trade regulation (Regulation (EU) No 995/2010 of the European Parliament and of the Council of 20 October 2010), which lays down the obligations of operators who place timber and timber products on the market. The measure, also known as the (Illegal) Timber Regulation, counters the trade in illegally harvested timber and timber products through three key obligations:

1. It prohibits the placing on the EU market for the first time of illegally harvested timber and products derived from such timber.
2. It requires EU traders who place timber products on the EU market for the first time to exercise 'due diligence'.
3. To facilitate the traceability of timber products traders have an obligation to keep records of their suppliers and customers.

Once on the market, the timber and timber products may be sold on and/or transformed before they reach the final consumer. While attempts at market reduction or control are to be welcomed, such measures are potentially vulnerable to fraud (e.g. false declarations) and abuse by traders as has been the case with other wildlife certification schemes, e.g. the CITES permit system. More problematic is the exploitation of natural resources where disputes over origin and ownership may be difficult to resolve.

Biopiracy: Contemporary Exploitation of Natural Resources

Biopiracy is concerned with the actions of biotechnology corporations involved in the (illegal) exploitation of natural products with medicinal and healing properties in a manner where doing so involves the exploitation of the resources of developing nations. South (2007) identifies how Western multinational corporations are dominant in exploiting natural resources often at the expense of the rights of indigenous peoples. Supporters of Western corporations' activities call this 'bio-prospecting', while opponents often refer to it as biopiracy. Zainol et al. (2011: 12395) argue that biopiracy is so defined because indigenous communities have increasingly had to contend 'with the misappropriation of their biological resources and associated traditional knowledge (TK) through the inappropriate exercise of intellectual property rights (IPRs)'. Such commercial exploitation routinely restricts the future use of medicinal plants while failing to pay fair compensation to the community from which it originates.

Biopiracy involves commercial development of naturally occurring biological materials, such as plant substances or genetic cell lines, in a manner that is arguably criminal; involving such activity as land theft, human rights abuses, bribery and fraud. In one sense it represents a crime of the powerful where illegal or at least unethical means are employed to pursue a legitimate goal; developing new pharmaceuticals and medicines. However, local people and indigenous peoples who have arguably contributed to the development of natural resources are often marginalized in the development of such projects and in some cases their rights are actively ignored. White and Heckenberg (2014) refer to this as the 'corporatization of agriculture', identifying that major corporations have begun to take control of agriculture to the extent that 'the basic means of life of humans is being reconstituted and reorganized through global systems of production' (2014: 146).

As an example of alleged biopiracy in action, Parry (2001) cites the case of the Bintangor tree, which contains a drug called Calanolide A. The drug once extracted from the tree's latex, reduces the levels of the Aids virus in the blood and also works against tuberculosis. If successfully developed in a way that allows it to be sold commercially, reportedly the drug derived from the Bintangor tree could potentially be worth as much as £250 million a year (Parry, 2001). However, exploitation of the Bintangor tree excludes the native Dyak people who still live in the area. Afreen (2008) identifies that bioprospectors rely on the local knowledge of indigenous people who have often been involved in the cultivation of plants and their habitat over several generations to the extent that such natural resources become valuable to biodiversity prospectors. However, the term biopiracy reflects the fact that business in developed world countries controls the wealth derived from indigenous knowledge while arguably acting illegally by violating international conventions and corresponding domestic regulations through their 'failure to recognise, respect and equitably compensate the rightful owners of appropriated bioresources' (Afreen, 2008: 5); a form of theft.

Lloyd Parry raises the prospect that much scientific research is in reality biological copyright infringement perpetrated upon native people – not so much bioprospecting as biopiracy. The issues are legally, ethically and politically complex. Aoki (1998) blames neoliberal markets, arguing that the principle of free trade means that Western multinational corporations are in a dominant position which allows them to exploit developing nations. However, in some cases, indigenous people and local farmers have developed the strains of natural products over generations, thus they arguably have some intellectual property rights over natural resources. Thus, for a transnational corporation to enter a region and generate profits arguably derived from indigenous people's labour without paying due compensation compounds theft with exploitation.

However, prosecuting biopiracy is problematic because it involves clearly identifying an offence for which there is no common definition. Most countries have legislation protecting natural resources and the Rio Declaration provides a framework under which exploitation of biodiversity should be controlled. However, not all countries currently have legislation that assigns intellectual property rights over natural resources, meaning that permission must be sought from a rights owner before a natural resource can be modified or exploited. In some cases, it is also unclear who actually 'owns' the plant or crop that is the subject of bioprospecting unless a state has passed a specific law protecting its biodiversity and making its unauthorized exploitation unlawful. Western corporations, familiar with legal systems and with resources at their disposal to pursue patent claims are also able to apply legal arguments to support their claims. In India, Monsanto and its Indian partners reportedly faced prosecution for biopiracy for violating the country's biodiversity laws over a genetically modified version of eggplant (Tencer, 2011). The National Biodiversity Board (NBA) and the Karnataka Biodiversity Board (KBB) filed a case for criminal prosecution of 13 individuals, including some top management officials of Mahyco or Maharashtra Hybrid Seeds Co. Limited, which is partly owned by Monsanto, for biopiracy. The authorities complained in 2012 that the company along with others had genetically modified local varieties of eggplant, the indigenous crop brinjal, without the mandatory approvals and then laid illegal proprietary claim to the genetically modified seeds. In other words, they were accused of biopiracy under India's Biological Diversity Act 2002, which protects natural resources from such exploitation.

In essence the case is about genetic modification of India's biological resources without permission. The case originated in a biopiracy complaint made by Environment Support Group, a Bangalore-based NGO in 2010. However, the authorities allegedly took no formal action for two years even after investigating and concluding that the circumstances of the case suggested a clear case of biopiracy. It was only when Environment Support Group, seemingly frustrated over alleged government inaction, filed a public interest litigation (PIL) complaint in the Karnataka High Court in 2012 seeking directions to compel the regulatory agencies to take action over the existing biopiracy complaints and to strengthen the regulatory processes to prevent any further acts of biopiracy, and also ensure that the Biological Diversity Act was implemented in its letter and spirit, that the authorities finally filed charges against the accused in November 2012.

Cases such as the Indian one are relatively rare, although various countries are now beginning to view biopiracy as something that requires them to take action; thus biopiracy may develop as a litigation or enforcement issue. The issue to be determined is how best to address biopiracy concerns, through natural resources legislation, criminal legislation, civil law or business legislation?

Despite the existence of international agreements on biological diversity, it is still largely left to the individual state to decide how it will implement biodiversity protection in its national law and how best to regulate the sharing of benefits from biodiversity exploitation and the use of indigenous knowledge and labour to create new intellectual property and compounds. Thus, the risk remains that in developing countries, dependent on the economic input of transnational corporations, biodiversity regulation could remain relatively weak or favour corporations over indigenous people.

Summary

This chapter illustrates the symbiotic relationship between the illegal and the legal within corporate exploitation of natural resources. Unlike mainstream criminology where mostly illegal actors are involved in activities defined as crimes by the criminal law, exploitation of natural resources often involves legal corporations operating with tacit or explicit approval of states who often benefit economically and politically from their actions. However, legal markets facilitate illegal ones, allowing organized crime to also operate under the cloak of legitimized markets and transnational flows of products. Corporations are also able to exercise considerable economic power to subvert regulations and avoid prosecution, particularly in developing world countries where local communities may lack the means to enforce the environmental rights outlined in Chapter 5 or to combat the legal resources available to MNCs well versed in such things as patent and intellectual property law. MNCs, in some cases, may simply be able to outspend local communities attempting legal action, thus effective recourse to justice systems may be denied to local communities.

However, this chapter also illustrates that where justice systems do attempt to deal with corporate wrongdoing associated with natural resource exploitation they may be ineffective in doing so. Partlett and Weaver's (2011) analysis of the Gulf Oil response and the official documents relating to compensation for the disaster identify the 'negotiated settlement' principle of regulatory justice identified in Chapter 5 to be in use in various ways. While it should be acknowledged that the use of plea agreements is not unusual in US courts and applies in other areas of criminal jurisprudence, its use here has allowed corporations to, in part, buy their way out of severe criminal consequences (i.e. prison) by deploying their financial resources. This is not to diminish the value of any compensation scheme or remediation measures aimed at addressing the harmful effects of the spill or the losses encountered by local communities. However, this chapter contrasts the response to this Global North oil spill with the responses to oil spills in Africa and other parts of the developing world and questions whether an equitable system of environmental justice exists.

Self-study Questions

1. What central difficulty exists in determining the obligations that corporations have towards acting responsibly and integrating strong principles of CER within their operating practices?

2. How should CER be enforced and what flaws are there with the current system of different standards and the mixture of voluntary and statutory regulation?

3. To what extent should corporate directors be liable for breaches of CER committed by their corporation? What benefits are there to making directors liable and subject to criminal sanctions?

4. How should corporations' false claims of environmental compliance be dealt with by justice systems? Should a false declaration be treated as 'criminal'?

5. In what ways is illegal or excessive exploitation of natural resources a crime of the powerful? Give reasons for your answer and consider the difficulties inherent in dealing with illegal actions carried out by legal actors as a 'crime'.

6. Critically discuss the forms of criminal activity involved in biopiracy. What are they and how do they take place?

7. To what extent is biopiracy a state issue, concerning how a country exercises control over or allows use of its biological resources rather than purely being a criminal justice issue?

7
CLIMATE CHANGE AND ENVIRONMENTAL DAMAGE

By the end of this chapter you should:

- Understand global warming and climate change as a form of crime and a core issue for green criminology.
- Be able to distinguish between climate change as crime and climate change as a cause of crime.
- Be able to identify climate change as a form of corporate crime and understand the impact of climate change via natural disasters.
- Understand a sociocultural perspective on climate change denial and the reasons why climate change remains a contested topic.
- Understand responses to climate change including the role of the courts and the contrasting perspectives of acceptance and mitigation.

Introduction

Given this book's focus on environmental crime as mainly being activities prohibited by law and which constitute offences (whether actual crimes or civil wrongs), climate change is potentially a topic that falls outside of the remit of green criminology. However, while discussions of climate change largely centre around its effects in the form of global warming and changed weather patterns; climate change is a consequence of a range of activities, some lawful and some unlawful. White and Heckenberg (2014) provide the following definitions of climate change and global warming:

> *Global warming* describes the rising of the earth's temperature over a relatively short time span. *Climate change* [emphasis in original] describes the inter-related effects of this rise in temperature: from changing sea levels and changing ocean currents, through to the impacts of temperature change on local environments that affect the endemic flora and fauna in varying ways (for instance the death of coral due to temperature rises in sea water, or the changed migration patterns of birds).
>
> (2014: 1)

These definitions clarify the far-reaching effects of global warming and climate change that identify them as causing significant environmental harm. Williams (2011: 500) identifies that 'the effects of rising global temperatures are likely to be experienced across every aspect of human life and will vary dependent on the extent of the temperature increase.' The IPCC (2014) identify that human interference with climate systems and the resultant climate changes pose risks for both human and natural systems. They identify that:

- glaciers continue to shrink worldwide as a result of climate change and that melting snow and ice are altering hydrological systems impacting negatively on water resources' quality and quantity;
- while only a few species extinctions can be directly attributed to climate change, many terrestrial, freshwater and marine species have altered their geographical ranges, seasonal habits and migration patterns;
- climate change has negatively affected wheat and maize yields for several regions and is having negative impact on crops.

(IPCC., 2014: 4–6)

Undoubtedly climate change is one of the most significant threats facing mankind and represents a major form of environmental harm, placing it firmly within the remit of a broad environmental harm-based green criminology. Yet White and Heckenberg (2014: 101) identify that it is only recently that criminology has paid attention to the issue despite scientific concern being expressed about global warming over several years. In part this reflects the prevalence of climate change denial (discussed later in this chapter) such that policymakers were able to consider climate change to be an issue of scientific dispute rather than a tangible, accepted phenomenon requiring a policy response. It also reflects the reality of climate change as being a primarily environmental issue concerned with the nature and impact of changing weather patterns and issues of environmental security including the integrity of ecosystems. This being the case, it is perhaps understandable that climate change would not automatically draw the attention of criminologists, particularly given the reality that much climate change is as a result of lawful activity, or at least the behaviour of legal actors (mainly corporations) albeit actors causing significant environmental harm (Lynch and Stretsky, 2014). The lack of a clear offender or specific criminal offence of 'climate change' would also place climate change outside the remit of mainstream criminology. Notwithstanding the efforts of such writers as Lasslett (2014), Green (2004) and Tombs and Whyte (2015) criminology has also been somewhat slow to consider corporate and state crimes; understandable given that not all jurisdictions provide for corporations to be treated as criminal actors (Nurse, 2014).

However, debates over the reality of climate change have largely been resolved, as Stallworthy states:

> evidence for climate change appears to now be unequivocal with a near consensus that global warming is accelerating, preponderantly as a result of increased greenhouse gas emissions (especially Co2 and methane) and related factors including the destabilising of natural balancing mechanisms such as the greenhouse gas sink effects of the rainforests and oceans.
>
> (2008: 199)

Most contemporary governments now recognize that climate change represents a problem that must be addressed although there may not be consensus on precisely how to achieve this. Although there are international agreements on climate change and individual states have passed their own legislation dealing with aspects of climate change (discussed later in this chapter), as with many other areas of environmental harm the enforcement of legislation and the development of appropriate policy are larger problems than the specifics of legislation. Effective enforcement of environmental laws and policy requires a regulatory or criminal justice regime able to appropriately deal with offences and enforce standards. As Chapter 1 outlines, green criminology's focus extends beyond consideration of traditional crime and considers a broader notion of green crime that incorporates environmental harms and damage (Lynch and Stretesky, 2014). But criminal justice policy often ignores harms lacking a clear, specified offender and a direct impact on a human victim whose harm can be punished via justice systems. Yet as the earth grows warmer, a range of issues such as land use, water rights, bio-security, and food production and distribution will continue to have far-reaching impact, and produce more opportunity for offenses by individuals and groups as well as political and corporate entities (White, 2012c). Indeed Kramer (2012: 1) goes so far as to suggest that 'any consideration of environmental crime and its victims should include an analysis of anthropocentric global warming and associated climate change. Outside of a nuclear war, there is no other form of environmental crime that can produce a wider range of victims.' He further explains that climate change has been variously described as 'an ecological catastrophe, an existential threat and an apocalyptic event' (2012: 1) thus from an ecocentric environmental harm perspective, climate change would undoubtedly constitute a green crime.

However, despite a general scientific consensus of climate change as the result of human action, meeting Lynch and Stretesky's (2014) criteria of being harmful human action that should be the subject of green criminological enquiry, the question remains whether climate change constitutes a crime? Notwithstanding the existence of some climate change deniers who contend that human action is not *directly* responsible for global warming (discussed later in this chapter) much climate change is likely the result of lawful activities. Legitimate business activities are the cause of some harmful impacts on the environment and greenhouse gas emissions are frequently a by-product of lawful operations, thus business' climate-change causing activities are not crime in the strict socio-legal sense (Situ and Emmons, 2000). Even where climate change is the result of regulatory breaches such as exceeding or ignoring pollution controls and other violations of environmental protections and clean air statues, it may not constitute crime, particularly where climate change is an incidental consequence of the regulatory breach. Such offences are often regulatory or administrative in nature and do not fall within the remit of the criminal law. However, within this chapter there is scope to discuss both climate change as a cause of crime, and climate change as crime where the specific characteristics of business activity breach existing laws.

Climate Change as a Cause of Crime

One area where criminology has paid attention to the impact of climate change, is as a *possible* cause of crime. Chapter 1 explains the importance of environmental criminology and Brantingham and Brantingham's (1991) criminological conception of environmental and context factors that influence criminal activity. Within this they discuss environment and geography as factors in criminality and the commission of crime and argue that the combination of space, time, law, offender and target or victim are integral to understanding why and how crime occurs. Theoretically, when certain combinations of environmental and human factors occur, crime is likely to increase and a number of criminologists, environmental economists and environmental scientists have examined the impact of climate change on weather and the resultant impact on crime (Barnet, 2006; Wachholz, 2007; Brown and McLeman, 2009; White, 2009; Agnew, 2011; Williams, 2011)

Agnew (2011: 27) argues that climate change potentially causes crime by increasing exposure to a range of strains conducive to crime, but also by 'affecting crime for reasons relating to social control/disorganization, social support, social learning, trait, opportunity and critical theories'. Climate change's impact on weather is the primary concern where rises in temperature and changing patterns of precipitation have an impact on our comfort levels within local environments. Broader climate change impacts (flooding, food and freshwater shortages and negative health effects) will contribute to social poverty and increased trauma that will adversely affect the poor and vulnerable groups who are traditionally more likely to turn to crime as a result of strain and relative deprivation. Where changing weather patterns and the resultant negative effects on food supplies and standards of living place communities in positions where legitimate opportunities diminish and survival is threatened or expected levels of comfort can only be maintained through unlawful means, crime is the likely result. At its most basic level, an argument can be made that increased heat, food and water poverty, and threats to health will likely cause people to turn to crime as a way out of their situation. Thus, where climate change causes these effects, it potentially becomes a cause of crime, although vulnerabilities and criminality associated with climate change are not evenly distributed either across or within affected countries (Blaikie et al., 1994; Denton, 2002; Wachholz, 2007).

Ranson (2014) used a 30-year panel of monthly crime and weather data for 2997 US counties in order to estimate the impact of climate change on the prevalence of criminal activity in the USA. Researchers had previously identified that higher temperatures caused increases in crime (Brunsdon et al., 2009; Horrocks and Menclova, 2011) with various explanations for why this might be the case. Agnew (2011: 21) identified that 'climate change will increase strain, reduce social control, weaken social support, foster beliefs favourable to crime, contribute to traits conducive to crime, increase certain opportunities for crime, and create social conflict.' At its most basic level, incorporating Becker's (1968) notion of rational choice as a prime factor in crime, with individuals considering the costs and benefits of committing crime before doing so, higher temperatures can provide greater opportunities in urban areas where situational crime prevention is reduced. During hot weather the routine activities perspective is more prevalent (Agnew, 2011: 27) as windows and doors are open and people may also be absent from their houses and in gardens, parks and beaches. Thus there may be increased opportunity combined with lower risk of being caught, providing greater incentive for the rational-thinking offender. Ranson theorized that by drawing on appropriate data on monthly weather patterns and crime rates across the USA together with climate change data on rising temperatures it would be possible to predict how climate change will affect crime rates in the USA. Ranson's data analysis concluded that 'in the year 2090, crime rates for most offense rates will be 1.5-5.5% higher because of climate change' (2014: 275).

Horrocks and Menclova (2011: 2–3) cite weather as being a factor both in the likelihood of getting caught when committing crime and as a causal factor in *affective* aggression; those forms of aggression that primarily manifest in injury to another person. Agnew also argues that negative emotions such as anger, frustration and fear increase as a result of climate change with crime being one possible response to escape or reduce strain. On the basis that the discomfort associated with climate change and uncomfortable weather patterns impacts negatively on rational thought and adherence to societal norms, prolonged exposure to unfavourable weather and its effects makes people uncomfortable and potentially increases aggression. Researchers have also noted a gendered dimension to climate-change related aggression. Enarson (1999) identified that violence against women increases in post-disaster communities. Wachholz (2007) whilst noting the difficulties of measuring climate-change related violence, analysed issues relating to violence against women following hurricanes, floods and drought. She concluded that in the years following sample hurricanes (Hurricane Andrew and Hurricane Mitch) violence against women, such as women battering, increased, while violence against women had probably increased in the communities affected by the 1993 Missouri Flood and 1997 Grand Forks Flood where men suffering from the impacts of the flood and associated strains were potentially more prone to violence, and an increase in crisis calls, protection orders and counselling was observed. Thus, 'life for many women after natural disasters is punctuated by violence and this fact needs to be more deeply integrated into discussions about climate change' (Wachholz, 2007: 178).

Arguably, more research needs to be done to better understand the relationship between climate change and crime, particularly crimes of violence. However, climate change can be situated within criminological discourse on strain and disadvantage as causes of crime, particularly the prevalence of crime within marginalized or poorer communities less able to adapt to or mitigate the consequences of climate change. In such communities, climate change is perhaps indirectly a cause of crime by creating the conditions under which crime may occur and criminality is a response to increased vulnerability. Wachholz argues that rather than being a technical problem, climate change 'must also be understood as a social process that is situated within the context of unequal distributions of power and privilege' (2007: 178). Thus in considering climate change as a criminological issue, it is also necessary to consider how those in positions of power and privilege respond to climate change and its effects.

Sociocultural Perspectives and Climate Change Denial

While a broad scientific consensus now exists that climate change constitutes a real phenomenon and is the consequence of human action, there remain some pockets of climate change denial. Such denial exists in the form of those who contest either the reality of climate change or the reality of climate change as having a direct human cause. Kramer argues that there has been political failure to act to regulate or mitigate emissions that cause climate change and a 'socially organized denial of climate change that shapes that failure' (2012: 1). The consequences of this denial has resulted in 'crimes of omission by individual states and the international political community' (Kramer, 2012: 1) which have failed to effectively consider climate change as an international crime.

Notwithstanding the reality that scientific disputes can and do occur with some frequency, the causes of climate change denial are also political, ideological and socio-economic in nature. In some respects climate change denial is socially constructed relating to cultural issues concerning restrictions on business and on the necessity of regulating environmentally damaging human activities. Stallworthy (2008) identifies that there is often a conflict between protection of the environment and economic interests. McCright and Dunlap (2011) identify that in the USA, conservative white males are significantly more likely than other Americans to endorse denialist views on climate change; even more so in the case of those conservative white males who self-report understanding global warming very well. Their study, which analysed ten Gallup opinion surveys from 2001 to 2010 focusing on five indicators of climate change denial, concluded that the views of conservative white males contribute significantly to the high level of climate change denial within the USA. In part, they identify that conservative think tanks, media and corporations have a vested interest in disputing climate change, given the likely consequences of emissions controls and curbs on business activities, and that conservative white males are receptive to such climate change denial views.

From a criminological perspective Kahan et al.'s (2007) view that individuals tend to form perceptions about risk shaped by their cultural worldviews (e.g., hierarchicalism, egalitarianism, individualism) also links with Sykes and Matza's theory on techniques of neutralization to explain sociocultural perspectives on climate change denial. Kahan et al. (2007) identify that individuals are likely to adopt shared beliefs according to socio-economic cultural and intellectual groups to which they belong or identify with 'often resisting revision of such beliefs when they are confronted with contrary information from perceived out-groups' (McCright and Dunlap, 2011: 3). Kahan et al. refer to this as 'identity-protective cognition', which serves as a protective mechanism for the status and self-esteem that individuals receive from group membership (2007: 470). Criminologically, neutralization techniques serve a similar function by allowing offenders to: appeal to higher loyalties such as membership of a deviant group or group which finds itself being stigmatized; deny the legitimacy of enforcement action or to challenge the motives of an enforcer; rely on tradition; or to claim that the alleged crime is victimless and not deserving of official attention (Sykes and Matza, 1957).

Bonfiglio (2012) also notes another form of denial, where people recognize that something untoward is happening but fail to act because they are emotionally uncomfortable or troubled about it. Thus a situation can arise where citizens and policymakers are sufficiently informed about an action like climate change but 'they take no action, make no behavioral changes and remain largely apathetic about it' (Bonfiglio, 2012). The lack of a direct personal impact can also be a factor; the effects of climate change as a global phenomenon may be disproportionately felt by developing world countries in the form of failed crops or the negative impacts of adverse weather patterns. Western communities may well be affected by changes in temperature or increased extreme weather events, but are generally either equipped to deal with these or are served by emergency services capable of preventing large scale loss of life and insurance and other services able to aid in the rebuilding process where negative impacts have been felt. Thus the effects of climate change and global warming might be seen as transient or temporary with the more severe impacts being felt by 'other' or future communities. Where people receive conflicting information from scientists, politicians and the media, a risk exists that they will either align themselves with the scientific and policy perspective that best matches their existing viewpoint and cultural beliefs or will be disincentivized to act due to uncertainty.

White and Heckenberg argue that climate change represents a form of state—corporate crime because corporate and state actors interact together to:

1. deny that global warming is caused by human activities;

2. block efforts to mitigate harmful greenhouse gas emissions;

3. exclude or prevent ecologically sound or just adaptations to climate change from the political arena;

4. adopt responses to climate change that have the effect of excluding marginalized communities and those likely to suffer most from climate change's harmful effects.

(2014: 112)

As White and Heckenberg illustrate, from a policy perspective, there is also an element of denial in determining how best to deal with climate change; whether through adaptation or mitigation. In this context, state—corporate crime is also a result of both act and omission. For example, policies that allow polluting activities to continue or approve new ones in the interests of short-term economic benefit are acts allowing climate change (whether intentionally or not). However, failure to control carbon emissions or to effectively act via effective environmental controls constitutes an omission that in some circumstances constitutes neglect by a state or failure to meet its obligations. State denial of the necessity of climate change action and increased regulatory control also indicates how Sykes and Matza's neutralization techniques (1957) are employed within climate change denial. As White and Heckenberg (2014: 113) illustrate, neutralization techniques include the following:

1. *Denial of responsibility* – particularly arguments that refute the anthropocentric notion of human activity as a direct cause of climate change.

2. *Denial of injury* – arguments that the effects of climate change are 'natural disasters' and thus no additional injury or harm has been caused by climate change.

3. *Denial of the victim* – failure to recognize that climate change has a range of victims and to differentiate between its mild or temporary effects in the Global North and the more severe consequences felt in the Global South.
4. *Condemnation of the condemners* – this includes attacks on climate change scientists and also attacks on those NGOs who argue for action to address climate change. Such attacks impugn both the integrity of the condemners and the ideological base on which they call for climate change action. NGOs, in particular, may be criticised for having an ecocentric view that denies or fails to understand the reality of contemporary industrial practices.
5. *Appeal to higher loyalties* – particularly claims that economic industries should predominate.

The politics of denial inform policy perspectives aimed at addressing climate change. Williams (2011: 499) identifies that some reporting 'into the human impact of climate change indicates that climate change is already responsible for 300,000 deaths each year and is affecting 300 million people worldwide.' This makes climate change a significant cause of environmental and social vulnerabilities and of greater importance than the majority of traditional criminal justice and criminological concerns. The existence of international agreements and contemporary scientific climate-change discourse dictates that policymakers must do something to deal with climate change. Yet there is a lack of coordinated policy on the extent to which climate change is dealt with either as a criminological issue or as a regulatory (environmental law) one. Climate change mitigation is perhaps the dominant policy perspective; that of reducing the impact of climate change through a process of emissions reduction and/or offsetting the effects of climate change and greenhouse cases through geoengineering, actual manipulation of the environment. Thus, mitigation takes an anthropocentric view, considering that significant human action targeted at reducing emissions is required to reduce the harmful emissions that cause climate change and global warming. From a criminological perspective, climate change mitigation employs a combination of rational choice and deterrence theories albeit linked to everyday behaviours that are likely not criminal. Thus by encouraging consumers to take (relatively) small steps that will reduce their carbon footprint; e.g. using the car less, recycling and reusing products, purchasing 'low emission' products and reducing product packaging, the cumulative effect will likely be quite large. Allied to individual mitigation activities, geoengineering or 'climate remediation' (Bipartisan Policy Center, 2011) suggests it might be possible to manipulate the earth's climate in order to minimize the harm from global warming.

By contrast, adaptation almost accepts the inevitability of global warming and involves measures to reduce human vulnerability to the effects of climate change. Thus at a micro level, increasing the strength of sun screen, for example, mitigates the increased harmful individualized effects of sun exposure caused by a reduction in the ozone layer. At a macro level, switching to renewable and low carbon energy sources, reforestation and greater home energy efficiency are all forms of mitigation. Weaknesses of mitigation are its anthropocentric nature and the associated failure to deal with climate change harms visited on the wider environment and non-human animals.

Adaptation and mitigation activities are sometimes enshrined in national law. For example, the UK's Climate Change Act passed in 2008 contains the following measures:

- A 2050 target on emissions reduction that commits the UK to reducing emissions by at least 80% in 2050 from 1990 levels.

- Carbon budgets. The Act requires the Government to set legally binding 'carbon budgets' which constitutes a cap on the amount of greenhouse gases emitted in the UK over a five-year period. The first four carbon budgets are enshrined in legislation and run up to 2027.

- The Committee on Climate Change, a specialist body that advises the Government on emissions targets, and reports to Parliament on implementation of greenhouse gas emission reduction measures. The Committee incorporates the Adaptation Sub-Committee (ASC) which scrutinises and advises on the Government's programme for adapting to climate change.

- A National Adaptation Plan requiring the Government to assess the UK's risks from climate change, prepare a strategy to address them, and encourage organisations considered critical to the success of climate change adaptation to do the same.

(Committee on Climate Change, 2014)

Other measures such as the US Clean Air Act and the UK's Environmental Protection Act 1990, although not explicitly or solely climate change legislation, also create regulatory and enforcement frameworks to deal with emissions. Arguably, adaptation fails to deal with existing harms caused by climate change and the impending threats to ecosystems. However, from a criminological perspective, adaptation and mitigation can be integrated into justice systems through regulatory and criminal justice measures that act as social controls. For example, emissions controls can have the effect of punishing those who drive fuel-inefficient vehicles via higher road taxes (where applicable). Excessive pollution, particularly that consisting of harmful emissions that contribute to climate change can be the subject of regulatory or criminal sanctions such that corporate activity that contributes to climate change becomes a crime or subject to regulatory control aimed at changing behaviour. Arguably a range of environmental legislation already serves this function such that while specific 'climate change' offences may not exist, polluting activities linked to climate are, in some cases, already environmental crimes.

Global Warming as Crime

Whether global warming is defined as a crime in the narrow sense (specifically defined as such by the criminal law) or in a broader sense (as an offence against legislation or accepted standards of behaviour whose harmful affects are globally damaging) is to a certain extent a matter of interpretation and debate. However, global warming by *direct* human action is arguably already prohibited by law, in some contexts, given a range of international and domestic law mechanisms that impose obligations to limit the prevalence of human activities which cause pollution and climate change.

Williams (2011) identifies the global nature and impact of climate change as requiring 'an international solution, one that reconciles the interests of different states and achieves a widespread agreement on an appropriate and effective plan of action' (2011: 503). At an international level, the United Nations Framework Convention on Climate Change (UNFCCC) entered into force on 21 March 2004 and at time of writing (mid 2015) has 196 signatories, which include all UN Member States with the exception of South Sudan. Article 1(2) of the Convention defines climate change as:

> ... a change of climate which is attributed directly or indirectly to human activity that alters the composition of the global atmosphere and which is in addition to natural climate variability observed over comparable time periods.

Article 2 of the Convention specifies that:

> The ultimate objective of this Convention and any related legal instruments that the Conference of the Parties may adopt is to achieve, in accordance with the relevant provisions of the Convention, stabilization of greenhouse gas concentrations in the atmosphere at a level that would prevent dangerous anthropogenic interference with the climate system. Such a level should be achieved within a time frame sufficient to allow ecosystems to adapt naturally to climate change, to ensure that food production is not threatened and to enable economic development to proceed in a sustainable manner.

Article 3 of the Convention specifies:

1. The Parties should protect the climate system for the benefit of present and future generations of humankind, on the basis of equity and in accordance with their common but differentiated responsibilities and respective capabilities. Accordingly, the developed country Parties should take the lead in combating climate change and the adverse effects thereof.
2. The specific needs and special circumstances of developing country Parties, especially those that are particularly vulnerable to the adverse effects of climate change, and of those Parties, especially developing country Parties, that would

have to bear a disproportionate or abnormal burden under the Convention, should be given full consideration.

3. The Parties should take precautionary measures to anticipate, prevent or minimize the causes of climate change and mitigate its adverse effects. Where there are threats of serious or irreversible damage, lack of full scientific certainty should not be used as a reason for postponing such measures, taking into account that policies and measures to deal with climate change should be cost-effective so as to ensure global benefits at the lowest possible cost.

Taken together, these conditions, accepted by states when ratifying the Treaty, amount to an obligation to prevent climate change irrespective of any doubts about the scientific case for climate change or the necessity of taking action based on scientific assessment. The Convention uses the language of the precautionary principle (Gullett, 1997) to specify that action is required to deal with climate change before it happens ('anticipate, prevent') as well as to take action where harmful activities are taking place ('minimize the causes of climate change and mitigate its adverse effects'). Employing the precautionary principle means adopting a 'risk based' regulatory approach that arguably requires proactive rather than reactive legislation, i.e. a legislative and regulatory response that prevent something from happening rather than responding after the event (Fazio and Strell, 2014). The first conference of the parties to the UNFCCC in 1995 commenced a negotiation process that resulted in the Kyoto Protocol of 1997 which 'committed industrialized states to quantified emission reductions and a timetable for their achievement'. This incorporates flexible mechanisms designed to make it easier for states to achieve their objectives including: Joint Implementation, the Clean Development Mechanism, and Emissions Trading (Williams 2011: 508–9).

However, despite the existence of such measures, climate change denial issues, referred to earlier in this chapter, combined with political and ideological differences persist and negatively impact on the effectiveness of climate change law. Weston and Bollier argue that:

> The ill-fated Copenhagen summit in December 2009 – the Fifteenth Conference of the Parties to the United Nations Framework Convention on Climate Change (COP 15) – never had a real chance of success. Participating States would not even adopt the nonbinding Copenhagen Accord drafted by Brazil, China, India, South Africa, and the United States, though touted as a 'meaningful agreement' by the United States. Developed countries refused to commit to legally binding emission reductions and to providing financing and technology for developing country climate mitigation and adaptation needs, and the so-called Basic Countries (the rising developing bloc of Brazil, China, India, and South Africa) were prepared to block any imposition of binding emissions reduction on them lest this curb their economic growth.

(2013: 47)

Thus self-interest and economic priorities overturned the potential for effective legally binding emissions-reduction targets. In addition, Kramer argues that 'for criminologists concerned with global warming and the environmental and social harms flowing from it, there is currently no established body of international or domestic law that offers a legal framework to bring these harms within the boundaries of criminology' (2012: 2). In part the problem is that while such agreements impose obligations on states, they do not contextualize a specific climate change crime within international law. Nor do they have the effect of defining specific activities causing climate change as amounting to international crimes given that strict definitions of international crime exist within the Rome Statute which sets up the International Criminal Court (ICC). While attempts have been made to add the term 'ecocide' (mass destruction of ecosystems) to the existing Rome statute definitions of genocide, crimes against humanity, war crimes, and crimes of aggression as international crimes, these attempts have thus far been unsuccessful (Johnston, 2014).

However, although climate change is not by itself recognized as a crime, certain actions that cause climate change are made unlawful and covered by national environmental legislation. Higgins has produced a definition of ecocide as 'the extensive destruction, damage to or loss of ecosystem(s) of a given territory, whether by human agency or by other causes, to such an extent that peaceful enjoyment by the inhabitants of that territory has been severely diminished' (2010: 63). Thus human action that causes climate change and results in damage to ecosystems would constitute ecocide were international law changed to accept ecocide as a crime against peace and international security. Provisions in domestic (national) law relating to damage to the environment or pollution already exist that provide for some pollution actions which cause climate change to be addressed. These include, for example, provisions of the US Clean Air Act (discussed later in this chapter) and the provisions of the UK's Environmental Protection Act 1990, which allow for enforcement action to be taken over pollution activities. Although practical enforcement of such measures may be predominantly directed at low-level emissions such as fumes or smoke that exceed permit levels, they provide a means through which enforcers might take action to address harms that have a cumulative effect.

White and Heckenberg argue that 'failure to act, now, to prevent global warming is criminal' (2014: 112) arguably reflecting the notion that states have a (international) legal obligation to address climate change yet frequently fail to do so. The failure is, in part, due to the vocal activities of industry and free-enterprise lobby groups who see climate change regulation as an unnecessary and excessive curb on business (Goldberg, 2014; Greenpeace, 2014). However, failures in climate change law have increasingly become a matter for the courts as the following section discusses.

Climate Change and the Courts

As this chapter identifies, in principle, climate change is regulated through international agreements that set the standard for allowable emissions that impact on the atmosphere, and by domestic legislation such as the US's Clean Air Act and the UK's Environmental Protection Act 1990 (amongst others). Such legislation generally allows regulators to take action where a corporation fails to adhere to pollution or emission limits, often providing regulators with tools that allow them to require remedial action, such that corporations may need to modify their processes to reduce environmental harm. Environmental statutes may contain criminal and civil sanctions although 'civil penalties are most typically involved as the legal remedy against environmental wrongdoers. Criminal penalties are usually invoked only when environmental statutes have been wilfully or knowingly broken' (Situ and Emmons, 2000: 38).

Tempus (2014) identifies environmental action through the courts as one route through which climate change might be addressed. However, while a number of lawsuits are underway in the USA effectively challenging US Environmental Protection Agency policies that would allow it to regulate greenhouse gas emissions by setting emission standards for new and existing power plants, Tempus (2014) quotes Michael Gerrard, Director of Columbia University Law School's Sabin Center for Climate Change Law as stating that 'the number of cases in which greenhouse gas emitters have been forced to pay money damages for their greenhouse gas emissions is zero'. Thus there remains a question concerning the extent to which court action is directly addressing breaches of greenhouse gas regulations, although regulatory action which imposes non-criminal sanctions will likely be the mechanism through which such actions are commonly addressed.

Case Study 7.1   Massachusetts v the Environmental Protection Agency 549 U.S. 497 (2007)

Based on respected scientific opinion that a well-documented rise in global temperatures and attendant climatological and environmental changes have resulted from a significant increase in the atmospheric concentration of 'greenhouse gases' in Massachusetts, a group of private organizations petitioned the Environmental Protection Agency (EPA) requesting that the EPA regulate emissions of carbon dioxide and other gases that contribute to global warming from new motor vehicles. The case hinged on an interpretation of the Clean Air Act which defines 'air pollutant' to include 'any air pollution agent ... including any physical, chemical ... substance ... emitted into ... the ambient air' subsection 7602(g). The Act requires that Congress via the administrative and regulatory functions of EPA 'shall by regulation prescribe ... standards applicable to the emission of any air pollutant from any class ... of new motor vehicles ... which in [the EPA Administrator's] judgment cause[s], or contribute[s] to, air pollution [and that can] reasonably be anticipated to endanger public health or welfare'. (Subsection 202(a)(1) of the Clean Air Act)

The EPA denied the petition arguing that the Clean Air Act did not authorize it to regulate greenhouse gas emissions. The EPA also argued that even if this was a correct interpretation of the Act, it had discretion to defer a decision until more research could be done on 'the causes, extent and significance of climate change and the potential options for addressing it'. The EPA further characterized any EPA regulation of motor-vehicle emissions as a piecemeal approach to climate change that would conflict with the president's comprehensive approach involving additional support for technological innovation, the creation of non regulatory programmes to encourage voluntary private-sector reductions in greenhouse gas emissions, and further research on climate change.

Following denial of the petition 12 states (Massachusetts and several others) appealed to the US Court of Appeals for the District of Columbia Circuit. The argument raised by Massachusetts and the other states was that carbon dioxide and other greenhouse gases caused by motor vehicles were pollutants defined by the Clean Air Act. Underlying the case was the perceived threat to the coast of Massachusetts from possible global warming issues. The state was arguably acting on research evidence that showed carbon dioxide and other emissions contributed to greenhouse gases that effect or cause global warming which in turn affects the water on the coast. The case ended up in the Supreme Court, which commented that:

The harms associated with climate change are serious and well recognized. The Government's own objective assessment of the relevant science and a strong consensus among qualified experts indicate that global warming threatens, *inter alia*, a precipitate rise in sea levels, severe and irreversible changes to natural ecosystems, a significant reduction in winter snowpack with direct and important economic consequences, and increases in the spread of disease and the ferocity of weather events. That these changes are widely shared does not minimize Massachusetts' interest in the outcome of this litigation. See Federal Election Comm'n v. Akins, 524 U.S. 11, 24.

(Continued)

(Continued)

According to petitioners' uncontested affidavits, global sea levels rose between 10 and 20 centimeters over the 20th century as a result of global warming and have already begun to swallow Massachusetts' coastal land. Remediation costs alone, moreover, could reach hundreds of millions of dollars. (Available online at: http://www.supremecourt.gov/opinions/06pdf/05-1120.pdf)

The US Supreme Court concluded that greenhouse gases (GHGs), which are widely viewed as contributing to climate change, constitute 'air pollutants' within the meaning of the US Clean Air Act. Meltz (2013: 2) identifies that as a result, the court concluded that 'the U.S. Environmental Protection Agency (EPA) had improperly denied a petition seeking CAA regulation of GHG emissions from new motor vehicles by saying the agency lacked authority over such emissions.' The consequence of this was that the EPA would be required to determine whether or not emissions of greenhouse gases from new motor vehicles cause or contribute to air pollution which may reasonably be anticipated to endanger public health or welfare (EPA, 2013).

Following the Massachusetts case, the EPA issued a series of greenhouse gas-related rules as follows:

- First, an Endangerment Finding, in which the EPA determined that greenhouse gases may 'reasonably be anticipated to endanger public health or welfare.'
- Secondly, the EPA issued the 'Tailpipe Rule' setting emission standards for cars and light trucks.
- Finally the EPA determined that the Clean Air Act requires major stationary sources of greenhouse gases to obtain construction and operating permits although it also issued the Timing and Tailoring Rules, in which it determined that only the largest stationary sources would initially be subject to permitting requirements.

The Massachusetts case and the EPA's subsequent actions are argued by the EPA to be a 'prerequisite for implementing greenhouse gas emissions standards for vehicles' rather than being measures that automatically implement burdens on industry or other entities (EPA, 2013). Markell and Ruhl (2012: 21) identify that there has been 'a rapidly building wave of litigation' in the USA, identifying that since the Massachusetts case 'EPA and other state and local agencies have put climate change law on the books in the form of regulations, permit issuances and denials, and other discrete decisions' (Markell and Ruhl, 2012: 21). Thus, separate from regulatory action aimed at polluting bodies and industry, litigation that seeks to enforce existing legislation and take action against state failures and the state—corporate crime identified by White and Heckenberg (2014) provides for contemporary climate change action. However, it should be noted that cases are taken on both sides of the climate change debate, both by business' seeking to challenge EPA decisions and resist climate change regulation, and by activists seeking to establish that the EPA has not done enough. Thus climate justice remains a contested paradigm as the following examples illustrate:

- In EME Homer City Generation v. EPA (United States Court of Appeals for the District of Columbia Circuit, August 21, 2012) the Court was asked to decide whether new EPA regulations defining emissions reduction responsibilities for SOX and NOX for upwind states that are major contributors to air quality problems in downwind states, exceeded the scope of the Clean Air Act. The court concluded that the emissions reduction requirements imposed on upwind states were disproportionate in relation to the states' contributions to downwind air pollution problems. The court also concluded that the EPA had exceeded its statutory authority by prematurely issuing Federal Implementation Plans to impose obligations on states.
- Resisting Environmental Destruction on Indigenous Lands v. EPA 42 ELR 20261 (Ninth Circuit, February 17, 2012). A coalition of environmental and Alaska Native groups filed an action in the Ninth Circuit seeking to overturn two air quality permits issued by the EPA to Shell for offshore Arctic drilling operations. The permit would allow Shell's ship and support vessels to operate in both the Chukchi Sea and the Beaufort Sea. As 'major source' permits the EPA authorization would also allow Shell to emit more than 250 tons of pollutants annually and to adhere to the Clean Air Act's prevention of significant deterioration requirements. The environmental groups argued that greenhouse gases and black carbon from the ships would accelerate the loss of snow and sea ice in the Arctic to the detriment of members of the Alaska Native communities and argued that the permits did not satisfy the Clean Air Act's air permit requirements. The court denied the petition for review, and upheld the EPA's decision to grant the two air permits, concluding that the EPA's interpretation of the statute, which concluded that best available control technology (BACT) does not apply to mobile support vessels unattached to the drill-ship, was permissible, reasonable, and entitled to deference.

Peeples (2015) identifies that 'several state and international [climate change] cases remain in the pipeline' concerning governments' failure to protect current and future citizens from the effects of climate change (see also Epstein, 2014). While it is beyond this book's scope to analyse climate change litigation in depth, it is clear that challenges to governmental inertia over climate change as well as to regulator's decisions either in favour of restricting emissions or in failing to rigorously enforce climate change laws, are increasingly being considered by the courts. Such cases will considerably develop our understanding of the obligations on government and business in respect of climate change while also clarifying issues of climate change law and the enforceability of climate change restrictions.

Summary

As this chapter illustrates, climate change becomes a green criminological issue given the significant environmental harms and marginalization of vulnerable communities it causes. However, its impact on criminal actors, increasing social vulnerabilities and causing strains from which criminality arise, also make it a cause of crime. Climate change is also a crime itself where activities that cause global warming contravene environmental protection regulations or where state failure to address climate change contravenes international agreements and customary international law.

Brisman (2014: 29) identifies that 'green criminology can help uncover the etiology of environmental crime' including the causes of environmental crime and harm including climate change. Environmental justice, discussed earlier in this book, contextualizes climate change as a crime of the powerful, particularly where the activities of wealthy corporations and the developed West impact negatively on the poor and marginalized and developing world countries. White and Heckenberg (2014: 115) argue that while the obvious and scientific-based answer to climate change is to minimize harmful emissions, there is also a need to criminalize carbon emissions and to forcibly shut down 'dirty industries' whose activities contribute to climate change and resultant global warming.

In essence, climate change illustrates Lynch and Stretesky's (2014: 24) view that 'the assumption that the environmental changes we are witnessing today are evolutionary, natural, and largely independent of human action permeates the general manner in which humans think about the environment and environmental problems.' Only recently has broad acceptance been achieved that humans are the primary cause of environmental problems and direct human action is required to address such problems. Yet despite the existence of both international and domestic legal mechanisms for addressing climate change, there remains a lack of willingness on the part of politicians and regulators to directly address climate change as a significant problem via existing or improved legal regimes and the criminalization that White and Heckenberg (2014) suggest may be necessary. Williams (2011: 503) identifies this as a climate justice deficit, arguing that ineffectual climate change law contributes to sites of social and economic insecurity. Indeed Williams goes so far as to state that 'it is becoming increasingly apparent that many of the legal, financial, and social structures created in response to climate change are doing little to ease the burden of insecurity, in fact in many cases they are further promoting insecurity and inequity' (2011: 510). Wealthy industrialized nations who bear significant responsibility for harmful greenhouse gas emissions are reluctant to criminalize and prosecute the actions of otherwise legal actors (mostly corporations) who contribute to economic growth, provide jobs and pay taxes and whose continued existence serves the interests of policymakers. Yet as other chapters of this book and the cases discussed in this chapter identify, it is often in enforcement of legal regimes that problems occur. In many areas of environmental harm well-meaning legislation exists on paper that is poorly enforced in practice. Part III of this book looks at these issues in more detail.

Self-study Questions

1. In what ways is climate change a green criminological issue?
2. Does international law provide for an effective means of dealing with climate change problems? How might such laws be improved to better achieve climate justice?
3. Given that much activity that causes climate change is the result of lawful activity, or at least is not intentional criminality, how should justice systems deal with otherwise legal corporate activities that cause climate change?
4. White and Heckenberg (2014) argue that climate change is state—corporate crime and should be considered as criminal. Evaluate this argument.
5. What challenges exist in prosecuting activities that cause climate change and global warming? Should this solely be a matter for criminal justice agencies or should other bodies be involved? If so, who?
6. Given its wide-ranging human impacts, consider the argument for climate change to be incorporated into the definition of international crime via creating a new offence of ecocide.

PART III
POLICING, PROSECUTING AND MONITORING ENVIRONMENTAL CRIME

8

THE GREEN MOVEMENT: NGOs AND ENVIRONMENTAL JUSTICE

By the end of this chapter you should:

- Have a firm understanding of what is meant by discussions of the green movement and the importance of green NGOs to environmental justice.
- Understand the importance of NGOs and the green movement to effective environmental justice and the development of policy.
- Understand the role of NGOs and necessity of their use as active participants in environmental enforcement.
- Understand the concept of the 'conservation corporation'; professional environmental organizations with considerable resources to influence policy and practice and determine the environmental enforcement agenda.
- Understand the extent to which 'extreme' activism by NGOs might be considered to be a legitimate environmental protection tactic from an ecocentric perspective but is considered otherwise by law enforcement and wider society.
- Understand the concept of 'eco-terrorism' and why this might be a contested term.

Introduction

This chapter examines the role of the 'green movement' considering the activity of NGOs in pursuing environmental justice at both political and practical levels.

Discussions of a homogenous 'green movement' are slightly misleading as far from there being one integrated movement, environmental NGOs come from different ideological and socio-economic perspectives and operate in different ways. Some NGOs employ fundraising and public-awareness campaigning as their main tool, others are heavily involved in political lobbying while others may employ an activist or even practical law-enforcement approach in order to achieve their goals.

Statutory enforcement failures and the perceived inadequacy of policy leave a vacuum that has increasingly been filled by Non-Governmental Agencies (NGOs) adopting policy development and practical enforcement roles in addition to sometimes taking direct action to prevent a green crime or to take enforcement action when the statutory regulator has failed to achieve this (Nurse, 2013b). NGOs in both the UK and USA already act as policy advisors, researchers, field investigators, expert witnesses at court, scientific advisors, casework managers, and, in the case of a small number of organizations, independent investigators and prosecutors. Acting together, NGOs also contribute greatly to public debates on wildlife crime, generating considerable publicity for the issue and coordinat- ing (and undertaking or funding) much of the research. Some NGOs take a hands-on approach to prosecution and challenging government enforcement inadequacies, while others view themselves as primarily having an advisory or scientific role (Nurse, 2013b). Thus NGOs such as Earthjustice and the Sierra Club who operate in a broader environmental field may differ from those such as Defenders of Wildlife or National Audubon who occupy a species—specific wild- life based remit or others such as WWF and Friends of the Earth operating as part of an international network rather than within a national framework.

However, the role of NGOs in environmental enforcement is sometimes subject to scrutiny and the effectiveness of NGOs can sometimes be called into question. For example, in the UK, the RSPCA has been criticized for wasting money on unnecessary prosecutions and for allegedly misusing the law to achieve its own ends operating from an ideological rather than purely criminal justice perspective (Hope, 2013). The UK government's 'Big Society' agenda, which envisaged greater use of NGOs in environmental law enforcement (Cabinet Office, 2011), risked over-reliance on NGOs; potentially problematic without considering why NGOs take on certain work, especially where their aims and objectives may not be compatible with those of government or public policy.

Elsewhere, some NGOs and activist groups have also begun to use more extreme direct-action mechanisms in order to achieve their goals reflecting the conception that 'one man's freedom fighter is another man's terrorist'. This chapter also explores the concept of extreme activism and what happens when NGO activity and environmental activism moves beyond enforcing the law and advocating certain policies and is alleged to constitute illegal activity. While some activists may consider it appropriate to use unlawful or 'violent' means in order to pursue environmental or animal protection, this raises the question of whether species justice or ecological concerns outweigh the limitations of the existing civil and criminal law.

Environmental Citizenship

The role of environmental NGOs is linked to notions of environmental citizenship and Beck's (1992) risk society theory. Beck argues that events such as the Chernobyl nuclear meltdown require us to reconsider our conceptual framework, the role of scientific knowledge and our policy responses. Thus our social and political institutions and mechanisms need to transform, particularly as regards how they deal with contemporary environmental risks. In this respect, there is a need for a new form of environmental citizenship that focuses not just on developing environmental policy to deal with obvious risks. In contemporary society there is a need for ecological citizenship which looks at the potential unity between legal, political and moral systems and it is here that a range of NGOs operate, from the small community grass roots group to the major 'conservation corporation' that combines professional activism and policy development with local action.

Contemporary NGOs sometimes combine policy development and advocacy with practical enforcement roles in addition to sometimes taking direct action to prevent a green crime or to address regulatory shortfalls. Nurse (2013b) examined the policies and practices of different NGOs involved in wildlife crime, identifying that NGOs could be categorized into the following different types:

1. Campaigning NGOs
2. Law Enforcement NGOs
3. Political Lobbying NGOs.

Although in principle NGOs can operate in more than one of these areas, NGOs generally adopt one of these functions as a primary role (e.g. direct law enforcement). The approach taken (campaigning, enforcement or lobbying) dictates how their environmental protection goals are pursued, even though a secondary objective (e.g. political lobbying to improve wildlife protection legislation) may be pursued alongside this.

NGOs and Ideology

On a broader level, environmental justice NGOs represent a varied set of interests that includes radical environmentalists (i.e. those with a 'pure' view of environmental protection) and middle-class movements who have a general environmental concern and the resources to 'indulge' those interests. Analysis of the available literature on NGO policies and their ideological perspectives reveals that environmental NGOs develop their policies from the primary ideological positions of:

1. Moral culpability – censuring activities that they believe are morally wrong;

2. Political priorities – censuring activities that they consider should be given a higher profile in public policy (which may include issues that they consider are worthy of a higher law enforcement priority or those which should be the subject of law enforcement activity and/or legislative change);

3. Environmentalism/Animal Rights – a belief in ensuring and protecting environmental rights or rights for animals which includes policies that demonstrate either the case for animal/environmental rights or which demonstrate breaches of these existing rights.

(Nurse, 2013b)

There is inevitably some overlap in these policy objectives but analysis of the background illustrates how NGOs develop their policing policies and priorities and whether active law enforcement or assistance to statutory agencies is pursued in order to give effect to policy objectives.

The Nature of Activism: NGOs as Agents of Social Change

In addition to addressing statutory enforcement failures or a perceived lack of attention to an issue, NGOs also act as agents of social change. NGOs primarily achieve their objectives through public campaigning to raise awareness of an issue, commonly commissioning or carrying out their own research to prove their issue-based case, to lobby for legislative change or manipulate public opinion on policy priorities or the need for government intervention. NGOs such as the ASPCA, RSPB, RSPCA, Defenders of Wildlife, Humane Society, League against Cruel Sports, and World Wildlife Fund (WWF) have expended much effort on publicity to ensure that the public is aware that environmental crime and specific aspects of wildlife crime are major priorities. So too have more broadly environment-based NGOs like the Sierra Club and Earthjustice. Glossy reports, press releases, direct mail campaigns, newspaper, television and radio advertisements, newspaper feature stories and extensive (often innovative) use of social media all contribute to the public's knowledge of NGO involvement in environmental crime and understanding of contemporary policy perspectives. Thus, unsurprisingly, UK members of the public wishing to report wildlife offences routinely telephone the RSPB, RSPCA, LACS and other similar organizations rather than mainstream policing agencies. This reflects both the perception that members of the public have that these are crimes that the police may not investigate and the success of the NGOs in promoting their involvement in wildlife crime investigation and their policy development. Such reporting, however, distorts the picture of wildlife crime somewhat as NGO publication of wildlife crime figures is naturally tailored to suit ideological, campaigning and policy needs. Thus reporting may reflect a species-specific conservationist message (e.g. number of wolves, birds, etc. illegally killed), a broad campaigning message (worsening levels of crime or inadequacies of legislation) or an ideological position (moral wrong of animal harm, demonization of hunters or other deviant groups) commensurate with the NGO's ideological stance as campaigning, policing or lobbying organization (Nurse, 2013b). Arguably it is generally in the interests of individual NGOs to produce figures that show a worsening picture of environmental crime given that many NGOs are also charitable organizations reliant on voluntary public donations in order to achieve environmental protection priorities.

Nurse (2013b) has identified that at one end of the spectrum there are large NGOs existing as 'conservation corporations' with legitimacy within social structures such that they are seen as part of the establishment. Such organizations gain legitimacy through Royal charters in the UK (e.g. the Royal Society for the Protection of Birds, Royal Society for the Prevention of Cruelty to Animals) in a manner that risks their being viewed by other, more activist, NGOs as 'illegitimate' by virtue of becoming part of the establishment. More activist NGOs are frustrated by the perceived lack of effectiveness of mainstream NGOs and a failure to use direct action or protest tactics as their drive for mainstream legitimacy distances them from grassroots activism (Carmin and Bast, 2009; Plows, 2008; Carter, 2007; Rawcliffe, 1998). Jasper (1997) in discussing 'postmaterial' social movements explained that mainstream environmental organizations are comprised mainly of people already integrated into their society's political, economic and educational systems and who by virtue of their affluence did not need to campaign for basic rights for themselves but could pursue protections and benefits for others. Major environmental NGOs illustrate this perspective, having grown from their activist roots to embrace animal protection and conservation corporations with considerable economic and political power.

Some NGOs and civil society groups employ direct action as a means of enforcing environmental laws (Nurse, 2013b); directly challenging actions that are either illegal or which they perceive as such through means such as interfering with the progress of fisheries operations, the planting of crops or the use of animals for scientific experimentation. Civil disobedience can be a useful tool in forcing governments to reconsider a policy or re-evaluate public support for a policy. Persen and Johansen (1998) argue that an action can be termed civil disobedience when it meets the five requirements of:

1. Openness;
2. Non-violence;
3. Breaking a law or norm;
4. Serious personal conviction;
5. Societal and/or ethical objectives.

In extreme cases violence is used to promote the animal rights or environmental cause, which raises questions about the legitimacy of NGO tactics. Lowe and Ginsberg (2002) concluded that the animal rights movement (in the USA) has a disproportionately well-educated membership reflecting what Parkin called 'middle class radicalism' (1968). The ability to undertake environmental activism and the means through which to do so are inextricably linked to socio-economic concerns. Ethnic minority groups are frequently disadvantaged when it comes to enjoying their environmental rights (Schlosberg, 2007) and disproportionately feel the effects of environmentally damaging development such as the citing of waste recycling plants. Stephens et al. (2001) identify that ethnic minority groups while suffering disproportionately from poor environmental conditions often lack access to processes which could affect these conditions, in part by being excluded by the language and perceptions of environmental groups (2001: 20). Nocella (2012: 142) also argues that the animal-rights movement remains dominated by people who identify as white with the consequence that people of colour remain marginalized within this form of activism.

White (2012b) applies contemporary regulation theory to environmental crime, recognizing the poor level of resources, meagre budgets and low staffing levels that exist in environmental law enforcement given the size and scale of environmental problems. Such statutory enforcement failures add to the marginalization of environmental crime and leave a vacuum that has increasingly been filled by NGOs adopting policy development and practical enforcement roles (Nurse, 2013b; White, 2012b), with a number of NGOs actively investigating and prosecuting environmental and wildlife crimes. While environmental NGO approaches often emphasize the importance of the criminal law and frequently include calls for tougher sentences and more punitive measures for wildlife crime (Nurse, 2011, 2012) they also employ a regulatory approach to compliance. Campaigns such as the campaign to end fox-hunting or the recent campaign against the badger cull in the UK identify the manner in which pro-environment or animal protection NGOs can influence the social construction of environmental or animal protection issues and the public policy that deals with it. A central feature of the campaign to end fox hunting and other forms of hunting with dogs was, for example, a moral objection to a form of animal control that was considered unnecessary and which could not be justified in terms of its apparent objective. But this was arguably a secondary objective with the primary objective being social condemnation of an activity considered to have no place in contemporary society. Through this condemnation a change in the law ultimately occurred when legislators accepted the need for new legislation to ban hunting with dogs and introduced the Hunting Act 2004. Thus the political and social campaigning by NGOs was instrumental in forcing the government to consider the issue and to 'officially' consider evidence from conflicting viewpoints that had been publicly aired for many years previously. Once the Hunting Act 2004 had been introduced, the LACS and other NGOs accepted a certain level of responsibility for enforcing the law through their investigations sections accepting that the police are unlikely to do so (see Chapter 9 for further discussion of environmental investigation perspectives). However, campaign groups opposed to such legislation exist and continue to press for repeal of the Act with some evidence that their calls meet sympathetic ears in government (Hope, 2014). Indeed, within two months of winning the May 2015 UK general election, the Conservative administration proposed amendments to the Hunting Act 2004 reportedly widely criticised as an attempt to partially repeal the Act. The proposals were, however, abandoned in the face of parliamentary and public opposition (Mason, 2015).

Willetts (2002) identifies that an artificial distinction exists between NGOs and different types of interest, campaigning and pressure groups and that there is no generally accepted definition of an NGO. However, environmental NGOs, in the context of mainstream environmental NGOs can usually be distinguished from pure campaigning groups by virtue of their active engagement in policy discourse where they conduct a role that the state arguably should fulfil and accepts as a matter of public interest. Arguably, many NGOs have developed to fulfil a societal need and due to failure in environmental governance. The classic example of this is the Love Canal incident that spawned a grassroots or community response that eventually gave birth to the Center for Health, Environment and Justice.

Case Study 8.1   The Love Canal Incident

Love Canal is an area of Niagara Falls, New York whose canal site became a dumping ground for petrochemical and military waste and subsequently a waste disposal site used in the 1940s and 1950s by its owners Hooker Chemicals and Plastics Corporation to dump an estimated 21,000 tons of toxins including: dioxin, chloroform and tetrachloroethylene. These toxins are associated with birth defects, cancer, narcosis of the central nervous system, kidney damage and cardiac problems. During the later 1950s and 1960s an elementary school and affordable housing projects were built on the site and in the 1970s reports on health problems, water contamination

(Continued)

(Continued)

and chemical residues resulted in an Environmental Protection Agency (EPA) investigation.

The EPA initially estimated that people living along Love Canal stood a 1 in 10 chance of getting cancer during their lives just from breathing the polluted air, but later revised this to say the increased risk was actually 1 in 100 and far less for people just a few blocks away. However, another EPA report found that some of the 36 residents who volunteered for tests showed signs of chromosomal damage – more than considered normal. Corroding waste-disposal drums could be seen breaking up through the grounds of backyards. Trees and gardens were turning black and dying. One entire swimming pool had popped up from its foundation, ending up afloat on a small sea of chemicals. Puddles of noxious substances were observed by some residents. Some of these puddles were in their yards, some were in their basements and others were on the school grounds. The air was also said to have a faint, choking smell and children reportedly returned from play with burns on their hands and faces. The EPA and New York State declared a health emergency and evacuated all residents who lived immediately above the toxic dump whereas the Love Canal Homeowners Association (LCHA, a local community group led by Lois Gibbs) began a campaign to have all residents evacuated.

LCHA highlighted potential impacts of various toxins produced by Hooker Chemicals on the health of Love Canal residents. When New York Department of Health officials were slow to react, LCHA conducted their own research together with health experts at the University of Buffalo and highlighted a range of health symptoms among residents that contradicted the official public health evidence. As a result of LCHA campaigning:

> on August 2, 1978, the New York State Department of Health (NYSDOH) issued a health order. The health order recommended that the 99th Street School be closed (a victory), that pregnant women and children under the age of two be evacuated, that residents not eat out of their home gardens and that they spend limited time in their basements. A few days later, the state agreed to purchase all 239 homes in the first two rings of homes closest to the canal.
>
> (Center for Health, Environment and Justice, 2014)

Continued campaigning and investigation by LCHA found increases in miscarriages, stillbirths, crib deaths, nervous breakdowns, hyperactivity, epilepsy, and urinary tract disorders. LCHA presented this evidence to residents and public health officials with the following results:

> On February 8, 1979, after the health department looked at the reproductive problems in the outer community, they confirmed the homeowners' findings and issued a second evacuation order for pregnant women and children under the age of two. This evacuation was a step in the right direction, but it was still not enough. It was not until October of 1980 that a total evacuation of the community was ordered by President Carter. Everyone who lived at the Love Canal had the option of moving away, with the government purchasing their homes at fair market value.
>
> (Center for Health, Environment and Justice, 2014)

Love Canal shows a particular notion of environmental citizenship and contextualizes the question of who is responsible for addressing environmental harm. Here, a grassroots community group took on the responsibility for proving health problems by collaborating with researchers and challenging the apathy of the political authorities. Subsequently Lois Gibbs went on to set up the Center for Health, Environment and Justice (CHEJ), a national NGO that works to empower people to build healthy communities, and prevent harm to human health caused by exposure to environmental threats. But where Love Canal and the subsequent establishment of the CHEJ might be considered a success, activists denied access to establishment tools and opposed to negotiations with corporations and bureaucratic structures may well establish non-mainstream activist networks dedicated to a policy of extreme direct action. This has resulted in the criminalization of some NGO groups and arguably a disproportionate law enforcement response aimed at direct environmentalism.

Extreme Activism and the Criminalization of NGOs and Environmental Activists

Cianchi (2015) argues that radical environmental groups are generally grassroots organizations that are committed to participatory forms of decision making and are strongly anti-institutional (Carter, 2007: 155–6; Doyle, 2000: 45). Yet the radical nature of such groups sometimes makes them a target of an extreme state response and subject to labelling as terrorists.

Terrorism is defined according to notions that view its goals and ideals as rooted in use of violence or threat of violence. Terry (2009) identifies that there is no single agreed-upon definition of terrorism, or of what constitutes a terrorist, noting also that terrorism can be domestic or international, based upon single issues or broad ideologies, with or without a religious foundation. Thus US law defines terrorism as an act 'calculated to influence or affect the government by intimidation or coercion, or to retaliate against government conduct' (US Code Title 18, subsection 2331) whereas Section 1 of the UK's Terrorism Act 2000 defines terrorism as 'the use or threat [of action] designed to influence the government or an international governmental organisation or to intimidate the public or a section of the public'. UK law also requires that 'the use or threat is made for the purpose of advancing a political, religious, racial or ideological cause'.

Thus a definition of eco-terrorism that defines groups such as the Earth Liberation Front (ELF) as such because of extreme activism committed for political or ideological reason is arguably consistent with some definitions of terrorism (Eagan, 1996). Thus American Justice agencies have pursued action against the ELF using US eco-terrorism laws (Deshpande and Ernst, 2012).

Loadenthall (2013), however, argues that defining the ELF as eco-terrorists is erroneous because the group does not employ violence against 'innocent victims' and has sought to damage property, not humans, and has broadly managed to avoid injuring individuals accidentally. In this context, the use of terrorism legislation and policing responses more appropriate to those seeking violent overthrow of state functions is arguably excessive. An argument might be made that the use of the emotive word 'eco-terrorism' is as much about demonizing radical environmental groups, notwithstanding the possible tragic consequences arising from use of tactics such as arson, and undermining their support networks as it is about dealing with the threat they represent, whether perceived or actual.

Ellefsen (2012) offers an analysis of the perceived threat that green movements pose to the state, observing that recently green movements have been criminalized and subject to state sanctions. He identifies a rise in threat assessments over the last 15 years evident in reports from US and European state institutions and private security firms. Ellefsen identifies how an anti-Mafia law intended to be used in respect of human trafficking was used against a prominent Austrian animal rights movement that had been successful in banning fur farming and pushing through progressive animal welfare legislation. Use of the law in this way arguably represents an attempt by the state to criminalize a civil society organization seen as challenging dominant social ideas or the established political order. White (2007) identifies that 'political economy' is at the heart of exploitation of animals and environments and that property values assigned to animals and the environment are important in a capitalist system. Thus animal rights and environmental organizations that threaten such rights risk being affected by crime control policies, especially where they use direct action techniques that go against social norms and break existing law. Ellefsen concludes that criminalization of animal rights movements reflects the fact that 'important societal interests are being challenged by the animal rights movement' (2012: 202) but also that animal advocates 'threaten the role and place of humans on our planet' (2012: 203). Thus state power is being used to criminalize animal activists as a means of political oppression and to prevent animal activists from challenging dominant ideas about animal exploitation. However, where animal or environmental activists are themselves using illegal means to address wider illegality the merits of using the criminal law to address their activities might be justified.

Case Study 8.2   Sea Shepherd vs Japanese Whaling

In principle the 1982 World Charter for Nature adopted by the United Nations provides a mechanism for protecting animals from harm by providing a conservation framework that would prevent animal harm through species protection measures (Nurse, 2013b). In practice implementation of the Charter relies on national animal protection legislation although Sections 21–24 of the Charter provide authority for individuals to enforce international conservation laws that could provide animal protection and has been used by NGOs as a basis on which to conduct direct action to prevent animal harm (Roeschke, 2009).

Sea Shepherd Conservation Society (SSCS) is an international non-profit, marine wildlife conservation organization. It states as its mission: an end to the destruction of habitat and slaughter of wildlife in the world's oceans. Sea Shepherd uses innovative direct-action tactics to investigate, document, and take action to expose and confront illegal activities on the high seas. This includes aggressive and violent action (Hoek, 2010) to combat perceived illegal action by the Japanese whaling fleet. In 1986, the International Whaling Commission (IWC) passed a temporary moratorium banning commercial whaling. However, Japan continues to whale on a commercial level thanks to a loophole in the Whaling Convention that allows for the take of whales in the name of research. Sea Shepherd contends that Japanese whaling is illegal and that the World Charter for Nature gives it authority to act on behalf of and enforce international nature conservation laws. In the absence of effective international law action (albeit in 2014 the ICJ eventually concluded that Southern Antarctic Japanese whaling was commercial whaling and in breach of the Convention) Sea Shepherd uses direct action to enforce the law and prevent Japanese whaling. However, it is arguable whether the direct action employed by Sea Shepherd is lawful; Roeshke identifies that Sea Shepherd techniques include 'chasing, harassing, scuttling and in some cases ramming illegal whaling and fishing vessels on the high seas' (2009: 99).

(Continued)

(Continued)

Hoek (2010) argues that it is likely that both the Japanese whaling fleet and Sea Shepherd are breaking the law. As of 2008 Sea Shepherd's Captain Watson had claimed responsibility for sinking 10 illegal whaling ships. Hoek identifies that the battles between Sea Shepherd and Japanese whalers are certainly 'life threatening' but that little has been done to regulate the actions of either party (2010: 161). The issue of legality is a complex one; the ICJ decision notwithstanding, Japan's whaling activities are theoretically legal because they are 'covered' by a loophole that allows whaling for research. However, Sea Shepherd and other conservation organizations have long contended that Japan is misusing the loophole to engage in commercial whaling and a whale meat trade that subverts the whaling ban and represents an 'abuse of right' (a position somewhat enforced by the ICJ judgment). Sea Shepherd on the other hand 'is arguably violating the law by engaging in eco-terrorism on the high seas' (Hoek, 2010: 162).

Both sides have used legal action. Sea Shepherd's Captain Paul Watson was reportedly arrested in Germany in 2012 on a warrant issued by Costa Rica for an alleged violation of ship's traffic in Costa Rica. The incident related to a confrontation with an illegal shark finning operation in 2002. Watson was released on bail but failed to report to Frankfurt police on a daily basis as he was required to do. Interpol (2012) issued a red notice requiring countries to identify or locate Watson with a view to his provisional arrest and extradition in accordance with the country's national laws. Japanese whalers have also been successful in obtaining injunctions against Sea Shepherd, making it illegal for SSCS ships to approach Japanese whaling ships where injunctions applied.

Sea Shepherd has also used legal action to press its case alongside its allegedly illegal action. For example, in 2010 Sea Shepherd lodged writs to sue the crew of Japanese whaling ship 'Shonan Maru 2' for piracy in the Dutch court system for threatening the lives of the six crew members of the Ady Gil and destroying their vessel. Sea Shepherd has also taken various legal actions in an attempt to have whaling activities declared illegal. However, in a recent US Court of Appeal ruling (*Institute of Cetacean Research, Kyoda Senpaku Kaisha Ltd, Tomoyuki Ogawa and Toshiyuki Miura v Sea Shepherd Conservation Society and Paul Watson* No. 12-35266 D.C. No.2:11-cv-02043-RAJ) Chief Judge Alex Kozinski of the 9th US circuit court of appeals stated:

> You don't need a peg leg or an eye patch. When you ram ships; hurl glass containers of acid; drag metal-reinforced ropes in the water to damage propellers and rudders; launch smoke bombs and flares with

> hooks; and point high-powered lasers at other ships, you are, without
> a doubt, a pirate, no matter how high-minded you believe your
> purpose to be.
>
> While the appeal ruling turns on some specific legal points and
> concerns an attempt by Japanese whalers to obtain an injunction it
> is nevertheless of interest in clarifying and contributing to the debate
> on the legitimacy of environmental activism.

Eco-terrorism is to a certain extent in the eye of the beholder and is both
socially constructed and subject to interpretation. Behind the labelling of NGOs
and activists as criminal lie complex questions about the role of the state and
NGO challenges to societal norms. But allegedly illegal actions by NGOs also
raise questions about the appropriateness and effectiveness of direct action,
especially extreme direct action.

Summary

The Sea Shepherd case and the, arguably more extreme, actions of groups like
the ELF illustrate both a theoretical and practical dilemma. Where an NGO
engages in civil disobedience which escalates into illegality can its activities be
justified as legitimate under environmental, ecological or species justice concerns? Does the 'alleged' or actual illegality of the NGO's actions negate the
legitimacy of the concern or should 'eco-terrorism' by an NGO, which nevertheless exposes wider illegality and serious environmental crimes, be exempt
from criminal prosecution?

Hoek (2010) acknowledges that extremists such as Sea Shepherd serve a
purpose by drawing attention to the issue of illegal whaling but argues that
'engaging in eco-terrorism is not helping to end Japanese whaling in the long-
term, but rather adding fuel to the fire' (2010: 193). However, given that
Southern Antarctic whaling has been ruled to be in breach of international law
(the Whaling Convention) arguably there is merit to the argument that extreme
measures are needed to enforce ineffective laws.

However, while NGOs committing minor transgressions or civil wrongs in
order to gain evidence of more serious conservation crimes may be able to claim
the legitimacy of civil disobedience, blatantly illegal acts or acts that endanger
life risk attracting undue attention from law enforcement and labelling as
eco-terrorists.

For environmental activists this raises the spectre that certain of their actions,
although deemed illegal, will not harm their cause, while more serious

transgressions will. So, environmental activists might, for example, trespass on private property to damage GMO crops or gain evidence of illegal killing of wildlife and the trespass would not by itself render any evidence inadmissible and could be defended as 'necessary' trespass. But allegedly illegal violent acts arguably undermine the legitimacy of any activity carried out under the guise of species justice concerns or which are argued as being enforcement action taken under the auspices of international environmental law.

While civil disobedience might be justified, a modern conception of eco-terrorism arguably applies when the use of illegal methods becomes an integral strategy not just in pursuit of the protection of the environment or wildlife but also a business or organizational strategy where the activist appears to consider themselves above the law. Where activists effectively prioritize some aspects of law over others and the allegedly illegal strategies used show disregard for the safety or well-being of others state agencies seemingly feel justified in applying both mainstream and environmental definitions of terrorism to their actions.

Self-study Questions

1. Thinking critically, what different types of NGO are active in the area of green crime (environmental and wildlife) and what different positions do they adopt? Consider the purpose and philosophy of NGO action in discussing this question.
2. What are the difficulties in considering NGOs collectively as a 'green movement'? Thinking critically, in what ways can it be said that NGOs share a common green perspective?
3. 'Enforcer NGOs misuse the law to pursue a political objective rather than acting in the interests of justice.' Critically evaluate this statement and consider the advantages, disadvantages and social importance of having NGOs act as law enforcers.
4. Thinking critically, consider the effectiveness of NGOs as: a) policy advocates or advisers; and b) agents of social change.
5. 'One man's terrorist is another man's freedom fighter.' Consider the appropriateness of this statement to evaluate the criminalization of environmental activists as eco-terrorists.

9
INVESTIGATING ENVIRONMENTAL CRIME

By the end of this chapter you should:

- Have a firm understanding of the manner in which environmental and wildlife crimes are monitored at both national and international levels.
- Understand the links between legal and illegal activity and the difficulties for investigators in establishing whether a crime has been committed.
- Understand the importance of NGOs as monitors and investigators and the regulatory justice theory that NGO involvement is essential for effective investigation of environmental crimes.
- Understand the complexity of prosecuting environmental crimes and the need for investigators and prosecutors to consider not just environmental offences but also associated business crimes which may sometimes be easier to bring before the courts.

Introduction

This chapter examines perspectives on the monitoring and investigation of environmental crime. Building on the previous chapter's discussion of the green movement, it examines the role of NGOs as active participants in environmental crime investigations and the role of different regulatory and enforcement bodies such as the EPA (USA), Fish and Wildlife Service (USA) and police action in relation to environmental crime (e.g. the UK's Wildlife Crime Officers network and the transnational environmental crime initiatives of Interpol and Europol).

The chapter also explores regulation theory (White, 2012b) and the contention that NGOs are an essential component of environmental enforcement given the general lack of criminal justice resources afforded to environmental and wildlife crime investigations. As previous chapters have identified, environmental governance structures often adopt a regulatory, 'prosecution as last resort' approach, designed to manage business' exploitation of natural resources. However, even where clear evidence of offending exists, for example in wildlife crime cases where there is an obvious 'victim', there remains a lack of resources for effective law enforcement and the required specialist knowledge that often 'standard' policing bodies do not possess (Nurse, 2012).

Whereas the previous chapter examined the role of NGOs as policymakers and agents of social change, this chapter examines their role as active enforcers of legislation, particularly those NGOs deemed to be field investigators and prosecutors. Thus this chapter explores how environmental law enforcement works in practice. It also discusses the availability of data on environmental problems, the dark figure of unrecorded environmental crime and the failure of justice systems to integrate environmental crime investigations into mainstream justice.

Practical Green Policing

Intervention on environmental crime involves a range of different activities involving complex legislative and regulatory measures combining international laws (treaties, conventions and customary law) together with national laws, regulations, voluntary and statutory schemes and codes of practice. Whereas accepted definitions of crime are generally concerned with punishment by the state through the criminal law (Barnett, 2011) environmental offending operates within a regulatory framework that, as previous chapters indicate, is more one of facilitation than punishment. It is rare for the state to solely exercise its coercive, criminal law powers in relation to environmental regulation (Gunningham and Sinclair, 1999; Hawkins 1984). Instead, a variety of measures are used to deal with environmental damage and environmental offending. The nature of the offence determines which agency has jurisdiction, and a cocktail of civil, administrative, and criminal measures might be used, determined also by the content of legislation/regulation and the public policy perspectives being employed. Environmental crime also involves both state and non-state actors, particularly in areas where failures in state action or the transnational nature of crimes dictates that international NGOs may be best placed to monitor and 'enforce' environmental crime problems. Where the cross-border nature of crimes means that it otherwise falls outside the remit (or interest) of nation states, this may also determine how a crime or environmental harm is dealt with.

Thus, at a micro level, local authority environmental health or planning departments administer planning and environmental protection legislation to ensure that development complies with land use rules. Where this is not the case they are empowered to take enforcement action, which sometimes involves the use of criminal penalties to secure compliance. At a macro level, statutory environmental regulators may enforce laws against companies harming the environment or states may take enforcement action against each other in international courts for breaches of international law. NGOs may also monitor and seek enforcement action where transnational problems occur and states appear unable or unwilling to act (see the discussion of the Basel Action Network later in this chapter).

As various scholars have observed, environmental enforcement broadly falls outside the remit of mainstream policing bodies and instead often falls to environmental regulators able to employ a mixture of civil and criminal law to achieve their goals (Hawkins, 1984; Nurse, 2015a; Stallworthy, 2008). Situ and Emmons (2000) identify the EPA and Department of Justice (DoJ) as the main enforcers of environmental law in the USA (The Fish & Wildlife Service deals with wildlife issues) with the EPA currently the main investigator and regulator. Specialist environmental protection agencies unencumbered by the confines of traditional punishment-based policing approaches can provide both regulatory and criminal enforcement options. However, limitations are often placed on these agencies by virtue of their enacting legislation and tightly defined jurisdiction (Stallworthy, 2008), which are determined by both political and practical considerations. Across jurisdictions, a range of problems have been identified within environmental law enforcement as follows:

1. Lack of resources
2. Inconsistency of legislation
3. Inconsistency in sentencing
4. Lack of police priority and inconsistency in policing approaches.

Investigatory and prosecutions philosophy is also a significant factor. White and Heckenberg (2014: 218) identify that environmental protection agencies[1] generally have a role to deal with pollution and waste offences; parks and fisheries departments deal with 'green' issues such as conservation, animal welfare and land use; whereas specialist animal welfare or animal control agencies may deal with animal abuse and domestic animal issues. The manner in which offences are dealt with and enforcement priorities determined is largely a matter

---

[1]For the remainder of this chapter the term 'environmental protection agencies' will be used as generic shorthand for all environmental regulators.

of law, policy, resources and priorities. Situ and Emmons (2000) identify that investigations and enforcement action is either proactive or reactive although the reality of environmental crime enforcement activity is that reactive enforcement approaches dominate. This is partly because the nature of offending is that it is not routinely under the eye of a public likely to report it to regulators, but also that unlike mainstream policing where the purpose of enforcement activity is prevention and detection, regulated environmental activity assumes that the activity is lawful. Thus, as Chapter 5 illustrates, the environmental protection agencies' role is not entirely to detect crime, but is instead to facilitate compliance in accordance with normative expectations of business behaviour. This is not to ignore those inspection regimes within regulated industries that may detect offences as part of regulatory inspections and permit monitoring and approval systems. However, Braithwaite and Pettit (1990) suggest that the regulatory compliance system that dominates polluting and waste industries is one of systematic negotiation albeit criminal enforcement remains an option. Yet, as with mainstream crime, problems in the enforcement regime and in the consistency of approach by enforcers undermine its effectiveness (Nurse, 2015a, 2012).

The reality of environmental enforcement is that it is subject to a range of factors determining whether an offence is detected and prosecuted or punished. Akella and Cannon (2004: 10) identify the following as the varied links in the enforcement chain:

- *Probability of detection* – corresponds to incentives given to enforcers, public knowledge of offences, availability of equipment and technical knowledge and skill of personnel.
- *Probability of arrest* – relates to public knowledge and awareness of a crime, police and other enforcer pay and reward structure, availability of equipment, quality of evidence.
- *Probability of prosecution* – rewards for prosecutors, capacity of the justice system, civil or criminal nature of the offence, social attitudes towards crime.
- *Probability of conviction* – corresponds to rewards for judges and magistrates, capacity of the justice system, nature of the crime, social attitudes towards the crime and quality of evidence.

Implicit in these various activities is the role of discretion among investigating and prosecuting agencies and the uncertainty of the detection, apprehension and punishment model (Bright, 1993) that dominates the environmental enforcement landscape. Akella and Allan argue that 'investments in patrols, intelligence-led enforcement and multi-agency enforcement task forces will be ineffective in deterring wildlife crime, and essentially wasted if cases are not successfully prosecuted' (2012: 11). Similarly within the broader environmental crime arena, the quality and timeliness of enforcement action is a factor in continued non-compliance. White and Heckenberg (2014) express concerns about how environmental cases are dealt with by the courts including:

- whether cases are heard in magistrates or superior courts;
- whether cases are heard in general or specialist courts;
- the types of penalty applied (fines, prison or action orders);
- what remedies are invoked for the harm caused.

(White and Heckenberg, 2014: 256)

Stallworthy argues that 'statutory regulation opens possibilities for proactive environmental protection, especially in targeting behaviour so as to pre-empt or limit harmful consequences' (2008: 76). However in practice; four basic enforcement models exist for environmental enforcement, as follows:

1. Enforcement by mainstream statutory police agency (including customs authority).
2. Enforcement by specialist environmental regulatory agency (EPA, Fish & Wildlife Service).
3. Enforcement by conservation, natural resource, parks agency.
4. Enforcement by NGO.

In some areas, specialist environmental investigators exist. For example, the UK has an excellent network of Police Wildlife Crime Officers, those officers identified in each municipal police force to specialize in wildlife crime, albeit many of these officers carry out their duties in addition to their 'main' duties (Kirkwood, 1994; Roberts et al., 2001). A national police wildlife crime unit also exists to provide a range of specialist support and facilitate intelligence sharing. Similarly, environmental protection agencies like the EPA will develop considerable expertise in identifying core non-compliance problems as well as developing their own case law on types of offending and appropriate remedies. Use of specialist environmental protection agencies arguably addresses some of the core problems identified by White and Heckenberg in environmental policing which include:

- the local and global nature of the crime;
- difficulties in detection;
- issues with jurisdiction and police inter-agency collaboration;
- the nature of investigative techniques and approaches;
- the need for specialist knowledge;
- the need for greater investment in enforcement policy, capacity and management;
- involvement of a range of criminal actors.

(2014: 222–3)

However, investigations policy and practice can only be effective if allied to effective prosecutions and policy, which is also arguably subject to considerable practical and procedural difficulties as follows:

1. Areas where there are difficulties in getting the statutory agencies to investigate crimes and where insufficient resources are provided for them to do so; for example a lack of available scientific or technical support in gathering evidence.

2. Difficulties in investigating cases due to the lack of specialist environmental or wildlife legislative knowledge on the part of wildlife and conservation investigators who, particularly in developing countries, are mostly part-time.

3. Perceived loopholes in legislation meaning that some illegal activities are similar to legal ones; the practical difficulty for investigators, therefore, is to determine whether or not a crime has actually been committed.

4. Difficulties in bringing cases to court due to a lack of expertise on the part of prosecutors and the low priority afforded to these cases in some areas.

5. The current use of the available sentencing options is often at the lower end of the scale meaning that for some offenders, fines can simply be absorbed as the cost of doing business.

(Nurse, 2015a: 146)

Bundy et al. (1999) argued that prosecutions activity in the USA plays a vital role in environmental protection by achieving the following functions:

1. Punish egregious violators, and assure local communities that the government is protecting the health of citizens and protecting natural resources.

2. Deter future violators, especially individuals.

3. Inform the regulated community that Federal enforcement sets a uniform standard for compliance; that no matter where a business operates in the United States, it must comply with federal environmental laws. This provides a level playing field for businesses that invest the time and money to comply with the law.

(Bundy et al., 1999: 1–2)

However, White (2012b) identifies that third parties such as NGOs often play a significant role in investigating and exposing environmental harm and offending and have become a necessity for effective environmental law enforcement.

The Role of NGOs

Active policing by NGOs is often a necessity where statutory policing has either failed or is inconsistent. In the UK at least, much wildlife crime is still reported directly to NGOs by members of the public, meaning that NGOs are often in the position of 'lobbying' the statutory agencies to have wildlife crimes investigated. Thus clear-up of wildlife crimes is dependent more on the public witnessing crimes and providing evidence that crime has taken place than on police detection of crimes, given that wildlife crime is frequently outside of the experience of most operational police officers (Nurse, 2013a). Nellemann et al. (2014) identify that in the field of illicit trafficking in wildlife, international collaborations exist such as the International Consortium on Combating Wildlife Crime (ICCWC), an inter-governmental consortium that includes CITES, UNODC, INTERPOL, the World Bank and WCO. Such networks, together with increased collaboration amongst agencies, such as with UNEP, and with individual countries provides a means through which at international level structured support can be given to countries in the fields of policing, customs, prosecution and the judiciary. In addition, much wildlife crime takes place in remote areas that fall outside police patrol areas and where observation of offences by the public is vital to ensuring they are reported. Thus, in the UK, birds of prey are monitored by volunteer raptor study group members, badgers are monitored by badger survey workers and illegal hunting activities are monitored by LACS Hunt Monitors. Similarly, in the USA, observation by Sierra Club members (and their regional affiliates), Defenders of Wildlife and Earthjustice members and activists such as PETA, HSUS and ASPCA officials, together with the many regional environmental or animal protection bodies and members of the public who report incidents to them is essential in identifying the occurrence of wildlife crime. Public cooperation is vital to green policing, and also helps provide some of the informal controls that may inhibit environmental crime from occurring in the first place.

NGOs also play a vital role because from the outset there are difficulties in enforcement due to the general lack of knowledge that most ordinary operational police officers have of environmental and wildlife law. This is not because of any particular lack of interest on the part of police officers in general, more that environmental law and crime often does not form a core part of police training and sometimes is not within police jurisdiction. Environmental and wildlife crime might also be seen by operational officers as 'rubbish' and not the sort of thing that the police should be involved in (Reiner, 2000). Active policing by NGOs, through the investigation and prosecution of environmental crimes, can thus serve the dual function of ensuring that legislation is properly enforced and offenders punished, while the provision of technical and expert advice as part of the policing function directly addresses the failures of mainstream policing to provide resources for environmental/wildlife investigations and operational officers' lack of expertise.

The role of NGOs as enforcers or campaigners varies according to the types of crime involved, with different policy perspectives pursued in respect of game offences and poaching, habitat destruction and pollution of rural environments, or offences involving domestic/farm animals and animal welfare and cruelty offences. The relationship between NGOs and policymakers also varies so that, for example, game offences are considered to be effectively policed within the UK's strong game and anti-poaching legislation, with good cooperation between police and game-rearing staff over poaching, but the same is not true of wildlife offences. Game-rearing staff regularly report poaching offences (which directly affect their livelihoods and the rural economy) to statutory agencies but may be reluctant to have the same involvement in wildlife offences such as bird of prey prosecution where game-rearing staff are often suspects. Thus, they may be in conflict with the police and conservationists over the appropriateness and legitimacy of enforcement action and rural crime policy.

The Wildlife Enforcement Monitoring System (WEMS)

WEMS is a United Nations Initiative with an objective to assist monitoring of trafficking and illegal wildlife trade via a joint effort carried out by United Nations bodies, national governments, private industries, civil society and research institutions. WEMS brings together national enforcement institutions to a common data collection and reporting mechanism through the WEMS 2.0 information system. The intention is that compiled data is analysed and made available online to enforcement bodies through the WEMS initiative website. According to the WEMS website, selected information is also shared with the public to increase awareness of wildlife crime. The primary objective of WEMS is to immediately address the following:

- absence of an official record on the amount of illegal trade of wild flora and fauna;
- poor reporting process regarding the compliance with Multilateral Environmental Agreements (MEA);
- absence of research data on illegal wildlife crime.

Other measures to address international environmental problems also exist. The CITES Secretariat monitors trade in regulated wildlife through its permit system and by keeping records on seizures, and there is an international monitoring system for toxic waste via the Basel Convention.

The Basel Convention and the Basel Network

In the field of e-waste, international monitoring measures are in place to address the negative consequences of globalization. White (2011) suggests that the commodification of waste can be traced back to a booming waste-removal industry in Europe following the Second World War. Italian organized crime families have trafficked in waste for decades with some estimates claiming mafia-style 'families' are responsible for the illegal transfer of over 35 million tons of garbage around the world each year (Liddick, 2011). The contemporary 'waste market' now includes toxic waste, and more specifically, electronic waste (e-waste). The relaxation of trade policies in the 1980s, the expansion of transnational organized crime and the concurrent development of environmental laws during this decade led to a substantial increase in the cost of responsible recycling practices (Liddick, 2011; White, 2011). This created the ideal environment for an illicit market in waste trading. Participation in illegal waste transfer is not limited to those considered typical 'criminals', but often includes corporate polluters, corrupt public officials and informal public and private markets. As a testament to its expansive range, the trafficking of hazardous and toxic waste has even been compared to the international drug trade in both its scope and profitability (Liddick, 2011).

The Basel Convention on the Control of Transboundary Movements of Hazardous Wastes and their Disposal was adopted in Basel, Switzerland on 22 March 1989. The Convention was initiated in response to numerous international scandals regarding hazardous waste trafficking that began to occur in the late 1980s. Although often criminal in nature, transnational trafficking in or illegal production of hazardous waste is not included in the definitions of international crimes, thus a specific international mechanism is required to criminalize it. The Convention entered into force on 5 May 1992 and regulates the transnational movement of hazardous waste. The 'Basel Ban' was adopted at the Second Conference of the Parties to the Basel Convention (COP2), 25 March 1994, Geneva Switzerland. The Basel Ban:

1. Required countries to immediately phase out all transboundary movements of hazardous wastes which are destined for final disposal from OECD to non-OECD States.
2. By 31 December 1997 phase out and prohibit all transboundary movements of hazardous wastes which are destined for recycling or recovery operations from OECD to non-OECD States.

The Basel Action Network (2011a) argues that 'in the current climate of trade liberalization, even for wastes it is vital to maintain the Basel Ban to avoid the great ESM [environmentally sound management] "escape" that economically motivated waste trade represents'. Until all nations cease to use waste trade as a means to gain economic advantage, instead of striving to become self-sufficient in hazardous waste management, it will be very dangerous and misguided to de-link ESM and the Basel Ban. The Basel Action Network (BAN) is a US registered charity that works to prevent the globalization of the toxic chemical crisis. BAN carries out the following:

- **Toxic Trade Monitoring** – BAN describes itself as an information clearing-house on the subject of waste trade for journalists, academics and the general public. BAN maintains the definitive website on international toxic trade (www.ban.org) and an e-mail newsletter, including electronic action alerts.
- **International Policy Advocacy** – BAN is recognized by the United Nations Environment Program (UNEP) as the leading organization dedicated exclusively to issues of 'toxic trade'. BAN provides advocacy and expert opinion and has also produced Model National Legislation on toxic waste trade for developing countries.
- **Research and Investigations** – BAN conducts field investigations in developing countries as well as providing photographic and video documentation of toxic trade.
- **Campaigns** – BAN engages in coalition campaigning with other NGOs to raise awareness on toxic trade.

Doyon (2014) examines how the booming industry of personal electronics has created a consequential market of electronic waste that has resulted in the transference of harm from the Global North to the Global South. Analysing the case of Executive Recycling Inc., Doyon highlights particular concerns about enforcement failures and a lack of prosecution within the USA as follows:

Case Study 9.1   Executive Recycling

Executive Recycling, Inc. was an electronics recycling company based out of Englewood, Colorado. Billed as a large-scale recycling firm, the company advertised a variety of recycling services giving clear assurances via its then website that its confidence in its ability to recycle old electronics and provide protection against identity theft from old hard drives was sufficiently high, that it would provide certificates of recycling and would transfer responsibility and any potential liability for disposal from consumers to the company.

Doyon (2014) notes that the company's website also exhibited awareness of the environmental dangers of improperly recycled e-waste, detailing the detrimental human and environmental health concerns related to the leaching of chemicals from e-waste (such as lead or mercury) into soil and waterways should they not be properly disposed of. The company also affirmed that its e-waste was recycled in the USA and not dumped elsewhere.

However, over a period of about 30 months BAN investigators followed and photographed shipping containers from loading docks at Executive Recycling, Inc., tracking them primarily into Chinese ports where the e-waste was subsequently processed in 'deadly, highly polluting operations' (BAN, 2011b: 1). The shipments were in direct violation of the US law as Executive Recycling, Inc. failed to file the notification of intent to export with the EPA, and also failed to obtain the consent of the receiving country. BAN alerted both CBS (whose 60 Minutes programme broadcast an expose), and the EPA. The EPA concluded that Executive Recycling, Inc. was the exporter in more than 300 shipping containers leaving the USA between 2005 and 2008; roughly 160 of these containers held a total of 100,000 illegally shipped CRTs. Doyon notes that Executive Recycling, Inc. profited twice in the process: first, by having consumers pay them to recycle their electronics and a second time when the shipping container arrived at the importing nation, earning the company an average of 35 dollars per unit (Doyon, 2014).

The case brought against the company by US justice authorities in 2011 was the first ever prosecution of an exporter for illegally exporting toxic electronic waste. CEO Brandon Richter and Vice President of Operations Tor Olson of Executive Recycling, Inc. were indicted on multiple charges, including wire and mail fraud, 'failure to file notification of intent to export hazardous waste', 'exportation contrary to law', and 'destruction, alteration, or falsification of records' (BAN, 2011b; Gluckman, 2011; United States District Court, 2011). Executive Recycling, Inc. and its directors Richter and Olson were convicted in criminal court on 21 December 2012 of six counts of wire fraud, one count of mail fraud, and one count of 'exportation contrary to law' (US District Court of Colorado, 2012). Brandon Richter, along with Executive Recycling, Inc. as a firm, was also convicted of U.S.C. Section 1519 'Destruction, alteration, or falsification of records in a Federal investigation' (US District Court of Colorado, 2012). However, Doyon (2014) notes that neither defendant was convicted of the specific hazardous waste offence although Executive Recycling Inc. was convicted on that count.

(adapted from Doyon, 2014)

The Quality of Justice

Doyon (2014: 66) argues that 'multiple changes need to take place in order to bring under control the illegal electronics recycling industry, including increased regulation and enforcement as well as producer and consumer responsibility.' The Executive Recycling case illustrates how national and international legislation regulating the transfer of electronic waste (e-waste) has been unable to keep up with the pace of technology and consumerism, and has led to the movement of this hazardous and toxic waste from developed nations into still-developing and undeveloped nations (Nurse, 2014).

The effective implementation of sanctions and processing of offenders through justice systems are key to successful environmental law enforcement. Some laws, such as the EU's Environmental Liability Directive and its associated laws and regulations in EU Member States establish an environmental liability framework intended to prevent and remedy environmental damage rather than purely punish it. The Directive and associated laws are based on the 'polluter pays' and precautionary principles (Mazurkiewicz, 2002; Turner, 1992), also used in US legislation regarding the prevention and restoration of natural-resource damage. Such laws provide a means for corporations to pay compensation for environmental damage (Hinteregger, 2008) making operators liable for significant environmental damage. In the EU Directive such damage is defined as 'a measurable adverse change in water, land and biodiversity quality', although the Directive does not apply to diffuse pollution, such as air pollution, or to 'traditional damage' such as personal injury and damage to goods and property. Where environmental damage creates harm to members of the public or affects their goods and property, national civil liability laws would be invoked across Member States. Thus the Directive's regulatory measures are specifically focused at environmental (including wildlife) harm.

The use of restorative measures in such a way is rare in pure criminal prosecution where punishments handed out to offenders are primarily intended to convey social disapproval. However, as Vincent (2014) observed in discussing wildlife crime, human–natural resource interaction incorporates a range of deviation from legal and regulatory rules, thus criminal justice punishment, which fails to address the harm caused by offending, is not the only solution to dealing with environmental and wildlife crime problems where these are broadly defined to include deviance that harms ecosystems and results in natural resource loss. Thus in the UK, the Law Commission's (2012) proposals for reviewing wildlife law include modifying the regime to make use of civil sanctions as an alternative to prosecuting the underlying criminal offence, based on the regime contained in Part 3 of the Regulatory Enforcement and Sanctions Act 2008 (Vincent, 2014: 74). This Act contains measures which include the opportunity for enforcers to apply enforceable undertakings measures whose aims are intended to achieve 'cessation of the conduct, redress for parties adversely affected, implementation of compliance measures to prevent further breaches', thus hopefully securing a change in offender behaviour by securing a means through which commitments are made in respect of future offending

(Peysner and Nurse, 2008: 204). The wide range of discretion allowed to enforcers to apply appropriate conditions on enforceable undertakings means that they can be used to implement restorative principles, i.e. requiring offenders to repair the harm they have caused in a manner determined by enforcers. Such powers (available in other jurisdictions and used, for example, in Australian competition law enforcement) provide an enforceable means through which harmful activity can be addressed, thus representing an alternative to pursue criminalization. However, Peysner and Nurse (2008) found some inconsistency in enforcers' use of such measures and recommended that they should be subject to criminal rather than civil enforcement as a means of ensuring they were used effectively and were truly enforceable. Where used alongside criminal justice powers regulatory action provides a possible means of remedying environmental harm albeit they are not universally incorporated into environmental enforcement regimes and may not be immune from the problems which infect other environmental and wildlife sanctioning and prosecution regimes.

Summary

Environmental investigation is a complex area only touched on here. State environmental investigation activity is usually characterized by the regulatory investigation approach, often characterized by a 'risk based' regulation approach of licensing, inspections and monitoring and which is largely designed to facilitate and manage rather than investigate and detect (Stallworthy, 2008).

These regulatory regimes often provide for a mixture of civil and criminal penalties although the idea of negotiated settlement dominates in certain areas of environmental crime (e.g. pollution offences) whereas criminal punishment may dominate in others (e.g. wildlife crime). As White (2012b) indicates in discussing regulation theory, NGOs are an integral part of certain environmental enforcement regimes. This is the case both where state bodies are deemed to be inadequate to the task, or where specialized knowledge often lacking on the part of state enforcers is required to ensure effective justice. However, dedicated environmental protection agencies have the benefit of developing expertise that allows them to develop specialist enforcement tools and techniques that may ultimately benefit environmental enforcement. They may also have discretion to employ a range of tools for addressing environmental harms such as deployment of restorative justice (discussed in the final chapter) or other means to remediate environmental damage.

A question remains, however, concerning whether specialist agencies should be used or whether environmental crime should be the remit of core policing bodies and considered alongside other forms of offending.

Self-study Questions

1. What barriers exist to effective international monitoring and enforcement of measures like the e-waste regulations and how might these be overcome?

2. Doyon notes that Executive Recycling Inc. was the first recycler to face charges in the USA for illegally exporting toxic waste and that the case took almost 30 months to prepare. What impression does this give you about the justice system response to such crimes?

3. What challenges potentially face investigators and prosecutors in prosecuting and investigating environmental crimes to the criminal standard where the prosecution is required to prove its case *beyond reasonable doubt*?

4. Given the potential scale of crimes such as illegal trading in e-waste, the profits involved and the potential for environmental disaster, what challenges exist in determining an appropriate penalty or sentence?

10

REPAIRING THE HARM:
RESTORATIVE JUSTICE AND
ENVIRONMENTAL COURTS

By the end of this chapter you should:

- Have an understanding of restorative justice theory and practice and the ways in which restorative justice principles can be applied to environmental harms.
- Understand the potential advantage of restorative justice as a tool for dealing with environmental harms that may fall outside of the criminal law.
- Understand the potential limitations of restorative justice and some of the criticisms of restorative justice as an integral part of justice systems.
- Understand the rationale for environmental courts and their use in dealing with environmental problems.
- Understand the rationale for alternate forms of justice such as ADR and mediation and their applicability in dealing with conflicts related to environmental exploitation.
- Understand the potential of Environmental Ombudsmen as an ADR mechanism for dealing with environmental harms.

Introduction

Unlike traditional crimes, environmental crimes (and environmental harms) frequently have long-lasting and irreversible effects. This raises questions about the effectiveness of justice systems in dealing with environmental offenders and the damage they cause. Lynch and Stretesky argue 'there is little doubt that humans produce an extraordinary amount of pollution and harm the world in numerous ways by damaging the environment' (2014: 8). Other green criminologists (Nurse, 2013a; Schneider, 2012; Wyatt, 2013) have commented on the negative, damaging impacts of the illegal trade in wildlife on rare and threatened species, with its knock-on effect on ecosystems. The reality is that environmental crime, and particularly those crimes that impact on nonhuman animals, represent an unsustainable attack on natural resources. WWF's 2014 *Living Planet Report*, which includes the Living Planet Index (LPI) measuring trends in thousands of vertebrate species populations, argues that there has been a decline of 52% between 1970 and 2010. Put another way, WWF argues that 'vertebrate species populations across the globe are, on average, about half the size they were 40 years ago' (2014: 8). Once a species has become extinct through human persecution there is little that can be done unless captive breeding programmes were already in place prior to extinction or genetic samples of sufficient quality exist in storage so that the species might be revived through scientific means.

Many environmental damage incidents such as major chemical or oil spills or widespread deforestation may also have severe and irreversible consequences beyond the initial event. Where this is the case, the criminal justice system, predicated on notions of punishing offenders rather than repairing harm, may be inadequate to deal with the consequences and alternatives may be required. This chapter discusses alternatives to the use of criminal justice as a potential solution to dealing with environmental harms (including wildlife crime) and explores the inadequacies of continued reliance on the criminal law and the law enforcement perspective (Bright, 1993). In part, it explores whether reactive detection, apprehension and punishment are effective as an environmental crime response. It also examines the use of mediation, reparation and restoration as effective tools for dealing with environmental conflicts (Brisman and South, 2013). The chapter examines the concept of restorative justice as applied to environmental crime, explicitly considering how justice systems need to do more than just provide punishment and social disapproval. Given the finite nature of environmental resources the notion of 'repairing the harm' should arguably be integral to green justice; incorporating a restorative element into any proceedings aimed at addressing environmental harm or crime. The ideal for effective environmental restorative justice is that offenders are held to account for what they have done, realize the harm that they have caused and are persuaded or compelled to repair that harm. Successful restorative justice also avoids the escalation of legal justice and its associated costs and delays (Marshall, 1999) by engaging both offender and victim in finding a resolution to environmental crime problems. Applied to environmental damage, restorative justice also provides for legal enforcement of Corporate Environmental Responsibility (CER) by requiring corporations to understand and mitigate their harms, offering hope of behavioural change. Examining arguments that traditional justice may be ill-equipped to deal with the specialized nature of environmental problems, this chapter also examines the use of specialist environmental courts and alternative dispute mechanisms (ADR) such as Environmental Ombudsmen. In doing so it specifically links to green criminology's exploration of environmental harm as a social problem requiring a harm-reduction rather than punitive response (Lynch and Stretesky, 2014).

Understanding Restorative Justice

Concerns about the effectiveness of traditional sentencing regimes led to the development of restorative justice, a theoretical model of justice that aims to repair the harm caused by criminal or offending behaviour. While various different conceptions on restorative justice exist, the UK's Restorative Justice Council provides the following broad definition:

> Restorative justice gives victims the chance to meet or communicate with their offenders to explain the real impact of the crime—it empowers victims by giving them a voice. It also holds offenders to account for what they have done and helps them to take responsibility and make amends. Government research demonstrates that restorative justice provides an 85% victim satisfaction rate, and a 14% reduction in the frequency of reoffending.
>
> (Restorative Justice Council, 2014)

As this definition indicates, a core aspect of restorative justice is the involvement of victims of crime who are often powerless in criminal justice systems, and for there to be some form of mediation or contact between victim and offender. In one sense, this 'pure' notion of restorative justice, predicated on victim/offender meeting and mediation creates an alternative justice system, one where redress and resolution of harm is directly in the hands of the participants in a crime (victim and offender) rather than wider criminal justice agents such as the police or courts. Effective victim/offender meeting and mediation can lead to:

- an apology;
- a chance for victims to get answers to questions;
- a chance for victims to tell offenders the real impact of their crimes and for offenders to understand this impact;

- a chance to achieve some form of reparation;
- a chance for victims to achieve some form of closure from events.

Thus the ideal for effective restorative justice is dialogue that allows for offenders to be held accountable for their actions and gain greater understanding of the harm they have caused. Personalizing the victim prevents offenders from distancing themselves from the consequences of their actions and may mitigate the use of neutralization techniques (Sykes and Matza, 1957) such as denial of injury or arguments that crimes such as burglary are victimless because householders can have goods replaced through household insurance. In successful restorative justice, victims are able to confront offenders, personalizing the harm, expressing in detail the long-term consequences of a crime and ensuring that offenders understand the social and long-term consequences of seemingly 'minor' crime incidents such as the theft of small items that may be replaceable in principle but which hold considerable sentimental value. Via victim/offender conferencing, victims are also often able to make sense of what has happened to them and to achieve some form of closure (Marshall, 1999).

However, beyond the 'pure' notion of restorative justice contained within mainstream criminal justice and 'standard' victim/offender conferencing, partial or modified restorative justice is possible. Thus, principles of restorative justice might be applied to areas where harm has been caused albeit the full menu of restorative justice techniques may not be possible or desirable. The following section discusses this, considering the read-across from traditional criminal justice system restorative justice to its application to other forms of crime or harm. Subsequently the chapter considers the application of restorative principles to environmental harms.

Restorative Justice and Criminal Justice

Restorative justice primarily operates in criminal justice systems as a means of achieving closure for victims of crime and giving offenders the motivation and insight to stop offending. Different conceptions on restorative justice exist across jurisdictions, commensurate with each jurisdiction's willingness to implement restorative techniques within its criminal justice processes and the applicability of restorative justice to jurisdiction-specific criminal justice policies and procedures. Restorative justice was introduced into the UK's youth justice system via the Crime and Disorder Act 1998 and has subsequently been introduced into the adult criminal justice system, although its use is not compulsory. But Part 2 of Schedule 16 to the Crime and Courts Act 2013 inserts a new section 1ZA into the Powers of Criminal Courts (Sentencing) Act 2000. This explicitly allows courts to use existing powers to defer sentence post-conviction, providing for a restorative justice activity to take place by imposing a restorative justice requirement (CPS, 2014). Courts can also adjourn sentencing to allow for restorative justice activities to take place where appropriate.

As of July 2007, 13 of the UK's (then) 42 local criminal justice boards had reported some adult restorative justice delivery (House of Lords, 2007). However, the UK's Ministry of Justice (2014: 2) notes that 'data on the use of RJ is not collected centrally' thus there is no formal justice system monitoring of restorative justice in the UK. However, the Ministry funded a seven-year research programme into restorative justice culminating in four reports by Professor Joanna Shapland. In the third report Shapland et al. (2007) concluded that:

- 78% of victims who took part in Restorative Justice (RJ) conferences said they would recommend it to other victims.
- 90% of victims who took part in an RJ conference received an apology from the offender in their case; as compared with only 19% of victims in the control group.
- Only 6 victims, and 6 offenders, out of 152 offenders and 216 victims interviewed, were dissatisfied with the RJ conference after taking part.
- Around 80% of offenders who took part in the RJ conference thought it would lessen their likelihood of re-offending.
- Victims who had been through a Restorative Justice conference were more likely to think the sentence the offender had received was fair, than victims in the control group who did not participate in RJ.

In the fourth report, concerning the impact of restorative justice on re-offending, Shapland et al. (2008), while noting that the restorative justice conferencing they assessed was too statistically small a sample on which to draw conclusions of statistical significance, concluded that offenders engaged in restorative justice do offend less. In particular Professor Shapland's team found that adult offenders' views on restorative justice and the extent to which restorative conferencing made them realize the harm they had done and whether they wanted to meet the victim at the start, had an impact on their re-offending. Shapland et al. (2008) also concluded that restorative justice was more cost-effective than pursuing convictions.

The UK research mirrors the belief widely held around the world that restorative justice, when carried out properly, can have a positive effect on re-offending. This has been demonstrated in a number of research studies (see for example Hayes, 2005; Nugent et al., 2003; Sherman and Strang, 2007) although it should be noted that success rates vary between offender groups and that different models for resolving the conflict can be employed. Victim—offender mediation, for example, can be carried out either directly (via face-to-face meetings) or indirectly (where the victim and/or offender do not wish to meet and the mediator conveys messages between the two parties to reach agreement). Family Group conferencing can involve the extended family so that the offender has support to address challenging behaviour. Restorative Conferencing involves intervention by a trained facilitator to enable a conflict to be resolved and for the offender to find a way of making reparation to the victim.

Although restorative justice is most often used in crime and criminal justice there is no reason why it cannot be used in civil and other cases. However, there may be a need to distinguish between 'pure' restorative justice and partial restorative justice where some of the principles are applied but not others. This chapter contends that the ability to apply some aspects of restorative justice to certain harm settings allows for a theoretical conception of restorative justice to be applied to activities such as environmental crime, while tailoring the use of restorative principles to the specific harm or crime in question. In fact restorative justice processes have already been implemented in schools, workplaces, care homes and health services where the principles can be readily applied (Peysner and Nurse, 2008).

Braithwaite (2002) describes restorative justice as 'a process whereby all the parties with a stake in a particular offence come together to resolve collectively how to deal with the aftermath of the offence and its implications for the future.' In discussing the implementation of restorative justice in criminal justice cases, attention often rests on the meeting between offender and victim and as a result the public perception of restorative justice is mostly based on this issue; the opportunity for a victim/offender meeting to facilitate understanding of the impact and consequence of their actions. This is in part because the focus in criminal justice is for victims to obtain answers and for offenders to face up to their crimes and begin the process of rehabilitation, thereby achieving the criminal justice system aim of reducing crime by preventing re-offending. But Llewellyn has argued that 'restorative processes are founded on a conception of justice as fundamentally concerned with restoring relationships' (2002). There need not be any face-to-face meeting between victim and offender but as long as there has been some mechanism through which the victim or 'wronged party' is able to communicate with the offender, even if via a third party or mediator, restorative principles have arguably been applied. Thus, restorative justice principles are also employed in some ADR and complaint investigation processes such as Ombudsman schemes where the aim is to put victims back into the position they would have been in had the fault not occurred and to allow the complainant to find some closure from events (Peysner and Nurse, 2008). The UK's public sector Ombudsman schemes, for example, routinely seek the views of complainants when considering a remedy and the 'injustice' caused to the complainant is a significant factor in determining the appropriate remedy. Thus a modified indirect form of victim—offender mediation/conferencing is applied with the victim being given an opportunity to identify the harm and injustice they have suffered, with the 'offender' given an opportunity to respond and apologize or otherwise provide a remedy.

Braithwaite (2004) argues for 'reintegrative shaming', disapproval of the crime act within a continuum of respect for the offender, as a means of preventing crime through forgiveness. Thus restorative justice serves to assist the offender. Braithwaite (2004) identifies restorative conferences as a means through which offender and victim discuss the consequences of a crime and draw out the feelings of those who have been harmed. But in accordance with Foucault's conception that power exists only when it is put into action, one aspect of restorative justice is to give power back to the victim (Dreyfuss and Rabinow, 1982). This is potentially problematic in environmental cases where the rights of the environment as crime victim may not be formally recognized. However, a number of mechanisms exist through which restorative justice, both 'pure' and partial, can be applied to environmental offences.

Applying Restorative Justice to Environmental Harm

In the House of Lords' debate on restorative justice, Lord Thomas commented on the effectiveness of restorative justice when compared with traditional forms of criminal justice, concluding that the aims of reduction of crime, rehabilitation of offenders and the making of reparation by offenders to their victims contained within the Criminal Justice Act 2003 had not been met. Lord Thomas commented that:

> It is interesting to compare the aims of that Act with the Macrory report published by the Better Regulation Executive a year ago. That report considered the purposes of sanctions for regulatory offences. The first aim was not punishment but changing the behaviour of the offender. The second aim was to eliminate any financial gain or benefit from non-compliance. The third aim was to be responsive and to consider what is appropriate for the particular offender. The fourth aim was for sanctions to be proportionate to the nature of the offence and the harm caused. Your Lordships will see that in the aims set out in the report, there is no mention of punishment simply for its own sake. Unfortunately, the report's recommendation that restorative justice techniques be applied in this field has not been carried into the Regulatory Enforcement and Sanctions Bill introduced on 8 November.

However, despite Lord Thomas's comments, the provisions of the Regulatory Enforcement and Sanctions Act 2008 do allow for the application of restorative practices. The Act contains provisions allowing for: the introduction of fixed financial penalties; enforcers to accept undertakings from offenders; enforcers to use discretionary measures, which could provide for restorative practices to be employed by enforcers. What will determine how effective these measures are in contributing to the development of a restorative enforcement culture in environmental cases is how they are used by enforcers and regulators. Although prosecution may be a practical means of dealing with individual offences it is an inefficient means of dealing with trade malpractice. Fines levied in individual cases may not provide a sufficient deterrent to prevent future wrongdoing and do not address any harm incurred by others in a similar position who may not have directly raised a complaint. As in some areas of crime, offenders may simply regard fines as the cost of doing business, and criminological theory (see for example Lemert, 1951; Merton, 1968) also explains how many business offenders do not see themselves as operating unlawful or criminal practices that need to be modified even when prosecuted. Restorative justice may, therefore, provide a means of changing business behaviour by ensuring that business becomes aware of the impact of their actions on consumers and the consequences of business practices that breach regulations, in much the same way that restorative conferencing requires burglars to see their victims as individuals whose lives have been severely affected as a direct result of their actions. The application of restorative practices to business regulation and compliance is possible where legislation allows enforcement authorities the tools to resolve complaints in addition to or as part of their enforcement or regulatory activities. In this regard, the UK has the Environmental Civil Sanctions Order and Regulations 2010, designed to provide for a range of sanctions to be applied to environmental offending.

Potentially it is in the area of achieving reparation for environmental harm and providing redress for aggrieved communities that restorative justice can best be applied to environmental cases. The core values of restorative justice are to secure healing for the victim, responsibility on the part of offenders and making amends for the offence. In environmental cases, this can be achieved as long as enforcers and designated regulators have the power to make binding awards and pursue negotiated settlements for complaints. Where legislation provides that regulators can decide not to take enforcement action if they can achieve compliance through negotiation and settlement with potential offenders, this option could be used by applying restorative principles. Although many corporations may embrace the concepts of social and environmental responsibility there are numerous examples of corporations who claim to act in a sustainable and responsible way while at the same time showing disregard for the communities in which they operate and causing considerable environmental damage. Where this is the case, standard criminal justice practices may be inadequate to deal with the harm that has been caused and so the 'polluter pays' principle has been developed as a means of ensuring that as part of any 'punishment' corporations are required to remedy the harm that they cause.

The use of the 'polluter pays' principle (see also Chapter 9) for environmental damage was adopted by the OECD in 1972 as a background economic principle for environmental policy (Turner, 1992). By making goods and services reflect their total cost including the cost of all the resources used, the principle required polluters to integrate (or internalize) the cost of use or degradation of environmental resources. However, environmental damage is not solely an issue of cost and, increasingly, legislators, regulators and the courts apply the basic principles of restorative justice that include the 'repair of harm' principle and mediation or contact between victim and offender as tools to remedy or mitigate corporate environmental damage.

A model for negotiated settlements exists within Australian consumer protection legislation. The Australian Competition and Consumer Commission (ACCC) has a power to use enforceable undertakings to formalize their decisions and to forego enforcement litigation if offenders agree to correct their misconduct and comply in the future. Parker (2004) argues that enforceable undertakings represent a means for applying restorative justice as an alternative to traditional regulatory enforcement action because the undertakings can facilitate the agreement of all parties involved in wrongdoing to correct a breach of regulations and prevent any further breaches. Parker cites as examples of enforceable undertakings, 'the selling of cots, sunglasses, bicycles and other goods that do not meet safety standards' (2004) and observed that most offences enforced by the ACCC are civil offences rather than criminal prosecutions. Australian legislation allows that the ACCC can accept undertakings after it has begun an investigation and will generally only accept an undertaking if there is evidence of a breach that would justify legal action or prosecution. Parker (2004) identifies the following criteria in the ACCC's decisions on whether to pursue enforceable undertakings:

1. the impact of the alleged breach on third parties and the community at large;
2. the type of practice;
3. the product or service involved;
4. the size of the corporation or corporations involved;
5. the history of complaints against the corporation and complaints concerning the practice complained of;
6. the nature of the product or industry and any relevant previous court or similar proceedings;
7. the cost-effectiveness for all parties of pursuing an administrative resolution instead of court action;
8. prospects for rapid resolution of the matter;
9. the apparent good faith of the corporation.

This provides possible criteria for achieving reparation via restorative justice. The provisions in the Regulatory Enforcement and Sanctions Act 2008 allow for enforcers to accept undertakings (Section 50 of the Act) although it is not currently clear whether these would be enforceable by the courts. DEFRA guidance (2010) suggests enforceable undertakings to be a means of negotiating compliance and achieving remediation. In this respect the idea of undertakings is intended to provide for restoration of harm. DEFRA note, for example, that 'practical steps could include, for example, cleaning up when non-compliance has caused nuisance in the form of dust or dirt, or restoring or providing actual amenities where these have been damaged' (2010: 27). But in practice, enforcers take such action already on an informal basis, as prosecution by trading standards is often a last resort with the aim being to secure compliance and punish offenders rather than achieving reparation for aggrieved consumers.

Environmental Courts

As this chapter identifies, traditional criminal justice with its focus on individualistic offending and punishment may be inadequate to deal with the problem of environmental crimes. Problems exist not just in the classification and investigating of environmental crimes (discussed in Chapter 8) but also in the presentation of cases at court. In particular, a lack of expertise on the part of prosecutors and jurists risk perpetuating a justice system that works as intended by punishing offenders but which fails to resolve the problems created by a particular environmental crime.

In a 1992 article and lecture entitled 'Are the Judiciary Environmentally Myopic?' Lord Woolf, at the time one of the most senior UK judges, questioned whether the judiciary was equipped to deal with environmental cases. Lord Woolf noted that a single environmental incident, for example pollution, could comprise of multiple offences under various different pieces of legislation. An incident that killed wildlife and resulted in human harm while also constituting regulatory breach by exceeding emission limits and other pollution controls could engage with criminal, civil and administrative laws and the need for punishment, remediation and civil damages. Such incidents could also engage with analysis and development of policy, which Lord Woolf contended the judiciary lacked competence to deal with and which were better dealt with by professional policymakers (Woolf, 1992).

The need to consider consequences beyond the initial direct impact requires consideration of a 'therapeutic jurisprudence approach' that makes offenders accountable for their actions and facilitates rehabilitation (Ward, 2014: 2). The 'therapeutic jurisprudence' concept incorporates focus on the therapeutic and anti-therapeutic benefits of consequences of the court process; the perception that court processes can go beyond pure punishment to incorporate reform and rehabilitation (Hoyle, 2012). The notion of specialist green courts reflects perceived benefits of specialism versus generalism (Stempel, 1995; Woolf, 1992). Lord Woolf's contention was that without specialist knowledge of environmental matters, judicial scrutiny through criminal law processes risked being inadequate. Similarly, White (2013a: 269) identifies that empirical evidence shows that when specialist courts are in place or when judicial officers with specialist environmental knowledge are placed within generalist systems, there is greater likelihood of both offender prosecution and use of appropriate sanctions. Accordingly, Lord Woolf's conclusion that a case exists for a special environmental tribunal with general responsibility for overseeing and enforcing environmental law that would be a 'multi-faceted, multi-skilled body which would combine the services provided by existing courts, tribunals and inspectors in the environmental field' has merit (1992: 14). Part of Lord Woolf's analysis related to the distinctive aspects of environmental crimes such as 'the possibility of a single pollution incident giving rise to many different types of legal actions in different forums—a coroner's inquest if deaths are involved; criminal prosecution, civil actions, and judicial review if public authorities are involved' (Macrory, 2010: 64). Similarly, within wildlife crime some incidents involve multiple offences, such as the poisoning of birds of prey on (UK) shooting estates, which can involve criminal offences relating to killing of wildlife, health and safety and prohibited substance offences in relation to handling and use of pesticides, and civil actions where non-target species (e.g. pets) are harmed. The implication of Lord Woolf's analysis was that a single specialized environmental forum with expertise to deal with all matters relating to the environmental incident would be better than the current system.

Since Lord Woolf's 1992 analysis, environmental courts have become a reality with Pring and Pring (2009) identifying over 80 Environmental Courts and Tribunals in 35 different countries. Environmental Courts are primarily concerned with 'mainstream' environmental issues; land use, planning law, pollution and regulatory environmental offences. Walters et al. (2013: 283) for example, describe the jurisdiction of the New South Wales Land and Environment Court (LEC) as being to compel compliance with environmental law through both civil and criminal enforcement. They describe the court's cases as including a range of matters; 'environmental planning and protection appeals, tree disputes, valuation, compensation and Aboriginal land claims, civil enforcement and judicial reviews' (Walters et al., 2013: 283) the nature of the case determining whether they are dealt with as criminal or civil matters.

Macrory and Woods (2003) identified a number of features that justified a separate environmental tribunal including:

- evidential and judgmental issues involving complex technical/scientific questions, usually of a quite different sort to those found in [ordinary environmental law] decisions;

- a challenging legislative and policy base, which is rapidly developing;

- the overlapping of remedies (civil and criminal) as well as interests (public and private). Environmental regulatory issues are also critically connected with the subsequent enforcement of environmental standards under criminal law;

- a powerful and increasing body of EC legislation and a growing number of interpretative judgments of the European Court of Justice (notably in areas such as IPPC, waste management, water pollution, genetically modified organisms and habitats protection. (Decisions of the European Court of Human Rights on the right to a healthy environment and biodiversity could also be added to this criteria);

- a substantial body of international environmental treaties and law covering issues such as trade in endangered species, pollution of marine waters, transnational shipments of hazardous waste and climate change;

- the development of certain fundamental environmental principles such as the precautionary approach, polluter-pays, prevention at source, and procedural transparency;

- the emergence of principles concerning third party access to environmental justice, and the requirement under the Aarhus Convention for review procedures that are timely and not prohibitively expensive;

- the emergence of the overarching principle of sustainable development which underpins contemporary policy approach.

(Macrory and Woods, 2003: 20)

Macrory and Woods' analysis is consistent with those of other scholars that the case for dedicated green courts incorporates a need for specialist expertise, not just in judicial consideration of cases but also as regards 'valuation of the harm degree of seriousness, extent and nature of victimization and remedies' (White and Heckenberg, 2014: 262). White (2013b: 270) identifies consistency in sentencing as being a special concern of the New South Wales LEC, which has also established a data base which provides sentencing information including judgments, recent law and other publications. Other environmental courts such as Vermont's Environmental Division also provide an online data-base of opinions. Specialist courts thus offer the benefit of evolving procedural norms suited to their jurisdiction and secure more effective jurisprudence through development of judicial and prosecutorial expertise, given that judges will have greater exposure to a homogenous legal policy regime and consistent consideration of specialist evidence and legal argument. Thus, in theory, specialist environmental courts will bring uniformity, consistency and predictability in developing the appropriate evidentiary base and robust decision-making. White (2013b) also comments that specialist environmental courts offer the hope of lower costs for enforcement agencies as well as the use of an array of alternative dispute resolution procedures including mediation. Arguably there are two conceptions on the specialist green court. One is the regulatory or dispute resolution environmental tribunal indicated by Macrory (2010) and which exists in several jurisdictions to deal with appeals and regulatory breaches and appeals against planning or land use decisions as a problem-solving court. The second is a specialist environmental court that arguably acts as a specialist criminal court considering a range of civil and criminal environmental offences. The former is more common within the environmental court model although Macrory and Woods' 2003 conception makes specific reference to trade in endangered species, the overlapping of civil and criminal remedies and sustainable development questions to which the latter model might be suited.

Calls have also been made for an international environmental court to be established. However, as earlier chapters establish, that function is partially fulfilled by the ICJ whose specialist environmental chamber was underused. A potential flaw in using the ICJ as an international environmental court is its requirement for states to bring action, whereas a broader international environmental court could be constituted to allow cases to be brought by NGOs and other recognized enforcers. However, short of establishing an international environmental court, national courts and ADR mechanisms such as Ombudsmen come into play.

Environmental Ombudsmen

Ombudsmen's schemes are now an established feature of consumer redress and the ADR system in the UK and their principles have been applied elsewhere. The Ombudsman principle is a Scandinavian one with Ombudsman meaning 'representative of the people' or 'grievance man'. In this context, Ombudsmen, often operating under statute, are responsible for examining procedural fault that has caused harm, albeit their precise jurisdiction to consider fault varies according to their enacting legislation and the industry/function under scrutiny. Generally, Ombudsmen are independent complaints investigators who can make recommendations to resolve a dispute. This includes requiring an organization to provide a service, pay compensation, change its policies and procedures and consider whether it also needs to provide recompense to others in a similar situation. The UK's former National Consumer Council (now Consumer Concern) estimated that in 2006/7 the combined efforts of the various UK Ombudsmen's schemes resulted in the resolution of nearly 150,000 cases (Brooker, 2008). Public sector Ombudsmen by virtue of public or administrative law provisions contained within their operating statute are public offices subject to scrutiny in the same way that other judicial and quasi-judicial functions are. Public Ombudsmen are usually funded by the taxpayer and have a specific jurisdiction while private sector Ombudsmen (mostly operating in the goods and services sector) are funded by industry participants who elect to join a scheme covering their industry.

Kirkham et al. (2008) broadly identify public sector Ombudsmen as being a particular kind of institution that is designed to uphold the rule of law, yet which operates outside of a mainstream understanding of legal practice. Thus Ombudsmen represent an alternative form of justice conversant with the idea that for some forms of dispute court processes may not be the best means of finding a solution (Brunsdon-Tully, 2009). Although the main role of the public sector Ombudsmen in the UK has primarily been that of complaint-handlers rather than enforcers of legal rights their scrutiny function often has the effect of enforcing rights and improving public service provision. The UK's public services Ombudsmen (The Local Government Ombudsman, The Parliamentary Ombudsman, the Health Service Ombudsman, The Commissioner for Local Administration in Wales and the Independent Housing Ombudsman) provide access to justice by dealing with complaints of maladministration brought by individuals against public authorities. In the area of criminal justice the UK also has a Prisons and Probations Ombudsman, providing for investigation of complaints surrounding a range of issues relating to prisoners' conditions and deaths in custody. The Independent Police Complaints Commission (IPCC) also provides for investigation of complaints against the police, including complaints concerning failures in investigation.

In some jurisdictions, Ombudsmen may enforce legal rights and state compliance with human rights norms or international law principles and obligations, including environmental ones. Ombudsmen provide for an independent and impartial quasi-judicial investigation of complaints. Ombudsman's services are generally free to use and lawyers are not required and while their decisions are not always legally binding, the existence of an impartial, statutory investigation and adjudication scheme provides a means through which complaints are often resolved. Given the statute-backed nature of public sector schemes, those organizations subject to an Ombudsman's jurisdiction are inclined to comply with any recommendation made on a complaint as failure to do so risks the Ombudsman's investigation and (mostly) public reports being used as evidence against the authority in court proceedings. Failure to comply with the findings of an impartial investigation also risks the authority being seen as intransigent or negligence in the way it addresses its faults once revealed.

Through the investigative process and provision of a remedy where fault in the decision-making process or procedure has caused injustice, Ombudsmen provide redress for complainants while also identifying areas of practice requiring improvement. This chapter identifies that environmental courts develop a repository of cases and decisions available to the public, scholars and business and which identify not only how the law is interpreted but also how it is applied to particular types of dispute. Ombudsmen's schemes offer the same service, many are required to make their reports and investigation findings public, but sometimes go further. One advantage of Ombudsmen's investigative processes is that they result in a distinct jurisprudence; unlike traditional policing or the courts, Ombudsmen are both investigator and 'judge' with both a fact-finding and adjudicator role. Thus, a body of evidence exists that allows for scrutiny of common fault found in the investigation process as well as areas where injustice or harm has been caused and a remedy is required. Thus Ombudsmen are in a position to identify mechanisms through which common problems can be avoided. Some have chosen to do so; the UK's Local Government Ombudsman, for example, enacts the duty to promote good administration enshrined in the Local Government Act 1974 by publishing guidance and advice notes on specific subjects within the Ombudsman's jurisdiction. It also publishes an annual digest of cases available to bodies under investigation and the public, making the Ombudsman's decisions and guidance public.

Environmental Ombudsmen have emerged in recent years as a way of resolving citizens' environmental complaints through independent investigation and adjudication. Pring and Pring (2009) identified a number of non-judicial bodies who used mediation and other forms of ADR with no decision-making or enforcement power (including those in Japan and South Korea), and also noted the existence of special environmental Ombudsmen who had standing and funding to represent complainants in court, citing Kenya and Austria as examples.

The Ombudsman concept has developed since Pring and Pring's initial analysis. For example, Hungary's Environmental Ombudsman (The Commissioner for Future Generations) was operational from May 2008 to January 2012 and acted as one of the country's four Parliamentary Ombudsmen before his functions were assigned to his legal successor, the Office of the Commissioner for Fundamental Rights. The Environmental Ombudsman had a remit to safeguard citizens' constitutional right to a healthy environment, providing for a mechanism through which citizens' complaints of environmental wrongdoing could be investigated. For example, the Environmental Ombudsman had jurisdiction to investigate a broad range of Hungarian environmental issues such as: the degradation of urban green areas; noise pollution by aviation; and licensing of individual industrial installations that might result in pollution and environmental harm. The Environmental Ombudsman also acted as a policy advocate for sustainability issues across all relevant fields of national or local legislation and public policy thus acting as an advocate for future generations and investigating the extent to which sustainability principles operated in practice. The Ombudsman also had a role to develop a strategic scientific research network through undertaking or promoting projects targeting the long-term sustainability of human societies. Other jurisdictions have also employed Environmental Ombudsmen recently. The Environmental Ombudsman Team was reactivated in May 2012 as part of the Office of the Public Ombudsman in the Philippines with a remit to handle cases filed with the office against government officials and individuals accused of violating environmental laws.

Public sector Environmental Ombudsmen's jurisdiction varies according to their enacting legislation and the civil code in which they operate but is generally concerned with some variation on decision-making fault. The mandate of the Philippines Environmental Ombudsman is to:

> take cognizance of any act or omission committed by any public official, employee, office or agency mandated to protect the environment and conserve natural resources that appears to be illegal, unjust, improper or inefficient, or any malfeasance, misfeasance or nonfeasance committed by any public officer or employee, including co-conspirator private individuals, if said act or omission involves any violation of environmental laws or concerns or relates to environmental protection or conservation considerations.

> (Office of the Ombudsman, 2014: 2)

Though broadly defined, this is similar to the concept of 'maladministration' used in the jurisdiction of bodies such as the Local Government Ombudsman and Parliamentary Ombudsman in the UK and the European Ombudsman, although what constitutes maladministration differs among Ombudsmen. For example the Local Government Act 1974 (the Local Government Ombudsman's governing legislation) does not specifically define maladministration, although in the Parliamentary debate on the Parliamentary Commissioner Act 1967 (House of Commons, 1966) Richard Crossman stated the characteristics of maladministration to include 'bias, neglect, inattention, delay, incompetence, ineptitude, perversity, turpitude, arbitrariness and so on'. Maladministration is thus concerned with bad administrative practice and fault in the decision-making process rather than the merits of a decision. In practice maladministration concerns such things as:

- unreasonable delay in taking appropriate action;
- taking incorrect action;
- a failure to provide adequate information, explanation or advice to customers/ service users;
- failure to take appropriate action;
- failure to follow an authority's own rules, the law or relevant codes of practice;
- the breaking of promises;
- failure in the decision-making process.

The Philippines Environmental Ombudsman's jurisdiction codifies some of these activities by specifically referring to action concerning natural resources that is 'illegal, unjust, improper or inefficient' (Office of the Ombudsman, 2014: 2). Thus a failure to take action to protect the environment, taking incorrect action or unreasonable delay in taking action (inefficiency) would all fall within the Environmental Ombudsman's jurisdiction.

Ideally an Environmental Ombudsman's investigation identifies fault and recommends a remedy for the harm caused. Where the nature of the events makes it impossible to put the complainant back in the position that they would have been in had the 'maladministration' not occurred, Ombudsmen are often empowered to recommend financial compensation and other remedies to address the harm caused. In environmental cases, this likely involves some action that mitigates the environmental damage or otherwise provides for positive environmental action. Thus in a pollution event where fault has been a factor in the nature and scale of the pollution a suitable remedy might be compensation for the affected community as well as meeting the costs of clean-up or mitigation work. A potential criticism of Ombudsmen is that in some jurisdictions their decisions on complaints are recommendations only, thus a public authority may not be required to accept the decision or take the action identified by an Ombudsman as necessary to remedy a complaint. As a result, a complaint can be upheld and tangible proposals for remedying the injustice made, yet the complainant still does not receive an effective remedy. However, Owen (1999) argues that the Ombudsman's ability to only recommend but also not enforce is a central strength of the Ombudsman model rather than a weakness as it 'requires that recommendations must be based on a thorough investigation of all facts, scrupulous consideration of all perspectives and vigorous analysis of all issues'. His contention is that complaint outcomes and remedy recommendations based on reasoned analysis rather than coercive power are more powerful, as a coercive process is more likely to create a 'loser' who is less likely to embrace change and carry out remedies. Studies of 'negotiated compliance' (Hawkins, 2002; Hutter, 1997) also demonstrate how the informal mediated practice can sometimes achieve better settlements and resolution than might have been achieved had an issue been pursued to enforcement (or court action).

It is perhaps worth pointing out that Ombudsmen are primarily a civil or administrative law option. Thus, their purpose is not to punish offenders but instead to resolve complaints and hopefully bring about some form of behavioural change. In doing so they embody the ecological and species justice notions of providing justice for the environment as a victim (Benton, 1998; Lynch and Stretesky, 2014). They also demonstrate practical implementation of the 'polluter pays' principle and the need for public authorities to consider environmental concerns in their decision-making and to be accountable for resulting environmental harm when they fail to do so.

Summary

This chapter has discussed both formal and informal conceptions on environmental justice, examining the need to consider how courts and other justice systems need to evolve to deal with environmental offending and disputes. Environmental harm cases represent a challenge for 'traditional' justice systems. As Lord Woolf identified (1992), jurists are not always familiar with the scope and technicality of environmental cases. The implications of such incidents also represent a challenge to punishment-based criminal justice systems.

As the discussion throughout this book has shown, environmental crime is a complex area where much offending is dealt with outside of criminal justice norms. In policy, enforcement, investigation and prosecution, there is a need to consider not just traditional punishment-based approaches centred on the role of the offender, but also mechanisms to repair environmental crimes that often have far-reaching consequences.

Self-study Questions

1. What are the advantages of applying restorative justice to environmental crime rather than using traditional notions of crime and punishment?
2. Should restorative justice be a voluntary process and how should restorative justice settlements be enforced in environmental cases?
3. What potential difficulties are there with applying restorative justice to environmental crimes? Give reasons for your answer.
4. What alternatives to traditional court processes exist in respect of environmental harms?
5. What potential benefits arise from having specialist environmental courts?

GLOSSARY

Anthropocentrism   the belief that human beings are the most significant on the planet, also refers to interpreting the world primarily in terms of human values, interests and experiences.

Biodiversity   the shortened and commonly used form of 'biological diversity', which refers to the community formed by living organisms and the relations between them. The phrase reflects the diversity of species and diversity of genes within species.

CER (Corporate Environmental Responsibility)   umbrella term both for the responsibility that corporations have towards the environment, and for the mechanisms they use to audit, measure and report on that responsibility.

CITES (Convention on International Trade in Endangered Species of Wild Fauna and Flora)   International Convention that regulates the trade in endangered species, largely via a classification and permit system and the implementation of its rules into national laws. Broadly, the rarer and more endangered the plant or animal, the greater the prohibition on trade.

Climate change   describes the inter-related effects of rises in temperature: from changing sea levels and changing ocean currents, through to the impacts of temperature change on local environments that affect the endemic flora and fauna in varying ways (for instance the death of coral due to temperature rises in sea water, or the changed migration patterns of birds).

Common law   a system of law that has developed through judicial decisions and precedents to arrive at a common understanding of law. Common law incorporates the system of case law where judges use the precedent from previously decided cases to decide how the law should be applied in current cases.

CSR (Corporate Social Responsibility)   umbrella term for corporate measures that assess and take responsibility for a company's effects on the environment and impact on social welfare. The term generally applies to company efforts that go beyond what may be required by regulators or environmental protection groups but can be used to refer to monitoring mechanisms.

Deforestation   in its negative sense the phrase has come to mean destruction of forests, although its correct technical usage is the permanent removal of forest cover which is not then replaced either by replanting or natural regeneration of trees.

ECHR (The European Convention on Human Rights),   originally framed as the Convention for the Protection of Human Rights and Fundamental Freedoms, is a human rights mechanism that provides for protection of human rights within the Council of Europe area.

ECtHR (The European Court of Human Rights),   principal court for considering claims of breaches of ECHR rights and for determining the limitations and scope of such rights.

Ecocentrism   a theoretical construction that identifies environmental concerns as being of primary importance.

Ecofeminism   a theoretical construction that connects the domination and exploitation of nature with the domination and exploitation of women.

Ecological justice   green criminological term referring to the idea of fairness to all, including nonhuman animals and ecosystems, with regard to the environment. Ecological justice argues for greater consideration of things that affect the environment within justice systems.

Ecosystem   used to describe the interdependent community of plants, animals and other organisms and their interaction with the natural world and habitats on which they depend.

Environmental law   umbrella term for a range of legislation concerned with the protection of the environment, natural resources and ecosystems.

EU (The European Union);   collection of 28 Member States which have formed a common market within Europe. The EU is distinguished from the wider Council of Europe area.

Exotic species   species not native to the geographical area.

Global North   refers to the North-South divide. Global North generally refers to the 'developed world' of North America, Western Europe and developed parts of East Asia.

Global South   generally refers to the developing countries of the Southern Hemisphere and incorporates Africa, Latin America, 'developing' Asia and the Middle East.

Global warming   describes the rising of the earth's temperature over a relatively short time span.

Habeas corpus   legal concept used to explore the unlawful detention of someone.

ICJ (The International Court of Justice);   the United Nations' primary court, which has jurisdiction over disputes between states, including on environmental matters.

Masculinities   theoretical conception on the role of 'maleness'.

Neoliberalism   pragmatic political theory that argues for maximizing personal liberty by limiting the interference of governments in free markets. Neoliberalism would argue for minimal environmental regulation on the grounds that, theoretically, markets generally regulate themselves and excessive regulation inhibits effective market operations.

NGOs (Non-Governmental Organizations)   usually created by individuals or companies with no participation or representation of government. The term is increasingly used to refer to think-tanks and voluntary sector agencies who carry out functions beyond pure fundraising and charitable concerns to include some aspects of a policy development or law enforcement role. NGOs vary in their methods. Some act primarily as lobbyists, while others conduct programmes and activities primarily to raise public awareness of an issue and actively carry out functions that the statutory sector are perceived as failing to carry out effectively (e.g. species protection or wildlife law enforcement).

NhRP (The Nonhuman Rights Project),   a campaigning group that pursues litigation to achieve legal rights and personhood for nonhuman animals.

Pollution   contamination of the soil, water or the atmosphere by the discharge of harmful substances that adversely affect the environment.

Private law   the law and legal system that governs relationships for the good of society and deals with resolving disputes between individuals (or individuals and companies). Private law can be further divided into contract law, family law and tort law (civil wrong).

Public law   the law and legal system governing the relationship between citizens and the state. Public law is divided into administrative law, constitutional law and criminal law. Public law is usually introduced by the government and applies to all citizens, whereas private law only applies to certain individuals and circumstances.

Species justice   considers the responsibility man owes to other species as part of broader ecological concerns. The principal idea is that man, as the dominant species on the planet, has considerable potential to destroy nonhuman animals, or, through effective laws and criminal justice regimes, to provide for effective animal protection.

UNEP (United Nations Environment Program)   United Nations initiative that aims to be the leading global environmental authority that sets the global environmental agenda and promotes ideas of sustainable development within the United Nations system.

UNODC (United Nations Office on Drugs and Crime)   United Nations body mandated to assist Member States in their struggle against illicit drugs, crime and terrorism.

Utilitarianism   a philosophy that determines moral worth by measuring its outcomes in terms of the greatest good for the greatest number of people.

Wildlife trafficking (illegal wildlife trade)   the phrase used to describe the illegal trade in wildlife that can include illegal trade, smuggling, poaching, capture or collection of endangered species or protected wildlife or derivatives. The terms wildlife trafficking or illegal wildlife trade are used interchangeably within green criminology and criminal justice discourse to refer to trading in animals whether alive or dead, primarily in contravention of CITES regulations and/or any national legislation which implements CITES.

FURTHER READING

As this book identifies, environmental crime and green criminology are umbrella terms that cover a range of different activities and the actions of different actors and agencies which have been the subject of academic and mainstream media writing. In addition, interest in green crimes as an area of criminological enquiry and the subject of NGO campaigning means that articles on environmental threats and environmental crime appear with relative frequency in the pages of mainstream criminology journals and in the popular press, many of whom employ an environment correspondent. Recent years have also seen a growth in online law, criminology and environmental law journals that cover issues relating to environmental crime and harms such as climate change, pollution and the illegal trade in wildlife. These publications provide a forum for academics, activists and students to discuss environmental and green criminological crime topics. In addition to the sources listed below, special green editions have been published of journals such as SAGE's *Theoretical Criminology*, Springer's *Crime, Law and Social Change*, *Criminal Justice Matters*, Waterside Press's *Crimsoc: The Journal of Social Criminology* and the *International Journal for Crime, Justice and Social Democracy* (Online). A selection of the key established journals and news services relevant to environmental crime and green criminology follows.

Animal Law Review

http://law.lclark.edu/law_reviews/animal_law_review/

A student-run law review based at Lewis & Clark Law School in Portland, Oregon, and published bi-annually. Each volume includes two issues: a fall/winter issue and a spring/summer issue.

Animal Legal and Historic Centre

http://animallaw.info/

Substantial online repository of animal law cases and legal articles housed at Michigan State University College of Law. The site contains both US and UK case law and over 1,400 US statutes.

British and Irish Legal Information Institute

http://www.bailii.org/

Free online searchable database of British and Irish case law and legislation, European Union case law, Law Commission reports, and other law-related British and Irish material.

Critical Criminology

http://link.springer.com/journal/10612

Peer-reviewed academic journal exploring social, political and economic justice from alternative perspectives. The journal has published green criminological articles and incorporates green criminology within its 'alternative' perspective.

Duke Environmental Law and Policy Forum

http://delpf.law.duke.edu/

Student-run environmental law and policy journal available online and covering a wide range of environmental topics.

Environmental News Network (ENN)

www.enn.com

An online resource for environmental news stories, contains a dedicated wildlife section, a peer news-sharing network and an email newsletter that delivers environmental news stories from around the globe free to its subscribers.

Environmental Protection Agency (US)

www.epa.gov

US governmental agency with a remit to ensure that the US federal laws protecting human health and the environment are enforced fairly and effectively. Details of US legislation and enforcement activities are published on the site.

Global Animal Law Project

https://www.globalanimallaw.org/

Online project that aims to create a framework for global discussion on animals in the law, the website also contains a database of animal laws (welfare and anti-cruelty) searchable by country and a matrix of proposals for new animal laws.

Global Journal of Animal Law

http://www.gjal.abo.fi/

The journal is a semi-annual online journal offered as a public service by Åbo Akademi University Department of Law, Finland. The journal brings together academics and other experts to define legal approaches to animals in different legal jurisdictions and to analyse the legal status of animals and the effectiveness of animal law. Articles from the journal are available for free download.

Green Criminology

http://www.greencriminology.org

Website of the International Green Criminology Working Group (IGCWG) providing information for academics, students and practitioners on green criminological subjects. The website hosts a blog, academic resources and member forums as well as articles published by Members through *The Monthly*, the IGCWG's online journal.

Harvard Environmental Law Review

https://journals.law.harvard.edu/elr/

Environmental law journal taking a broad view of environmental affairs, which includes land use and property rights; air, water, and noise regulation; toxic substances control; radiation control; energy use; workplace pollution; science and technology control; and resource use and regulation. The journal is edited by Harvard law students.

International Journal for Crime, Justice and Social Democracy

https://www.crimejusticejournal.com/

An open access, blind peer-reviewed journal that seeks to publish critical research about challenges confronting criminal justice systems around the world. The journal's focus is on: penal policy and punishment in the global era; policing, security and democratic freedoms; sex, gender and justice; eco-justice, corporate crime and corruption; crime, courts and justice institutions; counter colonial criminologies and indigenous perspectives. Volume 3, No. 2 (2014) is a special green issue.

Journal of Animal Welfare Law

http://alaw.org.uk/publications/

The journal of the UK's Association of Lawyers for Animal Welfare (ALAW); two main editions are currently published each year. Back issues of the journal from May 2005 (Issue 1) can be downloaded free of charge from this site.

Journal for Critical Animal Studies

http://www.criticalanimalstudies.org

The journal of the Institute for Critical Animal Studies is a peer-reviewed interdisciplinary academic (yet readable) journal published online by the Institute. The journal promotes academic study of critical animal issues in contemporary society.

Journal of Environmental Law

http://jel.oxfordjournals.org/

A peer-reviewed academic journal that looks at legal responses to environmental problems in national and international jurisdictions. The journal appears three times annually, publishing articles across a wide environmental law spectrum.

Pace Environmental Law Review

http://digitalcommons.pace.edu/pelr/

Scholarly journal on environmental law edited by J.D students at Pace Law School and linked to the activities of Pace's Centre for Environmental Legal Studies and the Pace Environmental Law Society.

Society and Animals Forum

www.societyandanimalsforum.org

The forum provides a number of resources relating to the field of human–animal studies, including a calendar of events for the Animals and Society Institute, links to *Society and Animals*, the Institute's journal, its book series and the *Journal of Applied Animal Welfare Science*.

Stanford Journal of Animal Law and Policy

http://sjalp.stanford.edu/

Online animal law journal covering a range of animal law and policy topics, articles and scholarship from around the world. The website includes access to past volumes.

Transnational Environmental Law

http://journals.cambridge.org/action/displayJournal?jid=TEL

Peer-reviewed academic journal dedicated to the study of environmental law and governance beyond the state (i.e. in a transnational context). The journal considers legal and regulatory developments and is also concerned with the role of non-state actors.

Vermont Journal of Environmental Law

http://vjel.vermontlaw.edu/

Online environmental law journal covering a wide range of environmental law and policy topics. The website includes access to past volumes.

William and Mary Environmental Law Review

http://scholarship.law.wm.edu/wmelpr/

Online environmental law journal covering a wide range of environmental law and policy topics. The website includes access to past volumes.

USEFUL ORGANIZATIONS

A number of organizations are actively involved in advocacy, campaigning or litigation aimed at reducing or eliminating the environmental crime topics covered by this book. While the following is not a comprehensive list it identifies those organizations firmly established in the field of environmental crime, wildlife crime, anti-corruption and corporate-crime monitoring and environmental law and justice. The precise nature of the organization's activity is defined by whether its focus is on particular types of environmental crime or has a subject-specific focus. The list does not endorse any particular organization but is intended to provide readers with some useful information sources and contacts from which they can explore specific topics further.

Animal Legal Defense Fund

170 East Cotati Avenue
Cotati
CA 94931
United States
Website: www.aldf.org

The Animal Legal Defense Fund (ALDF) campaigns within the US legal system to end animal suffering. A number of resources are available on its website including details of US animal abuse case law, bulletin boards and current news.

Association of Lawyers for Animal Welfare (ALAW)

PO Box 67933
London
NW1W 8RB
United Kingdom
Website: www.alaw.org.uk

ALAW is a UK-based organization of lawyers and legal academics with interest and experience in animal protection law. ALAW members provide advisory services and research on effective implementation of animal protection law and developing a better legal framework for the protection of animals.

ALAW also campaigns for better animal protection law and publishes the *Journal of Animal Welfare Law*, a legal journal dedicated to animal welfare topics while also carrying wildlife crime articles.

Centre for Public Integrity

910 17th Street, NW, Suite 700
Washington
DC 20006
United States
Website: www.iwatchnews.org

US-based non-profit organization working to investigate, analyse and disseminate information on national issues of importance to policymakers, academics and news organizations. The Centre investigates environmental issues and was co-author/publisher of Alan Green's investigation into the black market for rare and exotic species.

Coalition Against Wildlife Trafficking (CAWT)

The Chair of CAWT
c/o The Director
International Wildlife Trade Section
Australian Government Department of Sustainability, Environment, Water, Population and Communities
GPO Box 787
Canberra ACT2601
Australia
Website: www.cawtglobal.org/

International coalition of government partners and NGOs working together to eliminate wildlife trafficking and ensure the effective implementation and enforcement of CITES. UK-based organization, NGO partners include IFAW, IUCN, Save the Tiger Fund, the Smithsonian Institution, WCS, the Wildlife Alliance and WWF (among others).

Convention on International Trade in Endangered Species of Wild Fauna and Flora (CITES)

CITES Secretariat
International Environment House
11 Chemin des Anémones
CH-1219
Châtelaine
Geneva
Switzerland
Website: http://www.cites.org

The CITES Secretariat plays a coordinating, advisory and servicing role in the working of the Convention by assisting with communication and monitoring the implementation of the Convention to ensure that its provisions are respected, and by arranging meetings of the Conference of the Parties and of the permanent Committees at regular intervals and servicing those meetings. The CITES Secretariat also hosts the CITES Trade database and makes public a range of documents relating to the working of CITES.

Corporate Watch

c/o Freedom Press
Angel Alley, 84b Whitechapel High Street
London, E1 7QX
United Kingdom
Website: http://www.corporatewatch.org/

UK-based independent research group investigating the social and environmental impacts of corporations and corporate power.

Defenders of Wildlife

1130 17th Street NW
Washington
DC 20036
United States
Website: www.defenders.org

US-based not-for-profit organization founded in 1947 with a remit to protect and restore the USA's native wildlife and safeguard wildlife habitats. Defenders' main focus is restoring wolves to their surviving former habitats in the lower 48 states of the USA and to challenge efforts to reduce the protection afforded to wolves under US law. It also works to prevent the extinction of other North American wildlife and to prevent cruelty to wildlife. Defenders of Wildlife have offices in nine US states and Mexico, in addition to its Washington DC headquarters.

Department for Environment, Food and Rural Affairs (DEFRA)

Nobel House
17 Smith Square
London
SW1P 3JR
United Kingdom
Website: www.defra.gov.uk

The UK government department with responsibility for environmental issues, including: wildlife crime, sustainable development and rural communities. DEFRA's website contains a wildlife crime section covering aspects of UK wildlife crime and links to the website for its Partnership for Action on Wildlife Crime (PAW), the body that coordinates UK wildlife crime policy via a partnership between government and NGOs.

Earthjustice

50 California Street, Suite 500
San Francisco
CA 94111
United States
Website: http://earthjustice.org/

Earthjustice is a not-for-profit public interest law firm originally founded in 1981 as the Sierra Club Legal Defense fund. Earthjustice lawyers litigate on behalf of US citizens in environmental cases, in particular litigating in cases involving the Endangered Species Act, Clean Air Act, Clean Water Act and Natural Environment Policy Act. In addition, Earthjustice's campaigning work highlights current environmental threats and provides details of campaign work required to improve environmental protection. In addition to its San Francisco headquarters, Earthjustice has regional offices across the USA in Anchorage, Bozeman, California, Denver, Florida, Honolulu, New York, Seattle and Washington.

The Environmental Investigations Agency (EIA)

62–63 Upper Street
London
N1 0NY
United Kingdom
Website: www.eia-global.org

EIA is an international campaigning organization that investigates and exposes environmental crime primarily through the use of undercover investigations using the evidence gained in investigations in advocacy and lobbying campaigns. EIA has published investigative reports and policy documents on various wildlife and environmental crime issues and has also produced documentaries on various aspects of wildlife crime. In addition to its London office EIA has a US office in Washington.

Environmental Justice Foundation (EJF)

1 Amwell Street
London
EC1R 1UL
United Kingdom
Website: www.ejfoundation.org

The EJF is a registered charity that works on the protection of the natural environment and combating environmental abuses. EJF provides film and advocacy training to individuals and grassroots organizations (primarily in the Global South) and campaigns internationally to raise awareness of environmental issues facing its grassroots partners and vulnerable communities. EJF publishes a range of environmental research reports and campaign materials and in addition to its team of campaigners and film-makers based at its headquarters in London also works with partners in Brazil, Vietnam, Mali, Sierra Leone, Uzbekistan, Mauritius and Indonesia.

Environmental Protection Agency US (EPA)

Ariel Rios Building
1200 Pennsylvania Avenue, N.W.
Washington
DC 20460
United States
Website: www.epa.gov

The EPA is a US governmental agency with a remit to protect human health and the environment. The EPA is responsible for enforcing federal environmental laws, developing and enforcing these laws by writing regulations that states and tribes enforce through their own regulations. The EPA also publishes information on environmental crimes and its regulatory activities. The EPA has 10 regional offices across the USA, each of which is responsible for several states and territories.

The European Commission Environment Directorate

European Commission
Environment DG
B – 1049 Brussels
Belgium
Website: http://ec.europa.eu/dgs/environment/index_en.htm

The Environment Directorate of the EU publishes information on European wildlife trade regulations, threats to wildlife and wildlife trade issues in the EU.

Friends of the Earth

1100 15th Street NW
11th Floor
Washington, DC 20005
United States
Website http://www.foe.org

Friends of the Earth is a global campaigning organization employing advocacy, policy-analysis and litigation to achieve environmental protection and change or develop effective environmental policy. Friends of the Earth International has member groups in 76 countries covering Africa, Asia Pacific, Europe, Latin America and the Caribbean, North America and Russia.

Greenpeace (UK)

Canonbury Villas
London
N1 2PN
United Kingdom
Website: http://greenpeace.org.uk

Greenpeace is an independent global campaigning organization working to defend the natural world and promote peace by investigating, exposing and confronting environmental abuse, and championing environmentally responsible solutions. Greenpeace works on a range of issues including: climate change; marine protection; nuclear disarmament; anti-fracking; and an end to the use of toxic chemicals. Greenpeace has a range of country offices across the globe including: Australia, Belgium, Finland, France, Germany, India, Italy, Japan, The Netherlands, New Zealand, Norway, Portugal, Russia and South Africa.

Humane Society of the United States (HSUS)

The Humane Society of the United States
2100 L St., NW
Washington
DC 20037
United States
Website: www.humanesociety.org

US animal protection organization with approximately 10 million members and a network of regional offices across the USA.

Institute for Critical Animal Studies (ICAS)

PO Box 4293
Ithaca
NY 14852
United States
Website: www.criticalanimalstudies.org

The Institute for Critical Animal Studies (ICAS) is an interdisciplinary scholarly non-profit animal protection centre that provides education policy, research and analysis. The ICAS was originally formed in 2001 as the Centre on Animal Liberation affairs and changed its name to the ICAS in 2007. In addition to publishing the *Journal for Critical Animal Studies*, the ICAS organizes annual critical animal studies conferences in the USA and Europe.

International Fund for Animal Welfare (IFAW)

290 Summer Street
Yarmouth Port
MA 02675

United States

Website: http://www.ifaw.org/international

Animal Advocacy group based in the UK, originally formed to protest against the culling of seals in Canada but now working globally on animal welfare and animal cruelty issues. IFAW works to prevent the elephant ivory trade and the extinction of whales. In addition to its US international office there is a UK office based in London.

International Union for the Conservation of Nature (IUCN)

IUCN Conservation Centre

Rue Mauverney 28

1196, Gland

Switzerland

Website: www.iucn.org

The IUCN is a global environmental network and democratic membership union with more than 1,000 government and NGO member organizations, and some 10,000 volunteer scientists in more than 160 countries. Its priority work areas are biodiversity, climate change, sustainable energy, the development of a green economy and helping governments to understand the link between nature conservation and human well-being.

Nonhuman Rights Project (NhRP)

The Nonhuman Rights Project

5195 NW 112th Terrace

Coral Springs

FL 33076

United States

Website: http://www.nonhumanrightsproject.org/

NhRP employs education and litigation as tools to pursue legal rights for non-human animals. The NhRP describes its mission as changing the common law status of at least some nonhuman animals from mere 'things' that lack the capacity to possess any legal right, to 'persons' who possess fundamental rights including bodily integrity and bodily liberty. The NhRP files cases in the courts in order to pursue legal rights for animals via the common law. Founder and President Steven Wise also publishes extensively on legal rights for nonhumans.

Partnership for Action against Wildlife Crime (PAW)

PAW Secretariat

Zone 1/14

Temple Quay House

2 The Square

Temple Quay

Bristol
BS1 6EB
United Kingdom
Website: www.defra.gov.uk/paw

PAW is a UK-based multi-agency body comprising representatives of statutory agencies and NGOs involved in UK wildlife law enforcement. Its secretariat is hosted by DEFRA (see above) and maintains the PAW website, the distribution of PAW's email bulletins and publicizes PAW's activities.

People for the Ethical Treatment of Animals (PETA)

501 Front St.
Norfolk
VA 23510
United States
Website: www.peta.org

PETA is one of the largest animal rights organizations in the world with a global support base in excess of 3 million (members and supporters). PETA predominantly campaigns against animal cruelty on factory farms, in the clothing trade, in laboratories, and in the entertainment industry. Its work includes high-profile campaigning, advocacy, public education, cruelty investigations, animal rescue and legislative work aimed at changing animal protection laws.

The Royal Society for the Prevention of Cruelty to Animals (RSPCA)

Wilberforce Way
Southwater
Horsham
West Sussex
RH13 9RS
United Kingdom
Website: www.rspca.org.uk

A UK-based charity that works to prevent cruelty to, the causing of unnecessary suffering to and the neglect of animals in England and Wales. A uniformed Inspectorate investigates cruelty offences, while a plain-clothes and undercover unit called the Special Operations Unit (SOU) deals with more serious offences and 'low-level' organized animal crime such as dog-fighting and badger-baiting. The RSPCA has a network of branch offices across England and Wales.

The Royal Society for the Protection of Birds (RSPB)

The Lodge
Sandy
Bedfordshire
SG19 2DL

United Kingdom
Website: www.rspb.org.uk

The RSPB is a conservation charity that campaigns for the protection of wild birds and their environment. An in-house investigations section carries out investigations into wild bird crime and advises the police and others, as well as publishes annual reports on bird crime in the UK and a quarterly investigations newsletter on bird crime problems, sometimes with an EU slant. The charity is UK based but has international offices and is part of Birdlife International, a global network of bird conservation organizations.

The Scottish Society for the Prevention of Cruelty to Animals (SSPCA)

Kingseat Road
Halbeath
Dunfermline
Fife
KY11 8RY
Website – www.scottishspca.org

The SSPCA is the Scottish counterpart to the RSPCA. The SSPCA works to prevent cruelty to, the causing of unnecessary suffering to and the neglect of animals in Scotland.

Sierra Club

National Headquarters
85 Second Street, 2nd Floor
San Francisco
CA 94105
United States
Website: www.sierraclub.org

The Sierra Club is a US-based grassroots environmental organization with a remit to protect communities and wild places and to restore the quality of the natural environment. In addition to its national headquarters in San Francisco the Sierra Club has a legislative office in Washington DC and regional offices across the USA. In addition to campaigning and publishing research and policy documents on wildlife and environmental issues the Sierra Club has also employed strategic legal action and regulatory advocacy to protect US wildlife and the environment.

TRACE Wildlife Forensics Network

Royal Zoological Society of Scotland
Edinburgh
EH12 6TS
United Kingdom
Website: http://www.tracenetwork.org/

TRACE is an international NGO that aims to promote the use of forensic science in biodiversity conservation and the investigation of wildlife crime. The TRACE network brings together forensic scientists and enforcement agencies in order to exchange information on the latest challenges facing wildlife law enforcement and modern techniques for tackling them.

TRAFFIC

TRAFFIC International
219a Huntingdon Rd
Cambridge
CB3 ODL
United Kingdom
Website: www.traffic.org

TRAFFIC is the wildlife trade-monitoring arm of the World Wide Fund for Nature (WWF) and the International Union for the Conservation of Nature (IUCN). It mainly investigates compliance with CITES and related trade in endangered species, TRAFFIC has regional offices in Africa, Asia, the Americas, Europe and Oceania supported by a Central Secretariat based in the UK.

Transparency International

Alt-Moabit 96
10559 Berlin
Germany
Website: www.transparency.org

Transparency International is a campaigning NGO that describes its mission as to 'stop corruption and promote transparency', accountability and integrity at all levels and across all sectors of society. The NGO publishes a range of reports and makes anti-corruption resources freely available through its website.

The Whale and Dolphin Conservation Society (WDCS)

Brookfield House
38 St Paul Street
Chippenham
Wiltshire
SN15 1LJ
United Kingdom
Website: www.wdcs.org

WDCS is a global charity dedicated to the conservation and welfare of all cetaceans (whales, dolphins and porpoises). It has regional offices in the UK, Latin America, Germany, North America and Australasia. In addition to its campaigning work WDCS conducts investigations work to expose abuses of wildlife regulations and advises governments and regulatory bodies on the working of conventions and other mechanisms needed and intended to protect cetaceans.

World Animal Protection (WAP)

5th Floor
222 Grays Inn Road
London
WC1X 8HB
United Kingdom
Website: http://www.worldanimalprotection.org/

World Animal Protection (formerly the World Society for the Prevention of Cruelty to Animals) is an animal welfare and anti-cruelty charity with a global remit. WAP campaigns for the protection of companion animals, against commercial exploitation of wildlife and against intensive farming, long-distance transport and slaughter of animals for food. It has regional offices in the USA (Boston), Australia (Sydney), Asia (Thailand), Brazil (Rio de Janeiro), Canada (Toronto), Sweden, South America (Colombia), New Zealand (Auckland), the Netherlands, India (New Delhi), Germany (Berlin) and China (Beijing).

The World Wide Fund for Nature (WWF)

WWF International, Gland (Secretariat)
Av. du Mont-Blanc 1196 Gland
Switzerland
+41 22 364 91 11
+41 22 364 88 36
Website: www.wwf.org

The World Wide Fund for Nature is an independent conservation network working in more than 90 countries. A registered charity in the UK with campaigning interests in wildlife trade, threats to endangered species and their habitats. Its main regional offices are in the USA (Washington), Australia (Sydney), China (Beijing), Brazil (Brasilia), Canada (Toronto), France (Paris), Germany (Frankfurt), India (New Delhi), Japan (Tokyo), Sweden (Solna), South America (Colombia), New Zealand (Wellington), the Netherlands (Zeist), Pakistan (Lahore), Spain (Madrid), Switzerland (Zurich) and the United Kingdom (Godalming).

REFERENCES

Afreen, S. (2008) 'Biopiracy and Protection of Traditional Knowledge: Intellectual Property Rights and Beyond', Working Paper Series No. 629. Calcutta: Indian Institute of Management. Online at: https://facultylive.iimcal.ac.in/sites/facultylive.iimcal.ac.in/files/WPS-629_1.pdf (Accessed 19 March 2015).

Agnew, R. (2011) 'Dire forecast: a theoretical model of the impact of climate change on crime', *Theoretical Criminology*, 16 (1): 21–42.

Akande, D. (2003) 'The jurisdiction of the international criminal court over nationals of non-parties: legal basis and limits', *Journal of International Criminal Justice*, 1 (3): 618–50.

Akella, A.S. and Allan, C. (2012) *Dismantling Wildlife Crime*. Washington: World Wildlife Fund.

Akella, A.S. and Cannon, J.B. (2004) *Strengthening the Weakest Links: Strategies for Improving the Enforcement of Environmental Laws Globally*. Washington DC: Center for Conservation and Government, Conservation International.

Alcock, R. and Conde, C. (2005) 'Socially and environmentally responsible business practices: an Australian perspective corporate', *Governance Law Review*, 1 (2): 329–38.

Amao, O. (2011) 'Human rights, ethics and international business: the case of Nigeria', in A. Voiculescu and H. Yanacopulos (eds), *The Business of Human Rights: An Evolving Agenda for Corporate Responsibility*. London: Zed Books/The Open University, pp. 188–213.

Amnesty International (2009) *Nigeria: Petroleum, Pollution, and Poverty in the Niger Delta*. London: Amnesty International Publications.

Amnesty International and CEHRD (2011) *The True 'Tragedy': Delays and Failures in Tackling Oil Spills in the Niger Delta*. London: Amnesty International Publications.

Aoki, K. (1998) 'Neocolonialism, anticommons property, and biopiracy in the (not-so-brave) new world order of international intellectual property protection', *Indiana Journal of Global Legal Studies*, 6 (1): Article 2.

Arluke, A. and Luke, C. (1997) 'Physical cruelty toward animals in Massachusetts 1975–1976', *Society & Animals*, 5 (3): 195–204.

Ascione, F.R. (1993) 'Children who are cruel to animals: a review of research and implications for developmental psychopathology', *Anthrozoos*, 4: 226–7.

REFERENCES

Ascione, F.R (ed.) (2008) *The International Handbook of Animal Abuse and Cruelty: Theory, Research and Application*. Indiana: Purdue University Press.

Ascione, F.R., Weber, C.V. and Wood, D.S. (1997) 'The abuse of animals and domestic violence: a national survey of shelters for women who are battered', *Society and Animals*, 5 (3): 205–18.

Ayres, I. and Braithwaite, J. (1992) *Responsive Regulation: Transcending the Deregulation Debate*. New York: Oxford University Press.

Barnet, J. (2006) 'Climate change: insecurity and injustice', in N.W. Adger, J. Paavola, S. Huq and M.J. Mace (eds), *Fairness in Adaptation in Climate Change*. Cambridge, MA: MIT Press.

Barnett, H. (2011) *Constitutional and Administrative Law* (9th edn). Abingdon: Routledge.

Basel Action Network (BAN) (2011a) 'Environmentally sound management and the Basel ban amendment'. Online at: http://ban.org/library/esmban.html (Accessed 14 August 2015).

Basel Action Network (BAN) (2011b) 'Recycling news: first federal criminal charges brought against recycler for exporting toxic e-waste in Denver co.' Online at: http://www.ban.org/news (Accessed 14 August 2015).

Baumol, J. (1990) 'Entrepreneurship: productive, unproductive and destructive', *Journal of Political Economy*, 98 (5): 893–921.

Baumüller, H., Donnelly, E., Vines, A. and Weimer, M. (2011) *The Effects of Oil Companies' Activities on the Environment, Health and Development in Sub-Saharan Africa*. London: Chatham House.

BBC News Online (2010) 'Thames Water fine for toxic spill in River Wandle cut'. Online at: http://news.bbc.co.uk/1/hi/england/london/8524109.stm (Accessed 15 March 2015).

Beck, U. (1992) *Risk Society: Towards a New Modernity*. London: Sage.

Becker, G. (1968) 'Crime and punishment: an economic approach', *Journal of Political Economy*, 76: 169–217.

Beirne, P. (1999) 'For a nonspeciesist criminology: animal abuse as an object of study', *Criminology*, 37 (1): 1–32.

Beirne, P. (2004) 'From animal abuse to interhuman violence? A critical review of the progression thesis', *Society and Animals*, 12 (1): 39–65.

Beirne, P. (2007) 'Animal rights, animal abuse and green criminology', in P. Beirne and N. South (eds), *Issues in Green Criminology: Confronting Harms Against Environments, Humanity and Other Animals*. Cullompton: Willan, pp. 55–83.

Beirne, P. (2009) *Confronting Animal Abuse: Law, Criminology, and Human-Animal Relationships*. Lanham: Rowman & Littlefield.

Beirne, P. and South, N. (2007) (eds) *Issues in Green Criminology: Confronting Harms Against Environments, Humanity and Other Animals*. Cullompton: Willan.

Bentham, J. ([1789]1970) *Introduction to the Principles and Morals of Legislation* (eds J.H Burns and H.L.A. Hart). London: The Athlone Press.

REFERENCES

Benton, T. (1998) 'Rights and justice on a shared planet: more rights or new relations?', *Theoretical Criminology*, 2 (2): 149–75.

Berman, H. (2012) 'The Alien Tort Claims Act and the Law of Nations', Emory University School of Law Research Paper No. 05-5 (Forthcoming). Online at: http://papers.ssrn.com/sol3/papers.cfm?abstract_id=666146 (Accessed 23 September 2012).

Bipartisan Policy Center (2011) 'Geoengineering: a national strategic plan for research on the potential effectiveness, feasibility, and consequences of climate remediation technologies', Washington: Bipartisan Policy Center. Online at: http://bipartisanpolicy.org/wp-content/uploads/sites/default/files/BPC%20Climate%20Remediation%20Final%20Report.pdf (Accessed 2 March 2015).

Bisschop, L. (2012) 'Is it all going to waste? Illegal transports of e-waste in a European trade hub', *Crime, Law and Social Change*, 58 (3): 221–39.

Blaikie, P., Cannon, T., Davis, I. and Wisner, B. (1994) *At Risk: Natural Hazards, People's Vulnerability, and Disaster*. London: Routledge.

Bodansky, D. (1995) 'Customary (and not so customary) international environmental law', *Indiana Journal of Global Legal Studies*, 3 (1): 105–19.

Bonfiglio, O. (2012) 'Presidential candidates and the sociology of "climate change denial"', *Huffington Post*. Online at: http://www.huffington post.com/olgabonfiglio/climate-change-denial_1_b_1404412.html (Accessed 10 December 2014).

Braithwaite, J. (2002) *Restorative Justice and Responsive Regulation*. Oxford: Oxford University Press.

Braithwaite, J. (2004) *Restorative Justice: Theories and Worries*, Visiting Experts' Papers, 123rd International Senior Seminar, Resource Material Series No. 63, pp. 47–56. Tokyo: United Nations Asia and Far East Institute For the Prevention of Crime and the Treatment of Offenders.

Braithwaite, J. and Pettit, P. (1990) *Not Just Deserts. A Republican Theory of Criminal Justice*. Oxford: Clarendon Press.

Brantingham, P.J. and Brantingham, P.L. (1991) *Environmental Criminology*. Prospect Heights, IL: Waveland Press.

Brennan, A. and Lo, Y. (2008) 'The early development of environmental ethics', *Stanford Encyclopedia of Philosophy*. Online at: http://plato.stanford.edu/ (Accessed 6 October 2015).

Bright, J. (1993) 'Crime prevention: the British experience', in: K. Stenson and D. Cowell (eds), *The Politics of Crime Control*. London: Sage, pp. 62–86.

Brisman, A. (2014) 'Of theory and meaning in green criminology', *International Journal for Crime, Justice and Social Democracy*, 3 (2): 21–34.

Brisman, A. and South, N. (2013) 'Resource wealth, power, crime and conflict', in R. Walters, D. Westerhuis and T. Wyatt (eds), *Debates in Green Criminology: Power, Justice and Environmental Harm*. Basingstoke: Palgrave Macmillan, pp. 57–71.

Brockington, D., Duffy. R. and Igoe, J. (2008) *Nature Unbound: Capitalism and the Future of Protected Areas*. Abingdon: Routledge.

REFERENCES

Brooker, S. (2008) *Lessons from Ombudsmania*. London: National Consumer Council.

Brown, O. and McLeman, R. (2009) 'A recurring anarchy? The emergence of climate change and a threat to international peace and security', *Conflict, Security and Development*, 9: 298–305.

Brown Weiss, E. (1993) 'International environmental law: contemporary issues and the emergence of a new world order', *Georgetown Law Journal*, 81 (3): 675–710.

Brunsdon, C., Corcoran, J., Hoggs, G., Ware, A. (2009) 'The influence of weather on local geographical patterns of police calls for service', *Environment and Planning. B: Planning and Design*, 36 (5): 906–26.

Brunsdon-Tully, M. (2009) 'There is an A in ADR but does anyone know what it means any more?', *Civil Justice Quarterly*, 28 (2) :218–36.

Bundy, R., Devaney, E., Dowd, E. and Solow, S. (1999) 'Deterrence: a strong environmental crime program leads to industry compliance and a cleaner environment', *US Attorneys' Bulletin: Enforcement Issues*, 47 (5), Washington: Department of Justice.

Cabinet Office (2011) 'Red tape challenge'. London: Cabinet Office. Online at: http://www.redtapechallenge.cabinetoffice.gov.uk/home/index (Accessed 29 June 2014).

Campbell, A. (1993) *Men, Women and Aggression*. New York: Basic Books.

Carmin, J. and Bast, E. (2009) 'Cross-movement activism: a cognitive perspective on the global justice activities of US environmental NGOs', *Environmental Politics*, 18 (3): 351–70.

Carter, N. (2007) *The Politics of the Environment: Ideas, Activism, Policy*. Cambridge: Cambridge University Press.

Cavender, G., Gray, K. and Miller, K.W. (2010) 'Enron's perp walk: status degradation ceremonies as narrative', *Crime Media Culture*, 6: 251.

Center for Health, Environment and Justice (2014) *Love Canal*. Available at: http://chej.org/about/our-story/love-canal/ (Accessed 12 August 2015).

Chavis, B. (1991) 'The historical significance and challenges of the first national people of colour environmental leadership summit', in Proceedings of the First National People of Colour Environmental Leadership Summit. Washington DC: United Church of Christ Commission for Racial Justice.

Cianci, J. (2015) *Radical Environmentalism: Nature, Identity and Non-human Agency*. London: Palgrave Macmillan.

CITES (2010) *Activity Report of the CITES Secretariat: 2008–2009*. Geneva: CITES/ United Nations Environment Programme.

CITES (2013) 'Sixteenth Meeting of the Conference of the Parties', Bangkok (Thailand), 3–14 March, Geneva: CITES/United Nations Environment Programme.

Clapp, J. (2001) *Toxic Exports: the Transfer of Hazardous Wastes from Rich to Poor Countries*. Ithaca, NY and London: Cornell University Press.

Clawson, E. (2009) 'Canaries in the mine: the priority of human welfare in animal abuse prosecution', in A. Linzey (ed.), *The Link Between Animal Abuse and Human Violence*. Eastbourne: Sussex Academic Press, pp. 190–200.

REFERENCES

Committee on Climate Change (2014) *The Climate Change Act and UK Regulations*. London: Committee on Climate Change. Online at: http://www.theccc.org. uk/tackling-climate-change/the-legal-landscape/global-action-on-climate-change/ (Accessed 10 March 2015).

Connelly, J. and Smith, G. (1999) *Politics and the Environment: From Theory to Practice*. London: Routledge.

Convention on Biological Diversity (2014) *Strategic Plan for Biodiversity 2011–2020, Including Aichi Biodiversity Targets*. Montreal: Secretariat of the Convention on Biological Diversity/United Nations.

Cook, D., Roberts, M. and Lowther, J. (2002) *The International Wildlife Trade and Organised Crime: A Review of the Evidence and the Role of the UK*. Wolverhampton: Regional Research Institute, University of Wolverhampton.

Crowhurst, G. (2006) 'The commercial impact of environmental law', *Business Law Review*, 27 (4): 92–7.

CPS (The Crown Prosecution Service) (2014) *Legal Guidance: Restorative Justice*. London: CPS. Available at: http://www.cps.gov.uk/legal/p_to_r/restorative_justice/ (Accessed 10 December 2014).

Crowther, D. and Aras, G. (2008) *Corporate Social Responsibility*. Frederiksberg: Ventus Publishing.

Cudworth, E. (2005) *Developing Ecofeminist Theory: the Complexity of Difference*. Basingstoke: Palgrave Macmillan.

de Bohan, V., Doggart, N., Rryle, J., Trent, S. and Williams, J. (eds) (1996). *Corporate Power, Corruption and the Destruction of the World's Forests: the Case for a Global Forest Agreement*. London/Washington: Environmental Investigations Agency.

Defenders of Wildlife (2011) *Assault on Wildlife: the Endangered Species Act Under Attack*. Washington, DC: Defenders of Wildlife.

DEFRA (2010) *Civil Sanctions for Environmental Offences*. London: Department for Environment, Food and Rural Affairs. Available at: http://www.fwr.org/ WQreg/Appendices/Civil_Sanctions_defra-wag-guidance.pdf (Accessed 16 August 2015).

Denton, R. (2002) 'Climate change vulnerability: impacts and adaptation: why does gender matter?' *Gender and Development*, 10 (2): 10–20.

Deshpande, N and Ernst, H. (2012) 'Countering Eco-Terrorism in the United States: The Case of "Operation Backfire",' Final Report to Human Factors/ Behavioral Sciences Division, Science and Technology Directorate, U.S. Department of Homeland Security. College Park, MD: START. Available at: http:// www.start.umd.edu/start/publications/Countermeasures_OperationBackfire. pdf (Accessed 12 August 2015).

Dicey, A.V. ([1915] 1982) *Introduction to the Study of the Constitution*. Indianapolis, IN: Liberty Fund Free Press.

Dine, J. (2007) 'The capture of corruption: complexity and corporate culture', *Global Business and Development Law Journal*, 20: 1–26.

REFERENCES

Donaldson, S. and Kymlicka, W. (2011) *Zoopolis: A Political Theory of Animal Rights*. Oxford: Oxford University Press.

Doward, J. (2012) 'Women's alliance lobbies Clarke over legal aid reforms', *The Guardian*. Online at: http://www.guardian.co.uk/law/2012/apr/22/womens-groups-legal-aid-reforms?INTCMP=SRCH (Accessed 10 January 2015).

Doyle, T. (2000) *Green Power: the Environment Movement in Australia*. Sydney: University of New South Wales Press.

Doyon, J. (2014) 'Corporate environmental crime in the electronic waste industry: the case of Executive Recycling, Inc', in A. Nurse (ed.) *Critical Perspectives on Green Criminology*. Internet Journal of Criminology. Nottingham: New University Press/flashmousepublishing Ltd.

Dreyfuss, H.L and Rabinow, P. (eds) (1982) *Michel Foucault: Beyond Structuralism and Hermeneutics*. Chicago: University of Chicago Press.

Eagan, S.P. (1996) 'From spike to bombs: the rise of eco-terrorism', *Studies in Conflict and Terrorism*, 19: 1–18.

EIA (2013) 'Liquidating the forests: hardwood flooring, organized crime, and the world's last Siberian tigers', Environmental Investigation Agency. Online at: http://eia-global.org/images/uploads/EIA_Liquidating_Report__Edits_1.pdf (Accessed 20 March 2015).

Ellefsen, R. (2012) 'Green movements as threats to order and economy: animal activists repressed in Austria and beyond', in R. Ellefsen, R. Sollund and G. Larsen (eds), *Eco-global Crimes: Contemporary Problems and Future Challenges*. Farnham: Ashgate, pp. 181–205.

Ellefsen, R., Sollund, R. and Larsen, G. (eds) (2012) *Eco-global Crimes: Contemporary Problems and Future Challenges*. Farnham: Ashgate.

Enarson, E. (1999) 'Violence against women in disasters: a study of domestic violence programs in the United States and Canada', *Violence Against Women*, 5: 742–68.

Environmental Protection Agency (2013) 'Greenhouse gas court decisions'. Online at: http://www.epa.gov/climatechange/endangerment/ghgcourtdecision.html (Accessed 10 March 2015).

Environmental Protection Agency (2014) 'Plain English guide to the Clean Air Act: permits and enforcement', Washington: EPA. Online at: http://www.epa.gov/airquality/peg_caa/permits.html (Accessed 10 March 2015).

Epstein, H. (ed.) (2014) 'Climate change and the International Court of Justice', Yale Centre for Environmental Law and Policy. Online at: http://envirocenter.yale.edu/uploads/publications/Climate%20Change%20ICJ%208.23.13.pdf (Accessed 3 January 2015).

Ernst and Young (2014) 'Managing bribery and corruption risks in the oil and gas industry'. Online at: http://www.ey.com/Publication/vwLUAssets/EY-Managing-bribery-and-corruption-risk-in-the-oil-and-gas-industry/$FILE/EY-Managing-bribery-and-corruption-risk-in-the-oil-and-gas-industry.pdf (Accessed 20 March 2015).

REFERENCES

Fagan, N. and Thompson, L. (2009) 'Corporate responsibility and group redress mechanisms', *Business Law International*, 10 (1): 51–60.

Farone, A. (2014) 'Argentine court recognizes orang-utan as "non-human person"', *Jurist*, 22 December. Online at: http://jurist.org/paperchase/2014/12/argentina-court-recognizes-orangutan-as-non-human-person.php# (Accessed 23 December 2014).

Fazio, C.A. and Strell, E.I. (2014) 'Precautionary principle: a rational approach to climate change', *New York Law Journal*. Online at: http://www.clm.com/publication.cfm?ID=506 (Accessed 13 March 2015).

Felthous, A. and Kellert, S. (1987) 'Childhood cruelty to animals and later aggression against people: a review', *American Journal of Psychiatry*, 144: 710–17.

Fenwick, H. (2007) *Civil Liberties and Human Rights*. Abingdon: Routledge.

Flood-Page, C., Campbell, S., Harrington, V. and Miller, J. (2000) *Youth Crime: Findings from the 1998/99 Youth Lifestyles Survey*. London: Home Office.

Flynn, C.P. (2002) 'Hunting and illegal violence against humans and other animals: exploring the relationship', *Society & Animals*, 10 (2). Washington: Society & Animals Forum Inc.

Forsyth, C.J. and Evans, R.D. (1998) 'Dogmen: the rationalisation of deviance', *Society & Animals*, 6 (3). Washington: Society & Animals Forum Inc.

Frasch, P.D. (2000) 'Addressing animal abuse: the complementary roles of religion, secular ethics, and the law', *Society & Animals*, 8 (3). Washington: Society & Animals Forum Inc.

Friedman, M. (1970) 'The social responsibility of business is to increase its profits', *The New York Times Magazine*, 13 September.

Gallicano, T. (2011) 'A critical exploration of greenwashing claims', *Public Relations Journal*, 5 (3): 1–21.

Garrett, B.L. (2012) 'Habeas corpus and due process' *Cornell Law Review*, 98: 47–126. Online at: http://cornelllawreview.org/files/2013/02/Garrett-final.pdf (Accessed 20 January 2015).

Gluckman, P. (2011) 'Two charged in federal indictment with dumping e-waste illegally overseas; *Green Electronics Daily*, 09/20/11.

Goldberg, S. (2014) 'Conservative lobby group Alec plans anti-environmental onslaught', *The Guardian*. Online at: http://www.theguardian.com/us-news/2014/dec/02/alec-environmental-protection-agency-climate-change (Accessed 10 March 2015).

Goodey, J. (1997) 'Masculinities, fear of crime and fearlessness', *The British Journal of Sociology*, 37 (3): 401–18.

Green, P. (2004) *State Crime: Governments, Violence and Corruption*. London: Pluto Press.

Greenpeace (2014) 'Koch Industries: secretly funding the climate denial machine'. Online at: http://www.greenpeace.org/usa/en/campaigns/global-warming-and-energy/polluterwatch/koch-industries/ (Accessed 17 March 2015).

Groombridge, N. (1998) 'Masculinities and crimes against the environment', *Theoretical Criminology*, 2 (2): 249–67.

REFERENCES

Gullett, W. (1997) 'Environmental protection and the precautionary principle: a response to scientific uncertainty in environmental management', *Environmental and Planning Law Journal*, 14 (1): 52–69.

Gunningham, N. and Sinclair, D. (1999) 'Regulatory pluralism: designing policy mixes for environmental protection', *Law and Policy*, 21 (1): 49–76.

Haken, J. (2011) *Transnational Crime in the Developing World*. Washington DC: Global Financial Integrity.

Hall, M. (2013) 'Victims of environmental harm', in R. Walters, D. Westerhuis and T. Wyatt (eds), *Emerging Issues in Green Criminology: Exploring Power, Justice and Harm*. Basingstoke: Palgrave Macmillan, pp. 218–241.

Halsey, M. (2004) 'Against green criminology', *British Journal of Criminology*, 44 (6): 833–53.

Hampton, P. (2005) *Reducing Administrative Burdens: Effective Inspection and Enforcement*, London: HM Treasury.

Harland, K., Beattie, K. and McCready, S. (2005) *Young Men and the Squeeze of Masculinity: The Inaugural Paper for the Centre for Young Men's Studies*. Ulster: Centre for Young Men's Studies.

Harris, F. (2011) 'Brands corporate social responsibility and reputation management', in A. Voiculescu and H. Yanacopulos (eds), *The Business of Human Rights: an Evolving Agenda for Corporate Responsibility*. London: Zed Books/The Open University.

Hatchard, J. (2011) 'Combatting transnational corporate corruption: enhancing human rights and good governance', in A. Voiculescu and H. Yanacopulos (eds), *The Business of Human Rights: An Evolving Agenda for Corporate Responsibility*. London: Zed Books/The Open University, pp. 143–165.

Hawkins, K. (1984) *Environment and Enforcement: Regulation and the Social Definition of Pollution*. London: Clarendon Press.

Hawkins, K. (2002) *Law as Last Resort*. Oxford: Oxford University Press.

Hawley, F. (1993) 'The moral and conceptual universe of cockfighters: symbolism and rationalization', *Society and Animals*, 1 (2). Washington: Society & Animals Forum Inc.

Hayes, H. (2005) 'Assessing re-offending in restorative justice conferences', *Australian and New Zealand Journal of Criminology*, 38 (1): 77–101.

Henry, B.C. (2004) 'The relationship between animal cruelty, delinquency, and attitudes toward the treatment of animals', *Society & Animals*, 12 (3). Washington: Society & Animals Forum Inc.

Higgins, P. (2010) *Eradicating Ecocide: Exposing the Corporate and Political Practices Destroying the Planet and Proposing the Laws Needed to Eradicate Ecocide*. London: Shepheard-Walwyn Publishers.

Higgins, P. (2015) 'What is ecocide?' Online at: http://eradicatingecocide.com/the-law/what-is-ecocide/ (Accessed 20 March 2015).

Hillyard, P. and Tombs, S. (2011) 'From "crime" to social harm?', in Michael J. Lynch and Paul B. Stretesky (eds), *Radical and Marxist Theories of Crime*. The Library of Essays in Theoretical Criminology. Aldershot: Ashgate, pp. 13–29.

Hinteregger, M. (2008) *Environmental Liability and Ecological Damage in European Law*. Cambridge: Cambridge University Press.

Hobsbawm, E.J. (1969) *Industry and Empire from 1750 to the Present Day*. Harmondsworth: Penguin.

Hodges, C. (2008) *The Reform of Class and Representative Actions in European Legal Systems: A New Framework for Collective Redress in Europe*. Oxford: Hart Publishing.

Hoek, A. (2010) 'Sea Shepherd Conservation Society v. Japanese Whalers, the showdown: Who is the real villain?', *Stanford Journal of Animal Law and Policy*, 3: 159–193.

Hope, C. (2013) 'RSPCA warned on hunt prosecutions by charities watchdog', *The Telegraph*. Online at: http://www.telegraph.co.uk/news/politics/9809362/RSPCA-warned-on-hunt-prosecutions-by-charities-watchdog.html (Accessed 1 June 2014).

Hope, C. (2014) 'Tories to legalise fox hunting if they win 2015 general election', *The Telegraph*. Online at: http://www.telegraph.co.uk/news/general-election-2015/11307715/Tories-to-legalise-fox-hunting-if-they-win-2015-general-election.html (Accessed 25 April 2015).

Horrocks, J. and Menclova, A. (2011) 'The effects of weather on crime', New Zealand Association of Economics, Working Paper 45. Online at: http://nzae.org.nz/wp-content/uploads/2011/08/Horrocks_and_Menclova__The_Effects_of_Weather_on_Crime.pdf (Accessed 17 January 2015).

House of Commons (1966) Parliamentary Commissioner Bill. Available at: http://hansard.millbanksystems.com/commons/1966/oct/18/parliamentary-commissioner-bill (Accessed 12 August 2015).

House of Lords (2007) 'Restorative Justice', House of Lords, 17 July, Column 126.

Hoyle, C. (2012) 'Victims, the criminal process and restorative justice', in M. Maguire, M. Morgan and R. Reiner (eds), *The Oxford Handbook of Criminology* (5th ed.). Oxford: Oxford University Press.

Hutter, B. (1997) *Compliance: Regulation and Environment*. London: Clarendon Press.

Hutton, J.S. (1997) 'Animal abuse as a diagnostic approach in social work', in R. Lockwood and F. R. Ascione (eds), *Cruelty to Animals and Interpersonal Violence*. Indiana: Purdue University Press.

International Council on Human Rights Policy (2002) *Beyond Voluntarism: Human Rights and the Developing International Legal Obligations of Companies*. Versoix: International Council on Human Rights Policy. Online at: http://reliefweb.int/sites/reliefweb.int/files/resources/F7FA1F4A174F76AF8525741F006839D4-ICHRP_Beyond%20Voluntarism.pdf (Accessed 4 August 2015).

Interpol (2012) 'Red notice issued for Paul Watson at Japan's request', Lyon: Interpol. Online at: http://www.interpol.int/News-and-media/News-media-releases/2012/N20120914 (Accessed 1 May 2013).

IPCC (2014) Summary for policymakers. In: *Climate Change 2014: Impacts, Adaptation, and Vulnerability. Part A: Global and Sectoral Aspects Contribution of Working Group II to the Fifth Assessment Report of the Intergovernmental Panel on*

REFERENCES

Climate Change. [Field, C.B., V.R. Barros, D.J. Dokken, K.J. Mach, M.D. Mastrandrea, T.E. Bilir, M. Chatterjee, K.L. Ebi, Y.O. Estrada, R.C. Genova, B. Girma, E.S. Kissel, A.N. Levy, S. MacCracken, P.R. Mastrandrea, and L.L. White (eds.)]. Cambridge/New York: Cambridge University Press, pp. 1–32.

Jamison, A., Raynolds, M., Holroyd, P., Veldman, E. and Tremblett, K. (2005) *Defining Corporate Environmental Responsibility: Canadian ENGO Perspectives.* Canada: The Pembina Institute/Pollution Probe.

Jasper, J.M. (1997) *The Art of Moral Protest: Culture, Biography, and Creativity in Social Movements.* Chicago, IL: The University of Chicago Press.

Johnston, I. (2014) 'Campaign to put ecocide on a par with genocide in attempt to curb environmental destruction', *The Independent*. Online at: http://www.independent.co.uk/environment/green-living/campaign-to-put-ecocide-on-a-par-with-genocide-in-attempt-to-curb-environmental-destruction-9789297.html (Accessed 17 March 2015).

Kahan, D.M., Braman, D., Gastil, J., Slovic, P., Mertz, C.K. (2007) 'Culture and identity-protective cognition: explaining the white-male effect in risk perception', *Journal of Empirical Legal Studies*, 4: 465–505.

Kean, H. (1998) *Animal Rights: Political and Social Change in Britain since 1800.* London: Reaktion Books.

Kirkham, R. Thompson, B. and Buck, T. (2008) 'When putting things right goes wrong: enforcing the recommendations of the ombudsman', *Public Law* (3): 510–30.

Kirkwood, G. (1994) *The Enforcement of Wildlife Protection Legislation: A Study* of *the Police Wildlife Liaison Officers' Network.* Leicester: De Montfort University.

Kishor, N. and Lescuyer, G. (2012) 'Controlling illegal logging in domestic and international markets by harnessing multi-level governance opportunities', *International Journal of the Commons*, 6 (2): 1–10.

Knottnerus J.D., Ulsperger, J.S., Cummins, S. and Osteen, E. (2006) 'Exposing Enron: media representations of ritualized deviance in corporate culture', *Crime, Media and Culture* 2 (2): 177–95

Kramer, R. (2012) 'Climate change: a state-corporate crime perspective', Washington: Institute for Environmental Security. Online at: http://www.envirosecurity.org/ecocide/nov2012/Kramer,R.C.%282012%29-ClimateChange_A_state-corporate_crime_perspective.pdf (Accessed 9 January 2015).

Ladan, Muhammed Tawfiq (2011) 'Access to environmental justice in oil pollution and gas flaring cases as a human right issue in Nigeria'. Online at SSRN: http://ssrn.com/abstract=2336093 or http://dx.doi.org/10.2139/ssrn.2336093 (Accessed 6 October 2015).

Lasslett, K. (2014) *State Crime on the Margins of Empire: Rio Tinto, the War on Bougainville and Resistance to Mining.* London: Pluto Press.

Law Commission (2012) 'Wildlife Law: a Consultation Paper', London: Law Commission. Para 4.46.

Lea, J. and Young, J. (1993 rev. edn) *What Is To Be Done About Law & Order?* London: Pluto Press.

REFERENCES

Lemert, E.M. (1951) *Social Pathology: Systematic Approaches to the Study of Sociopathic Behaviour*. New York: McGraw-Hill.

Liddick, D.R. (2011) *Crimes Against Nature: Illegal Industries and the Global Environment*. Santa Barbara, CA: Praeger.

Lindsey, P.A., Frank, L.G., Alexander, R., Mathieson, A. and Romanach, S.S. (2006) 'Trophy hunting and conservation in Africa: problems and one potential solution', *Conservation Biology*, 20: 880–3.

Linzey, A. (ed.) (2009) *The Link Between Animal Abuse and Human Violence*. Eastbourne: Sussex Academic Press.

Llewellyn, J. (2002) 'Dealing with the legacy of native residential school abuse in Canada: litigation, ADR, and restorative justice', *The University of Toronto Law Journal*, 52 (3): 253–300.

Loadenthall, M. (2013) 'The Earth Liberation Front: a social movement analysis', *Radical Criminology*, (2): 15–45.

Lockwood, R. (1997) *Deadly Serious: An FBI Perspective on Animal Cruelty*. Washington DC: The Humane Society of the United States.

Lough, R. (2014) 'Captive orangutan has human right to freedom, Argentine court rules'. Online at: http://www.reuters.com/article/2014/12/21/us-argentina-orangutan-idUSKBN0JZ0Q620141221 (Accessed 10 March 2015).

Lowe, B.M. and Ginsberg, C.F. (2002) 'Animal rights as a post-citizenship movement', *Society & Animals* 10 (2). Washington: Society & Animals Forum Inc.

Lowther, J., Cook, D. and Roberts, M. (2002) *Crime and Punishment in the Wildlife Trade*. Wolverhampton: WWF/TRAFFIC/Regional Research Institute (University of Wolverhampton).

Lubinski, J. (2004) *Introduction to Animal Rights* (2nd edn). Michigan: Michigan State University.

Lynch, M. and Stretesky, P. (2003) 'The meaning of green: contrasting criminological perspectives', *Theoretical Criminology*, 7 (2): 217–38.

Lynch, M. (1990) 'The greening of criminology: a perspective on the 1990s', *Critical Criminologist*, 2: 1–5.

Lynch, M. and Stretesky, P. (2014) *Exploring Green Criminology: Toward a Green Criminological Revolution*. Farnham: Ashgate.

McBarnet, D. (2006) 'After Enron will "whiter than white collar crime" still wash?', *British Journal of Criminology* (November), 46 (6): 1091–109.

McCright, A.M. and Dunlap, R.E. (2011) 'Cool dudes: The denial of climate change among conservative white males in the United States', *Global Environmental Change*, doi: 10.1016/j.gloenvcha.2011.06.003 (Accessed 10 January 2015).

McGrew, A. (ed.) (1997) *The Transformation of Democracy : Democratic Politics in the New World Order*. Milton Keynes: The Open University.

Macrory, R. (2010) 'Environmental courts and tribunals in England and Wales – a tentative new dawn', *Journal of Court Innovation*, 3 (1): 61–78.

REFERENCES

Macrory, R. and Woods, M. (2003) *Modernizing Environmental Justice: Regulation and the Role of an Environmental Tribunal*. London: Centre for Law and the Environment, University College.

Maguire, M. (2000) 'Researching "street criminals": a neglected art', in R.D. King and E. Wincup (eds), *Doing Research on Crime and Justice*. Oxford: Oxford University Press, pp. 121–152.

Markell, D. and Ruhl, J.B. (2012) 'An empirical assessment of climate change in the courts: a new jurisprudence or business as usual?', *Florida Law Review*, 64 (1): 15–72.

Marshall, T.F. (1999) *Restorative Justice: An Overview*. London: Home Office.

Mason, R. (2015) 'Government shelves foxhunting vote after SNP opposition', *The Guardian*. Online at: http://www.theguardian.com/uk-news/2015/jul/14/foxhunting-vote-shelved-by-tories-in-face-of-snp-opposition (Accessed 12 August 2015).

Matza, D. (1964) *Delinquency and* Drift. New Jersey: Transaction.

Mazurkiewicz, P. (2002) *Corporate Environmental Responsibility: is a Common CSR Framework Possible?* Washington DC: World Bank.

Meltz, R. (2013) *Federal Agency Actions Following the Supreme Court's Climate Change Decision in Massachusetts v. EPA: A Chronology*. Washington DC: Congressional Research Service.

Merton, R.K. (1968) *Social Structure and Social Theory*. New York: Free Press.

Mill, J. (1993) *On Liberty*. New York: Bantam.

Ministry of Justice (2014) *Restorative Justice Action Plan for the Criminal Justice System for the Period to March 2018*. London: Ministry of Justice. Available at: https://www.gov.uk/government/uploads/system/uploads/attachment_data/file/375581/restorative-justice-action-plan-2014.pdf (Accessed 15 August 2015).

Mountain, M. (2014) 'Appellate Court Hearing in Tommy Case'. Online at: http://www.nonhumanrightsproject.org/2014/10/09/appellate-court-hearing-in-tommy-case/ (Accessed 10 March 2015).

Nelken, D. (1994) 'White-collar crime', in M. Maguire, R. Morgan and R. Reiner (eds), *The Oxford Handbook of Criminology*. Oxford: Oxford University Press, pp. 355–92.

Nellemann, C., Henriksen, R., Raxter, P., Ash, N. and Mrema, E. (eds) (2014) *The Environmental Crime Crisis – Threats to Sustainable Development from Illegal Exploitation and Trade in Wildlife and Forest Resources. A UNEP Rapid Response Assessment*. Nairobi/Arendal: United Nations Environment Programme and GRID-Arendal.

Nieuwoudt, S. (2007) 'How to turn the curse of oil into a blessing', Inter Press Service. Online at: http://www.ipsnews.net/2007/05/trade-africa-how-to-turn-the-curse-of-oil-into-a-blessing/ (Accessed 13 August 2015).

Nocella, A. J. II (2012) 'Challenging whiteness in the animal advocacy movement', *Journal for Critical Animal Studies*, 10 (1): 142–54.

Norland, S., Wessell, R.C. and Shover, N. (1981) 'Masculinity and delinquency', *Criminology*, 19 (3): 421–33.

Nugent, W.R., Umbreit, M.S. and Williams, M. (2003) 'Participation in victim-offender mediation and the prevalence and severity of subsequent delinquent behavior: a meta-analysis', *Utah Law Review* (1): 137–66.

Nurse, A. (2003) 'The nature of wildlife and conservation crime in the UK and its public response', Working Paper No. 9. Birmingham: University of Central England.

Nurse, A. (2009) 'Dealing with animal offenders', in A. Linzey (ed.), *The Link Between Animal Abuse and Human Violence*. Eastbourne: Sussex Academic Press, pp. 238–49.

Nurse, A. (2011) 'Policing wildlife: Perspectives on criminality in wildlife crime', *Papers from the British Criminology Conference*, 11: 38–53.

Nurse, A. (2012) 'Repainting the thin green line: the enforcement of UK wildlife law', *Internet Journal of Criminology*, October: 1–20.

Nurse, A. (2013a) *Animal Harm: Perspectives on Why People Harm and Kill Animals*. Farnham: Ashgate.

Nurse, A. (2013b) 'Privatising the green police: the role of NGOs in wildlife law enforcement', *Crime Law and Social Change*, 59 (3): 305–18.

Nurse, A. (2014) 'The beginning of the end? The International Court of Justice's decision on Japanese Antarctic whaling', *Journal of Animal Welfare Law*, Spring: 14–17.

Nurse, A. (2015a) *Policing Wildlife: Perspectives on the Enforcement of Wildlife Legislation*. Basingstoke: Palgrave Macmillan.

Nurse, A. (2015b) 'Creative compliance, constructive compliance: corporate environmental crime and the criminal entrepreneur,' in Gerard McElwee and Rob Smith (eds), *Exploring Criminal and Illegal Enterprise: New Perspectives on Research Policy and Practice: 5 (Contemporary Issues in Entrepreneur Research)*. Bingley: Emerald Publishing, pp. 97–120.

Nurse, A. and Ryland, D. (2014) 'Cats and the law: evolving protection for cats and owners', *Journal of Animal Welfare Law*, December: 1–6.

Office of the Ombudsman (2014) 'Environmental Ombudsman: a briefing paper', Quezon City: Office of the Ombudsman. Online at: http://www.ombudsman.gov.ph/docs/investmentOmbudsman/EnviTeam.pdf (Accessed 20 December 2014).

Office of the UN High Commissioner for Human Rights (2015) 'Universal Declaration of Human Rights – in six cross-cutting themes'. Online at: http://www.ohchr.org/EN/UDHR/Pages/CrossCuttingThemes.aspx (Accessed 20 March 2015).

Organ J.F., Geist, V., Mahoney, S.P., Williams, S., Krausman, P.R., Batcheller, G.R., Decker, T.A., Carmichael, R., Nanjappa, P., Regan, R., Medellin, R.A., Cantu, R., McCabe, R.E., Craven, S., Vecellio, G.M. and Decker, D.J. (2012) 'The North American model of wildlife conservation', *The Wildlife Society Technical Review*, 12-04. Bethesda, MD: The Wildlife Society.

REFERENCES

Orian, A. (2011) *The Declaration of Animal Rights*. Online at: http: declarationofar. org (Accessed 25 October 2015).

Owen, S. (1999) 'The Ombudsman: essential elements and common challenges,' in L.C. Reif (ed.), *The International Ombudsman Anthology: Selected Writings from the International Ombudsman Institute*. The Hague: Kluwer Law International, pp. 51–72.

Pardo, I. and Prato, G. (2005) 'The fox-hunting debate in the United Kingdom: a puritan legacy?', *Human Ecology Review*, 12 (1): 143–55.

Parker, C. (2004) 'Restorative justice in business regulation? The Australian competition and Consumer Commission's use of enforceable undertakings', *Modern Law Review*, 67 (2): 209–46.

Parkin, F. (1968) *Middle Class Radicalism: the Social Bases of the British Campaign for Nuclear Disarmament*. Manchester: Manchester University Press.

Parry, R.L. (2001) 'Bio-Pirates raid trees in the swamps of Borneo', *The Independent*, Thursday, 2 August.

Parsons, E.C.M., Clark, J., Wharam, J. and Simmonds, M.P. (2010) 'The conservation of British cetaceans: a review of the threats and protection afforded to whales, dolphins, and porpoises in UK waters, Part 1', *Journal of International Wildlife Law & Policy*, 13: 1–62, 201.

Partlett, D.F. and Weaver R.L. (2011) 'BP oil spill: compensation, agency costs, and restitution', *Washington & Lee Law Review*, 68 (3): 1341–75.

Patterson, C. (2002) *Eternal Treblinka: Our Treatment of Animals and the Holocaust*. New York: Lantern Books.

Pearce, F. and Tombs, S. (1998) *Toxic Capitalism: Corporate Crime and the Chemical Industry*. Aldershot: Dartmouth.

Peeples, L. (2015) 'Teens Take Politicians To Court Over Climate Change', *Huffington Post*. Online at: http://www.huffingtonpost.com/2015/01/17/climate-change-lawsuit-teens-oregon_n_6490036.html (Accessed 14 March 2015).

Persen, A.B. and Johansen, J. (1998) *The Necessary Disobedience*. Oslo: Folkereisning Mot Krig.

Peysner, J. and Nurse, A. (2008) *Representative Actions and Restorative Justice: a Report for the Department for Business Enterprise and Regulatory Reform*. Lincoln: University of Lincoln Law School.

Pirjatanniemi, E. (2009) 'Desperately seeking reason—new directions for European environmental criminal law', *Scandinavian Studies in Law*, 54: 409–30.

Plows, A. (2008) 'Towards an analysis of the "success" of UK green protests', *British Politics*, 3: 92–109.

Potoski, P. and Prakash, M. (2004) 'The regulation dilemma: cooperation and conflict in environmental governance', *Public Administration Review*, 64 (2): 152–63.

Potter, G. (2010) 'What is green criminology?', *Sociology Review*, November: 8–12.

Pring, G. and Pring, C. (2009) 'Specialized environmental courts and tribunals at the confluence of human rights and the environment', *Oregon Review of International Law*, 11 (2): 301–30.

Quinney, R. (1970) *The Social Reality of Crime*. Boston, MA: Little Brown.

Rachman, G. (2009) 'The crude realities of diplomacy', *Financial Times*, 8 September, p.13.

Radford, M. (2001) *Animal Welfare Law in Britain: Regulation and Responsibility*. Oxford: Oxford University Press.

Ranson, M. (2014) 'Crime, weather, and climate change', *Journal of Environmental Economics and Management*, 67 (3): 274–302.

Rawcliffe, P. (1998) *Environmental Pressure Groups in Transition (Issues in Environmental Politics)*. Manchester: Manchester University Press.

Regan, T. (2004) *The Case for Animal Rights*. Berkely, CA: University of California Press.

Regan, T. (2007) 'Vivisection: the case for abolition', in Peirs Beirne and Nigel South (eds), *Issues in Green Criminology: Confronting Harms Against Environments, Humanity and Other Animals*. Devon: Willan Publishing, pp. 114–39.

Reiner, R. (2000) *The Politics of the Police*. Oxford: Oxford University Press.

Restorative Justice Council (2014) 'What is restorative justice? Online at: http://www.restorativejustice.org.uk/what_is_restorative_justice/ (Accessed 7 January 2014).

Reuters (2014) 'Sandra the orangutan granted limited human rights', *The Telegraph* Online: http://www.telegraph.co.uk/news/worldnews/southamerica/argentina/11307205/Sandra-the-orangutan-granted-limited-human-rights.html (Accessed 10 March 2015).

Rhodes, W.M., Allen, E. and Callahan, M. (2006) *Illegal Logging: a Market-Based Analysis of Trafficking in Illegal Timber*. Washington: ABT Associates/US Department of Justice.

Roberts, M., Cook, D., Jones, P. and Lowther, D. (2001) 'Wildlife crime in the UK: towards a national crime unit', Wolverhampton: Department for the Environment, Food & Rural Affairs/Centre for Applied Social Research (University of Wolverhampton).

Roeschke, J.E. (2009) 'Eco-terrorism and piracy on the high seas: Japanese whaling and the rights of private groups to enforce international conservation law in neutral waters', *The Villanova Environmental Law Journal*, 20 (1): 99–136.

Rollin, B.E. (2006) *Animal Rights and Human Morality*. New York: Prometheus Books.

RSPCA (2015) 'Facts and figures'. Online at: http://media.rspca.org.uk/media/facts (Accessed 15 March 2015).

RSPCA Australia (2014) 'RSPCA Australia national statistics 2013-2014'. Online at: http://www.rspca.org.au/sites/default/files/website/The-facts/Statistics/RSPCA_Australia-Annual_Statistics_2013-2014.pdf (Accessed 20 March 2015).

Ruhl, J.D. (1997) 'The case of the Speluncean polluters: six themes of environmental law, policy, and ethics', *Environmental Law*, 27: 343–73.

Schaffner, J. (2011) *An Introduction to Animals and the Law*. New York: Palgrave Macmillan.

REFERENCES

Schlosberg, D. (2007) *Defining Environmental Justice: Theories, Movements, and Nature*. Oxford/Basingstoke: Palgrave Macmillan.

Schneider, J.L. (2008) 'Reducing the illicit trade in endangered wildlife: the market reduction approach', *Journal of Contemporary Criminal Justice*, 24 (3): 274–95.

Schneider, J.L. (2012) *Sold into Extinction: The Global Trade in Endangered Species*. Santa Barbara, CA: Praeger.

Scruton, R. (2006) *Animal Rights and Wrongs*. London: Continuum.

Shapland, J., Atkinson, A., Atkinson, H., Chapman, B., Dignan, J., Howes, M., Johnstone, J., Robinson, G. and Sorsby, A. (2007) 'Restorative justice: the views of victims and offenders, the third report from the evaluation of three schemes', Ministry of Justice/University of Sheffield.

Shapland, J., Atkinson, A., Atkinson, H., Dignan, J., Edwards, L., Hibbert, J., Howes, M., Johnstone, J., Robinson, G. and Sorsby, A. (2008) 'Restorative justice: does restorative justice affect reconviction. The fourth report from the evaluation of three schemes', Ministry of Justice Research Series 10/08. London: Ministry of Justice. Online at: www.justice.gov.uk/publications/restorative-justice.htm (Accessed 13 February 2015).

Sherman, L.W. and Strang, H. (2007) *Restorative Justice: The Evidence*. London: The Smith Institute.

Singer, P. (1975) *Animal Liberation*. New York: Avon.

Situ, Y. and Emmons, D. (2000) *Environmental Crime: the Criminal Justice System's Role in Protecting the Environment*. Thousand Oaks, CA: Sage.

Skjærseth, J. (2010) 'Exploring the consequences of soft law and hard law: implementing international nutrient commitments in Norwegian agriculture', *International Environmental Agreements: Politics, Law and Economics*, 10 (1): 1–14.

Slapper, G. (2011) 'Violent corporate crime, corporate social responsibility and human rights', in A. Voiculescu and H. Yanacopulos (eds), *The Business of Human Rights: an Evolving Agenda for Corporate Responsibility*. London: Zed Books/The Open University, pp. 79–100.

Smith, J., Obidzinski, K. and Suramenggala Subarudi, I. (2003) 'Illegal logging, collusive corruption and fragmented governments in Kalimantan, Indonesia', *International Forestry Review*, 5 (3): 293–302.

Smith, R. (2010) *Texts and Materials on International Human Rights*. Abingdon: Routledge.

Solinge, T.B. (2008) 'Eco-crime: the tropical timber trade', *Organized Crime: Culture, Markets and Policies*, 7: 97–111.

Sollund, R. (2012) 'Speciesism as doxic practice versus valuing difference and plurality', in R. Ellefsen, R. Sollund and G. Larsen (eds), *Eco-Global Crimes: Contemporary Problems and Future Challenges*. Farnham: Ashgate, pp. 91–113.

South, N. (2007) 'The corporate colonisation of nature: bio-prospecting, bio-piracy and the development of green criminology', in P. Beirne and N. South (eds), *Issues in Green Criminology: Confronting Harms Against Environments, Humanity and Other Animals*. Willan, Devon, pp. 230–47.

South, N. (2010) 'The ecocidal tendencies of late modernity: transnational crime, social exclusions, victims and rights', in R. White (ed.), *Global Environmental Harm: Criminological Perspective*. Devon: Willan, pp. 228-47.

South, N. and Beirne, P. (1998) 'Editors' Introduction', *Theoretical Criminology*, 2 (2): 147–8.

South, N. and Wyatt, T. (2011) 'Comparing illicit trades in wildlife and drugs: an exploratory study', *Deviant Behavior*, 32 (6): 538–61.

Spence, D.B. (2011) 'Corporate social responsibility in the oil and gas industry: the importance of reputational risk', *Chicago-Kent Law Review*, 86 (1): 59–85. Online at: http://scholarship.kentlaw.iit.edu/cklawreview/vol86/iss1/4 (Accessed 20 March 2015).

Stallworthy, M. (2008) *Understanding Environmental Law*. London: Sweet and Maxwell.

Steiner, R. (2010) *Double Standard: Shell Practices in Nigeria Compared with International Standards to Prevent and Control Pipeline Oil Spills and the Deepwater Horizon Oil Spill*. Amsterdam: Friends of the Earth Netherlands.

Stempel, J.W. (1995) 'Two cheers for specialisation', *61 Brook. Law Review*, 67: 88–9.

Stephens, C., Bullock, S. and Scott, A. (2001) 'ESRC global environmental change programme (2001) environmental justice: rights and means to a healthy environment for all', Special Briefing No.7. Brighton: University of Sussex.

Stone, R. (2010) *Civil Liberties and Human Rights*. Oxford: Oxford University Press.

Sunstein, C.R. (2004) 'Introduction: What are animal rights', in C.R. Sunstein and M.C. Nussbaum (eds), *Animal Rights: Current Debates and New Directions*. New York: Open University Press, pp. 3–15.

Sutherland, E.H. (1973) *On Analysing Crime* (K. Schuessler, ed.). Chicago, IL: University of Chicago Press (original work published 1942).

Sykes, G.M. and Matza, D. (1957) 'Techniques of neutralization: a theory of delinquency', *American Sociological* Review, 22: 664–73.

Tannenbaum, J. (1995) 'Nonhuman animals and the law: property, cruelty, rights', in Mack, A. (ed.) *Humans and Other Nonhuman Animals*. Columbus, OH: Ohio State University Press.

TCEQ (2012) 'Environmental crimes investigators pursue worst willful polluters', *Natural Outlook*, February. Online at: https://www.tceq.texas.gov/assets/public/comm_exec/pubs/pd/020/2012/Outlook-Feb-2012-x.pdf (Accessed 20 March 2015).

Tempus, A. (2014) 'Environmental lawyers gear up for fighting climate change in the courts', *Vice News*, 21 October. Online at: https://news.vice.com/article/environmental-lawyers-gear-up-for-fighting-climate-change-in-the-courts (Accessed 9 January 2015).

Tencer, D. (2011) 'Monsanto, world's largest genetically modified food producer, to be charged with biopiracy in India', *Huffington Post*. Online at: http://www.huffingtonpost.ca/2011/10/03/monsanto-india-biopiracy-farmers_n_992259.html?ir=Green&just_reloaded=1 (Accessed 12 August 2015).

REFERENCES

Terry, K. (2009) 'Terrorism', *Oxford Bibliographies*. Online at: http://www.oxfordbiblio graphies.com/view/document/obo-9780195396607/obo-9780195396607-0023. xml (Accessed 12 August 2015).

The Economist (2015) 'The Petrobas scandal: he's got a little list'. Online at: http://www.economist.com/news/americas/21645703-now-brazilian-politicians-will-face-investigation-hes-got-little-list (Accessed 20 March 2015).

Tombs, S. and Whyte, D. (2003) 'Unmasking the crimes of the powerful', *Critical Criminology*, 11 (3): 217–36.

Tombs, S. and Whyte, D. (2015) *The Corporate Criminal: Why Corporations Must Be Abolished*. Abingdon: Routledge.

Transparency International (2015) 'Corruption by topic: oil and gas'. Online at: http://www.transparency.org/topic/detail/oil_and_gas (Accessed 20 March 2015).

Turner, R.K. (1992) *Environmental Policy: An Economic Approach to the Polluter Pays Principle*. Norwich: University of East Anglia.

United Nations (1999) 55th Session of the Commission on Human Rights (22 March to 30 April 1999) – Documentation. Online at: www.ohchr.org/EN/HRBodies/CHR/55/Pages/Documentation.aspx (Accessed 30 October 2015).

United Nations (1992) Framework Convention on Climate Change Online at: https://unfcc.int/resource/docs/convkp/conveng.pdf (Accessed 20 October 2015).

UNECE/UNEP (2006) 'Your right to a healthy environment'. New York and Geneva: United Nations Economic Commission for Europe/United Nations Environment Programme.

United Nations Environment Programme (2011) 'Environmental assessment of Ongoniland'. Kenya: United Nations Environment Programme. Online at: <http://postconflict.unep.ch/publications/OEA/UNEP_OEA.pdf> (Accessed 14 December 2014).

United Nations Human Rights Council (2011) 'Guiding principles on business and human rights: implementing the United Nations "protect, respect and remedy" framework'. New York: The United Nations. Online at: http://www.business-humanrights.org/media/documents/ruggie/ruggie-guiding-principles-21-mar-2011.pdf (Accessed 20 March 2014).

UNODC (2012) *Wildlife and Forest Crime Analytic Toolkit*. Vienna: UNODC.

US Department of State (2009) *Against Wildlife Trafficking: Working Together to End the Illegal Trade in Wildlife*. Washington DC: US Department of State (Bureau of Oceans and International Environmental and Scientific Affairs).

United States District Court of Colorado (2012) Criminal Case No. 11-cr-00376-WJM. Verdict Form – *United States of America v. Executive Recycling Inc., Brandon Richter, Tor Olson*. Filed December 21, 2012.

Vincent, K. (2014) 'Reforming wildlife law: proposals by the Law Commission for England and Wales', *International Journal of Crime Justice and Social Democracy*, 3 (2): 68–81.

Viñuales, J.E. (2008) 'The contribution of the International Court of Justice to the development of international environmental law: a contemporary assessment',

Fordham International Law Journal, 32 (1): 232–58. Online at: http://ir.lawnet. fordham.edu/ilj/vol32/iss1/14 (Accessed 18 March 2015).

Voiculescu, A. and Yanacopulos, H. (eds) (2011) *The Business of Human Rights: An Evolving Agenda for Corporate Responsibility*. London: Zed Books/The Open University.

von Essen, E., Hansen, H.P., Källström, N.H., Peterson, N.M. and Peterson, T.R. (2014) 'Deconstructing the poaching phenomenon: a review of typologies for understanding illegal hunting', *British Journal of Criminology*, 54 (4): 632–51.

Wachholz, S. (2007) '"At risk": climate change and its bearing on women's vulnerability to male violence', in P. Beirne and N. South (eds) *Issues in Green Criminology*. Cullompton: Willan, pp. 161–85.

Waddington, P.A.J. (2013) 'A trial of criminology'. Online at: http://blog.oup. com/2013/07/policing-criminology-modern-state/ (Accessed 25 April 2015).

Walters, R. (2007) 'Crime, regulation and radioactive waste in the United Kingdom', in Piers Beirne and Nigel South (eds), *Issues in Green Criminology: Confronting Harms Against Environments, Humanity and Other Animals*. Cullompton: Willan, pp. 186–205.

Walters, R., Westerhuis, D. and Wyatt, T. (eds) (2013) *Emerging Issues in Green Criminology: Exploring Power, Justice and Harm*. Basingstoke: Palgrave Macmillan.

Ward, J. (2014) 'Are problem-solving courts the way forward for justice? Howard League What is Justice?' Working Papers 2/2014. London: Howard League.

Webb, T. and Pilkington, E. (2010) 'Fears for BP's future as US launches criminal inquiry', *The Guardian* 2 June. Online at: www.guardian.co.uk/environ ment/2010/jun/02/bp-criminal-inquiry-gulf-of-mexico (Accessed 19 June 2015).

Weber, M. (1964) *The Theory of Social and Economic Organization*. (Talcott Parsons, ed.). New York: The Free Press.

Webster, D. (1997) 'The looting and smuggling and fencing and hoarding of impossibly precious, feathered and scaly wild things', *New York Times Magazine*, 16 February 1997.

Welch, M. (1996) 'Critical criminology, social justice, and an alternative view of incarceration', *Critical Criminology*, 7 (2): 43–58.

Wellsmith, M. (2010) 'The applicability of crime prevention to problems of environmental harm; A consideration of illicit trade in endangered species', in R. White (ed.) *Global Environmental Harm; Criminological Perspectives*. Cullompton: Willan Publishing, pp. 132–49.

Wellsmith, M. (2011) 'Wildlife crime: the problems of enforcement', *European Journal on Criminal Policy and Research*, 17/2: 125–48.

Weston, B.H. and Bollier, D. (2013) *Green Governance: Ecological Survival, Human Rights and the Law of the Commons*. New York: Cambridge University Press.

White, R. (2007) 'Green criminology and the pursuit of ecological justice', in P. Beirne and N. South (eds) *Issues in Green Criminology*. Cullompton: Willan Publishing, pp. 32–54.

REFERENCES

White, R. (2008) *Crimes Against Nature: Environmental Criminology and Ecological Justice*. Cullompton: Willan.

White, R. (2009) 'Dealing with climate change and social conflict: A research agenda for eco-global criminology', in K. Kamngaspunta and I.H. Marshall (eds), *Eco-crime and Justice*. Turin: UNICRI, pp. 13–35.

White, R. (2011) *Transnational Environmental Crime: Toward an Eco-Global Criminology*. New York: Routledge.

White, R. (2012a) 'Land theft as rural eco-crime', *International Journal of Rural Criminology*, 1 (2): 203–17.

White, R. (2012b) 'NGO engagement in environmental law enforcement: critical reflections', *Australasian Policing*, 4 (2): 7–12.

White, R. (ed.) (2012c) *Climate Change from a Criminological Perspective*. New York: Springer.

White, R. (2012d) 'The foundations of eco-global criminology', in R. Ellefsen, R. Sollund and G. Larsen (eds) *Eco-global Crimes: Contemporary Problems and Future Challenges*. Farnham: Ashgate, pp. 15–31.

White, R. (2013a) 'Environmental crime and problem-solving courts', *Crime Law and Social Change*, 59: 267–78.

White, R. (2013b) 'The conceptual contours of green criminology', in R. Walters, D. Westerhuis and T. Wyatt (eds), *Emerging Issues in Green Criminology: Exploring Power, Justice and Harm*. Basingstoke: Palgrave Macmillan, pp. 17–33.

White, R. and Heckenberg, D. (2014) *Green Criminology: an Introduction to the Study of Environmental Harm*. London: Routledge.

Wiessner, D. (2014) 'NY court questions lawyer's novel bid to win rights for chimps'. Online at: http://www.gmanetwork.com/news/story/382787/news/world/ny-court-questions-lawyer-s-novel-bid-to-win-rights-for-chimps (Accessed 10 March 2015).

Willetts, P. (2002) 'What is a non-governmental organization?' London: City University. Online at: http://www.staff.city.ac.uk/p.willetts/CS-NTWKS/NGO-ART.HTM (Accessed 25 April 2015).

Williams, A. (2011) 'Climate change law: creating and sustaining social and economic insecurity', *Social and Legal Studies*, 20 (4): 499–513.

Wilson, J.Q. (1985) *Thinking about Crime* (2nd edn). New York: Vintage Books.

Wilson, S., Anderson, L. and Knight, A. (2007) *The Conservation of Seals Act 1970: The Case for Review*. Scotland: Seal Forum.

Wise, S. (2000) *Rattling the Cage: Towards Legal Rights For Animals*. London: Profile.

Wise, S. (2014) 'Tommy's Appeal – What the Judges May Say'. Online at: http://www.nonhumanrightsproject.org/2014/11/10/tommys-appealwhat-the-judges-may-say/ (Accessed 6 August 2015).

Wise, S. (2015) 'That's One Small Step for a Judge, One Giant Leap for the Nonhuman Rights Project'. Online at: http://www.nonhumanrightsproject.org/2015/08/04/thats-one-small-step-for-a-judge-one-giant-leap-for-the-nonhuman-rights-project/ (Accessed 6 August 2015).

REFERENCES

Wood, M. (2009) 'Advancing the sovereign trust of government to safeguard the environment for present and future generations (Part 1): Ecological realism and the need for a paradigm shift', *Environmental Law*, 39: 43–89.

Woolf, H. (1992) 'Are the judiciary environmentally myopic?' *Journal of Environmental Law*, 4 (1): 1–14. doi: 10.1093/jel/4.1.1.

WWF (2014) 'Living Planet Report 2014'. Switzerland: WWF International. Online at: http://wwf.panda.org/about_our_earth/all_publications/living_planet_report/ (Accessed 2 January 2015).

Wyatt, T. (2011) 'Criminal Involvement in Wildlife Smuggling'. Online at: http://ips.cap.anu.edu.au/sites/default/files/IPS/IR/TEC/WYATT_Criminal_involvement_in_wildlife_smuggling.pdf (Accessed 12 August 2015).

Wyatt, T. (2013) *Wildlife Trafficking: a Deconstruction of the Crime, the Victims and the Offenders*. Basingstoke: Palgrave Macmillan.

Young, J. (1994) 'Incessant chatter: recent paradigms in criminology', in M. Maguire, R. Morgan and R. Reiner (eds), *The Oxford Handbook of Criminology*. Oxford: Oxford University Press, pp. 69–124.

Zainol, Z.A., Amin, L., Akpoviri, F. and Ramli, R. (2011) 'Biopiracy and states' sovereignty over their biological resources', *African Journal of Biotechnology*, 10 (58): 12395–408. Online at: http://www.academicjournals.org/AJB (Accessed 20 April 2015).

Zimmerman, M.E. (2003) 'The black market for wildlife: combating transnational organized crime in the illegal wildlife trade', *Vanderbilt Journal of Transnational Law*, 36: 1657–89.

INDEX